THE *garden* INTERIOR

Advance praise for

THE *garden* INTERIOR
A Year Of Inspired Beauty

In this book David Jensen joins the ranks of garden writers whose words come from the soul as well as the soil. Written as a seasonal diary in the voice of a true place maker, his passion for the mid-Atlantic garden he calls home shines through on every page.

—**Elizabeth Barlow Rogers**, president of
The Foundation for Landscape Studies and author of
Writing the Garden, A Literary Conversation Across Two Centuries

Don't take this book to bed—treat yourself to a quiet moment with a cup of coffee and David Jensen as your warm, witty, and wonderful companion. *The Garden Interior* is a generously personal account of the gardening year, which eloquently reminds us that it's not so much about what we gardeners do for Nature, but what Nature does for us.

— **Angelica Gray**, author of *Gardens of Marrakesh*

Reading David Jensen makes me want to sit right down and start writing or go do some planting in my own garden. He declares in the Introduction that his book is about "…how a garden grew and how a gardener grew as well, and how they formed and cared for each other." Gardening how to—and how not to—is in these pages but what is unique is the author's discoveries of *why* we garden. Bravo!

— **Elvin McDonald**, author of more than 50 gardening books and former garden editor of *House Beautiful, Family Circle, Traditional Home* and *Better Homes and Gardens*

David Jensen is an American Gardner who is a long-time contributor at EverythingZoomer.com and has earned the handle "The Spiritual Gardner". With this beautiful book, more readers will get know what our readers already do: that there are wonderful interior changes that happen to serious gardeners on the joyful journey of discovery that is the gardening art.

—**Suzanne Boyd**, Editor-in-Chief of
Zoomer Magazine and EveythingZoomer.com

I could tell immediately from reading David Jensen's delightful book that we are kindred spirits. Reading these pages is like having an intimate and engaging conversation with a wise and interesting friend, one who shares my personal passion for gardening.

—**Barbara Paul Robinson**, author of
Rosemary Verey: The Life and Lessons of a Legendary Gardener

A heartfelt and deeply personal account of one man's gardening life. Delicious recipes accompany wise words of horticultural advice from a skilled and devoted gardener.

—**Alex Ramsay**, photographer for *Japanese Zen Gardens*
and *The Gardens of Venice and the Veneto*

THE *garden* INTERIOR

A YEAR OF INSPIRED BEAUTY

DAVID JENSEN

New York

THE *garden* INTERIOR
A YEAR OF INSPIRED BEAUTY

© 2016 DAVID JENSEN.

Published in New York, New York, by Morgan James Publishing. Morgan James and The Entrepreneurial Publisher are trademarks of Morgan James, LLC.
www.MorganJamesPublishing.com

The Morgan James Speakers Group can bring authors to your live event. For more information or to book an event visit The Morgan James Speakers Group at www.TheMorganJamesSpeakersGroup.com.

Shelfie

A **free** eBook edition is available with the purchase of this print book.

CLEARLY PRINT YOUR NAME ABOVE IN UPPER CASE

Instructions to claim your free eBook edition:
1. Download the Shelfie app for Android or iOS
2. Write your name in **UPPER CASE** above
3. Use the Shelfie app to submit a photo
4. Download your eBook to any device

ISBN 978-1-63047-682-3 paperback
ISBN 978-1-63047-683-0 eBook
Library of Congress Control Number:
2015909394

Cover Design by:
Rachel Lopez
www.r2cdesign.com

Interior Design by:
Bonnie Bushman
The Whole Caboodle Graphic Design

In an effort to support local communities and raise awareness and funds, Morgan James Publishing donates a percentage of all book sales for the life of each book to Habitat for Humanity Peninsula and Greater Williamsburg.

Get involved today, visit
www.MorganJamesBuilds.com

Peninsula and
Greater Williamsburg
Building Partner

For Debbie, Mimi and Nick, with love

— Qui plantavit florebit

He who knows the most, he who knows what sweets and virtues are in the ground, the waters, the plants, the heavens, and how to come at these enchantments, is the rich and royal man....The difference between landscape and landscape is small, but there is great difference in the beholders. There is nothing so wonderful in any particular landscape, as the necessity of being beautiful under which every landscape lies. Nature cannot be surprised in undress. Beauty breaks in everywhere.

—Ralph Waldo Emerson

Table of Contents

Foreword

by Barbara Paul Robinson

I could tell immediately from reading David Jensen's delightful book that we are kindred spirits. Reading these pages is like having an intimate and engaging conversation with a wise and interesting friend, one who shares my personal passion for gardening.

This memoir is a marvelous mix of "how-to" tips from an experienced hands-on gardener with astute observations about the beauty of nature, along with musings about life and philosophy, all lightened with a touch of wit. As a bonus, David enriches the mix by inserting mouth-watering recipes here and there to further whet the reader's appetite.

The Garden Interior is an apt title for what proves to be a collection of the inner thoughts and ruminations of an intelligent, thoughtful man as he works in his garden. Although the book is structured over the twelve months of a single year, it clearly reflects a much longer composite of memories and experiences. There are flashbacks to earlier years, different homes and gardens and personal anecdotes about his family life. I suspect that his tongue-in-cheek reference to his wife as "She Who Must Be Obeyed" suggests that he actually doesn't often obey and that she is in reality long suffering. Endearingly, he is devoted to his dog, his constant companion in the garden.

David Jensen believes that "gardens are inherently about beauty" and his descriptions of flowers, sunsets and the joys of scent on the air are pure poetry. His thoughts about the quality of silence in the garden were particularly meaningful to me. He also concludes that the garden is a profound teacher about life. Among the lessons he has learned are the three basic virtues of "hope, persistence and stoicism." In the garden, he believes we learn to make allowances and even to love our favorite plants despite their flaws and that is "pretty good training for coping with people one comes across in a long life." We also learn that gardening has nothing to do with "subduing nature or even changing nature; it is about *cooperating* with nature." In fact the best results are often what I like to call "happy accidents," when "volunteers" self-sow in places they most want to grow, creating compositions that are far better than any the gardener intentionally planned.

What David refers to as the Tao of gardening makes it appear to the uninitiated or casual observer that "the gardener is making the garden, but the greater reality is that the garden is all the while making the gardener." I share that view of reality as well as his thought that no hired professional "can achieve what you yourself can do by actually getting in amongst your own garden and getting your hands dirty on a regular basis," as this is certain to provide a "strong feeling of connection, satisfaction and well-being." In my own professional life as a lawyer, I am sure that my hours in the garden have been the best form of therapy possible.

It is clear that David has a day job that forces him to drive into the City, dragged reluctantly away from his garden, but he doesn't tell us that he is a highly successful executive in the media and communications industry. While he describes a trip with his son to England where the reader learns he studied at Magdalen College, Oxford, it is only in the final chapter that he reveals he was there as a Rhodes Scholar. That modesty no doubt reflects his conclusion that gardening is a work that is endlessly in process and never finished, that the "gardener goes on being instructed and humbled over the years."

Introduction

I am a ten-year-old boy. It is early January and I am driving in a car, in the snow, with my mother. We live in a small western town in Colorado, where the foothills of the Rocky Mountains begin to give way to the alkali flats and sage brush barrens that, in their turn, eventually break up into the red rock country and canyonlands of central and southern Utah. We are driving into our small town, where there is a pet shop, and at the back of this shop, there is a bank of warm and brightly lit aquariums, filled with brilliantly exotic tropical fish. It is a magical wall of color and light, like something in a movie, and I have always been fascinated by it. I got an aquarium for Christmas a week ago and have set it up, carefully following the directions. The water is purified and heated, and today I am going to buy my first fish. I am very excited in a way that only ten-year-old boys can be. I am a newly minted ichthyologist. Ick-thee-ologist: my ten-year-old tongue tries out the new word I have just learned from the book, thick with fantastic pictures of tropical fish, that came with the aquarium.

The Monkeys' raucous hit "I'm a Believer" is playing on the radio and I love it. I smile. The catchy song fuses with my happiness and excitement. For the rest of my life, whenever I hear that song, this day will be called vividly to mind, and I will (briefly) be ten again. I have a garden at home too, but it is very small and now, in January, it is blasted by our harsh western winter: a patch of ground around the base of a small Russian olive tree, with a few irises and some destroyed remains of annuals I scrounged from my mom and some neighbors. Some common red geraniums and some coleus with their amazing foliage. I planted this first garden last spring and this is the first of many winters to come as a gardener. While we drive through the blanketing snow on our bright tropical errand, my mind wanders back home to that tiny patch of wintry ground and I think about each individual plant and how it is faring; what it will be like when the spring comes, and then summer; what else I can plant; how I can make this garden better, more interesting, bigger. I am lost in alternate reveries of tropical waters, winter gardens, and summer gardens: the mind of a ten-year-old boy in his interior world, which is simultaneously small and large, precisely defined, but also ecstatically unbounded.

Half a century later, I am an international television executive, of all the improbable things, and I work for a big media company. I am married and we have raised two children, now in college. I have been educated far beyond my station in life, lived and studied in Australia and Europe, worked in government and media. In the course of a long career, I have met and worked with all sorts of unusual people: presidents, cabinet members, Members of Congress, heads of state, ambassadors, movie stars, television personalities, and some of our current age's most entrepreneurial business people. But I am still somehow that same boy, pottering about in his little garden, tending his small earth. We live now in a historic, pre-revolutionary small town in southern New Jersey in a rambling Arts and Crafts bungalow set in about an acre of mature gardens that are a joy to behold, to live in, and to be the guardians of. This is the story of that garden, and what it is like and how it came to be. Inevitably, too, it is obliquely the story of what happened to that ten-year-old boy, and how he came to the present day. It is the story of how a garden grew and how a gardener grew as well, and how they formed and cared for each other.

Gardening for most people—most non-gardeners, that is—seems to be about growing nice flowers for the house or vegetables for the kitchen table; a way of staying active, perhaps, or of having something to do outdoors on the weekend. They consider it a somewhat eccentric pastime, as flowers and vegetables are so much easier to come by at the grocery store, and indeed they are. Other people, who are somewhat more reflective, may perceive some of the esthetic side of gardening and intuit that it has something to do with beauty, art, and design; but again, they will generally only be seeing the external result of gardening. What most people completely overlook is the most important and satisfying part of gardening: its *interior* aspect; that it is a way of internal living more than mere external activity; that it is, in short, a spiritual discipline with profound metaphysical qualities.

And so this book is about the garden interior. It is about what goes on in the heart and mind of a gardener and how gardens change, educate, and raise up the gardener as much as the gardener forms, tends, and raises up the garden. It will be part memoir and part garden journal, part nostalgic memoir, and part foodie journal. It will be eclectic and idiosyncratic, and made up of many parts and pieces and ornaments, just like any good garden is. Hopefully, it will also form a coherent whole and so make a kind of holistic sense too. It will be an attempt to explain those gardeners for whom the purpose of gardening, the *point* of it, is not the external affect—the flowers and plants and vegetables, or the general landscape and all that a passerby sees in strolling casually past the garden gates—but rather what no one sees and what is far more subtle and interesting, really; and that is, what is going on inside the gardener's head and in the gardener's heart.

Our gardens make us more than we make them, and that is the simple, profound truth of it. The plants will come and go, we may move from garden to garden, our skill and energy levels will change over a lifetime and the local conditions where we find ourselves planted may change radically. But the garden interior is subtly accretive and durably everlasting, its beauty and glory unseen and unknown to others, and in many ways not even understood by the gardener himself. But the garden interior of each of us is real all the same, and it is gorgeous indeed, and it rejoices Him who is the Gardener of all.

January

New Year's and Ladybugs

It is a severe and bitter, perfectly classic, early January morning when I awake at 4:00 a.m. I am propelled out of bed by a host of thoughts and ideas that sit gibbering on the headboard of my bed…all the usual things that disturb the rest of parents these days, perhaps at any time in history, and can cause them to stagger to the kitchen for a badly needed cup of coffee. These are the things that are sent to try us, I suppose, and remind us that earth is not our home. The person known ominously around here as She Who Must Be Obeyed is still asleep, although I would just say that, here in America where we have a right of free speech, we are allowed to add (mentally) the surname "But Against Whom Passive Resistance Is Tolerated, Though Strongly Discouraged." She would tell me to stop being such a Shetland sheepdog and go back to bed, but in this case, I resist and stay up with my thoughts.

My dog, Cosimo, who actually *is* a sheltie, is trailing at my heels, looking rather surprised by the early hour, but with nothing more on his mind than the pretty certain hope of an early breakfast. It is only ten degrees* outside and still dark for hours yet. None of the Christmas lights, indoors or out, have yet tripped their timers and come on. It is not exactly the dark night of the soul, but all the same, it is very dark.

The furnace thermostats are still set to night time and so the downstairs rooms are chilly, but I have a mug of strong, hot, milky coffee in my hands, and in the reading room, I open the large illustrated coffee table book that I got for Christmas this year, *English Country House Interiors.* What superb, superlative rooms these are: wealth, taste, antiquity, tradition, and eccentricity all combined in a lovely materialist accretion and encrustation that seems to go on and on. My mind wanders in this fantasyland of wealth and taste and privilege for a long time, the whole "Downton Abbey" thing, before I am recalled to the more straitened present. I try to suppress the cares that disturbed my sleep, and think instead about the frozen garden outside.

Hours later, our two kids in their late teens are still nowhere to be seen, sleeping off their considerable exertions from a New Year's Eve that mysteriously involved some seriously illegal fireworks and a box of kitchen pots and pans. Sometimes a parent, in his growing wisdom, does not want to know what exactly his children are up to, and last night was just such a time.

---

* For our non-U.S. readers, all temperatures used in this book are Fahrenheit and not Celsius.

Outside in the frozen garden, the hyacinths are an inch or two out of the ground, in their unflagging optimism, and so are hundreds of leaf-spears of daffodils. The extremely sharp cold of these bitter days will certainly kill off most of the pests in the garden, so we must rejoice over that, though of course, it is hard on the birds. I try to remember to put bread out for them and sometimes, when it is very cold, a dish of warm water, as water is more critical to them than food on a cold day when all water sources are frozen solid. Almost all the insect pests perish in cold like this, and just think of all the slugs and Japanese beetles that are doomed, though their successors will all be here next year. Many ladybugs survive all but the cruelest winters in our garden, or rather many survive in the garden and others prefer to find their way inside our rambling, not very airtight old house. I am forever catching them indoors and putting them carefully back outside. In weather like this, only these escapees will have survived the cold, plus a few with the good fortune or good sense to have burrowed deep into garden debris near a south-facing wall.

The first couple of years we lived here, I went out each spring to buy small containers of ladybugs to release into our garden, to establish this small friend with such a ravenous appetite for aphids and other pests. You release them at night so they get acclimated to your garden and don't fly away, and then by morning (in theory, anyway), they like their new abode and they and their descendants will be your allies and assistants forever after. Years later, they are legion here and I never see aphids in our garden any more. Victory!

When my son was very small, I took him to the garden center once on a ladybug errand and he was fascinated with the little cardboard container they come in, like the containers you get fishing worms in, but with screen over the top. He held the ladybugs while I was pushing the shopping cart through the garden center, and when I wasn't looking, he poked out the screen to see the bugs better. Of course they all escaped, and we left a long trail of ladybugs through the store. While I ineffectually tried to scoop at least some of them back into the container, he giggled with delight at all the escaped bugs and Daddy's manic antics.

This weekend was just barely warm enough to get out and do the last of the weeding before the year ended, and I ruthlessly cleaned the long herbaceous border of its infestation of a tiny but vigorous weed that looks something like watercress. Then I raked up the last of the autumn leaves, adding them to the mulch pile so the snows and rains of winter can create the dark, rich leaf mold that is worth its weight in gold in the spring garden. I am so greedy for this stuff that I would treat all the leaves that fall in our yard in this way if I could, but alas, then no other indoor chores or parenting—not to mention my day job in the city— would ever get done. So one does what one can.

But what a rich harvest this is and it does so much good in the garden, especially if you don't want to use chemical fertilizers. The soil in this garden has—just in the space of eight years of treating it with respect, strictly abstaining from chemicals of any kind, especially pesticides—gone from impoverished and clay-like stuff to dark, rich, and crumbly garden soil. You can turn over a spadeful of garden earth or sod and find it teeming with earthworms—and, yes a few grubs too, we must take the rough with the smooth after all—and what a joy it is to think of having rehabilitated this one fine acre of garden in so short a time. Weeding this last bed and getting the leaves all raked up once and for all were the last two chores I wanted to get done this year, and it is a nice feeling to have them accomplished.

I notice with joy that the pink 'Knock Out' roses are still blooming, and enthusiastically too, while their red cousins have completely given up, and it reminds me of what a weak color red is, overall, in the garden. Or rather, the color is not weak, but the plants that bear it generally are. I do not know why this is so, but the red version of any flower seems to be much less robust than its other exemplars. Perhaps there is a botanical theory that explains this. Red roses are typically much less florid than other colors, so too with peonies, daylilies, red rose mallows, red irises and on and on. It does not mean they are not worth growing but it is odd that a particular color should be associated with lack of vigor, or perhaps I am just imagining this, as I am fond of red in the garden and can never seem to get enough of it.

I feel the same way about blue, which also seems to me to be associated with lack of vigor, but I love it all the more too. Pastel colors, and whites and yellows in particular, seem not to suffer at all from this debility. I do like a bit of color variety in a species, and how boring a place the garden would be if every flower only came in one or two colors. But I also think that plant breeders tend to go too far and cannot rest until, merely for novelty, every plant is available in every color of the rainbow. Do we really need yellow and orange azaleas, for example? To me, they look hideous in the spring woods, blighting the bright green landscape with their toxic haze of mustard gas bloom. A golden holly is unusual and striking the first time one sees it, but would anyone really prefer it to the classic red, year in and year out for fifty years? Unthinkable.

One day last spring, at the end of a long walk around our town, I came upon a small planting at my neighbor's house where, among a festive and traditional gathering of fresh pink and white azaleas, they had planted a splendid, tall group of *orange* irises. And not apricot orange either, which would have been awful enough, but pumpkin orange. Have you ever seen such a thing? And the combination with pink and white was a premeditated insult to the eye. It stopped me in my tracks and I was thunderstruck by their unseemliness; I had to wonder who had seen fit to inflict this awful plant on the world and on unsuspecting and relatively innocent passersby.

I am all for letting people do whatever they want to do in their gardens, and to indulge their enthusiasms and whims as much as they like, however odd. That's part of the fun of gardening, after all. But honestly, there are limits. In the old days, in the live-and-let-live west, they used to say: "Around here, you can do whatever you want, so long as it doesn't startle the horses." And I think that's a pretty good way to organize a civilized society. But orange irises would definitely be in the horse-startling category and therefore should be outlawed. Or rather, not outlawed exactly, but I do think it would be okay for the sensible, steady sort of gardener to give a sniff of disapproval and move along, shaking his head in wonder at the folly of mankind.

Manure beyond the Dreams of Avarice

Perhaps it is time to tell you about the secret sauce, the gold at the end of the gardener's rainbow, the manna from heaven. For this gardener, it is: *horse manure.* My greed for the magical ingredient has finally led me to ask my daughter's formidable horse barn owner for some manure, a commodity he has in great supply, and of which I have a great need. One of the fine things, surely, about owning a horse, and there are many, is the free supply of manure, which is like precious gold in the garden. As my daughter's horse boards at his barn, some of the manure he has on his farm must, I think, belong to us, at least arguably. So I drove out to his farm, and there it was, piles and piles of it, all lovely and aged and available for the taking. But first I had to overcome my shyness in asking for it from Claude, the forbidding Swiss taskmaster who owns the barn and runs it with an iron fist, a sort of equestrian Bismarck (but Swiss, not German; you see how my metaphor is getting a bit muddled). And to my delight, he was happy to oblige.

I backed my truck up to his vast manure pile, and he very cordially steered me to an even more valuable pile, which had been aged and cured in the sun for years and was a mountain of black gold, a veritable Fort Knox of garden goodness. The light of pure, unguarded greed lit up my eyes. As Henry Mitchell says of people too foolish to use manure in their gardens: "It is no use to say you haven't got any; get some." So I now take our daughter to and from the barn when she is home, each way happily acquiring two huge trash barrels of the stuff, the largest containers that will fit in my SUV. I hesitated at first, thinking it was a bit unseemly somehow, but not for long, concluding cheerfully with the English poacher that I "may as well be hung for a sheep as a lamb." Or was it "in for a penny, in for a pound"? Anyway, I am as pleased as a dog with two tails, to use an expression closer to home.

Most sensible people, and nearly all serious gardeners, perceive in the rich smell of well-rotted manure one of the great perfumes we humans are able to savor on this good earth. To us, it smells like the very essence of a healthy, life-giving soil, which indeed it is. My dog, Cosimo, for example, who is widely celebrated for his extremely good judgment, thinks it is just fine and in fact rather interesting. He is called The Wonder-Dog by those who know him and love him; I call him The Assistant Gardener, and his help in the garden and unwavering friendship are beyond price. He has been my constant companion in the manure caper, and he loves to frisk about the stables and visit the horses in his friendly way while I load my SUV with the golden stuff.

Unaccountably, however, other people who are important in our household have an unreasoning prejudice against the bouquet given off by this precious commodity. My teenage son, who has always had a hair-trigger gag reflex, can now scarcely bear to drive my car. And She Who Must Be Obeyed had quite a lot to say on the subject of horse droppings as we were going out to dinner one night, saying that she "would never again be taken out on a dinner spree in a foul manure-mobile," and adding quite a lot of further conversation that drifted volubly along this same rhetorical line. She embroidered this theme with numerous riffs about the pig-headedness of certain gardening folk and their greedy, selfish folly and so on, and I could not help thinking these subtle barbs may have been *aimed* at me. Still, we gardeners are past masters at putting up with adversity and prejudice, and we plough doggedly forward with the right and the true and the good, just as we were meant to do. We persevere, do we not?

When I got home from each trip to the stables, the wholesome stuff went right into the gardens, and my intention this winter is to put a rich layer of it over every inch of my garden. With the stock market now as uncertain as ever, hoarding manure seems a very sensible precaution and a perfectly viable alternative investment strategy.

We cannot, of course, stop gardening just because it is a revolting day in the dead of winter. So, inspired by a picture in a Penelope Hobhouse book of Russian sage blooming with yellow yarrow, I dug all the mangy grass out of the 4x7 bed on the street corner where we live, and where I started two Russian sages last summer to fill that hot and prominent spot with bright and lasting summer color. Today, I put down landscaping fabric around the center, leaving the edges empty for the yarrow that I will move from the crescent bed in the spring, when such tender plants may safely be moved. The two should bloom together a long time and stop traffic at that intersection. In my imagination, anyway. I added my secret ingredient, the manure, and covered the whole in bark chips for now, then was driven indoors by the pelting, freezing rain.

Inside, we have a huge red amaryllis open, with *three* bloom stalks, and it looks grand in the reading room, where you can look through it at the Christmas tree that is still up in the front room. Some friends gave us a second Christmas-red camellia as a gift, uncannily detecting that I had always had an ambition to have another camellia and, in fact, had been recently thinking of looking for one to place on the north side of the house, where it should do well. I intend to plant it beneath a kitchen window so that, when it is grown, it can peep in and watch me wash dishes and I can be cheered by its Renoiresque red blooms.

Outside, in welcome breaks of more mild weather, I have been cutting decades' worth of dead wood out of the rhododendrons in the hedgerow, as I can't do much else in the yard in the dark of January, and this is a job that badly needs to be done. Recently, I saw our old friend the resident cardinal, who seems to be sheltering in the dense yew by the trash bins, whence he explodes in startled flight if, in his opinion, you make too much noise on a trash bin errand. What a delight to see him again, after a mysterious absence of some time, dressed all in his Christmas red and adding some much-needed color to a dull winter landscape.

Also today, I got two large terra cotta pots for future tomatoes and filled them with manured soil, placing them by the corner of the garage next to the shaped yew, where they should get plenty of heat and sun this summer. If it ever becomes warm again. For now, the manure can rot nicely in the winter wet. Foul weather and rot and decay become new life before our eager eyes; delicious! After a hot shower, I re-read a favorite gardening book and extracted from it more than a full page of ideas for changes in my own garden. The winter gardener lives a rich and forward-looking interior life, planning for and savoring the sunlight and beauty to come.

So much for the garden in the dark of January as the New Year comes on strong. Inside the house, the mind of the gardener turns to penitent thoughts of the great excesses of the holiday season that concluded the year: the chocolates, the baked goods, the huge meals following each other in regular and unbroken procession, washed down by rivers of lovely wine and far too frequent depth charges of port and single malt whiskey…and on and on. And let us not even mention the platefuls of almond butter toffee, shall we? (It was Enstrom's toffee, by the way, and it is the best in the world.) And so we find ourselves longing for food that is fresh, light, and wholesome to begin the year on the right note.

A good place to start is with a lovely piece of salmon that we slow roast with colorful winter vegetables, bursting with wholesome goodness and flavor, and here is the simple recipe, designed as a one-dish marvel.

Slow-Roasted Salmon

1 butternut squash
1 celery root
2 pink grapefruits
¾ cup olive oil
¼ cup brown sugar
¼ cup soy sauce
1 Tbsp. hot sauce
1 large bunch of red kale
2 lbs. of salmon
Salt and pepper

Pre-heat oven to 350 degrees. Peel the squash and halve it lengthwise; scrape out the seeds and halve each piece again; cut the quarters into pieces smaller than one inch thick and put them in a large bowl. Peel the celery root and cut it into pieces smaller than one inch, and add to the squash. Cut the grapefruits in half and use a small sharp knife to cut each segment, as if you were going to eat them with a spoon. Spoon out the grapefruit gems and reserve them in a small bowl; squeeze the juice from the grapefruit halves into a small saucepan; the four halves should yield about half a cup of juice. To the juice, add the olive oil, sugar, soy sauce, and hot sauce and cook over a low heat, whisking until it is combined.

Pour half a cup of the sauce over the squash and celery root mixture and toss to coat. Turn this mixture into a large (10 x 15 inch) baking dish that has been coated with olive oil and bake for 55 minutes. Remove from oven and reduce temperature to 275 degrees; put the squash and celery root in a large bowl. Wash and trim the kale, at least 12-15 large leaves of it, and then cut the leaves in half horizontally. Re-coat the baking dish with more olive oil, then line it with the kale. Top the kale with the squash and celery root and add the gems of grapefruit on top of the vegetables. Reserve half a cup of the remaining sauce, and pour the rest over the vegetables and grapefruit.

Lay the salmon on top of this and pour the last half-cup of sauce over the fish. Season the salmon with salt and pepper to taste. Slow-roast the salmon until it is cooked but tender, 30-40 minutes. Thirty minutes yields a fish that is a little underdone, which is how we like it, but suit yourself. Serve with generous hunks of artisanal bread for mopping up the insanely delicious broth, and stop worrying so much about your excesses of the holiday season. You have started the New Year right by turning over a new leaf, and happily it is a brilliantly red-veined leaf of healthy kale. And with all the manure scattered in the winter garden, you can tell it is going to be a good year.

Oh To Be in England...

Our large holly trees were sheeted with festive red berries all during the Christmas season and now, with the colder weather, the robins by their dozens are feasting on them. I put some sand and fireplace ash on the mulch piles, to add to the delicious stew of rot that I am brewing there this winter. One recent evening, I heard a hawk cry and went outside to see this sleek and fat bird of prey at the very top of the tallest pine tree next door, transfixed in the last rays of rose sunlight, a magical moment. Today, as I go about the garden, my loyal dog, Cosimo, is at my side and what excellent company he is. I hope it does not make me sound too misanthropic to say that, honestly, he is more intelligent and certainly more pleasant than half the people I know.

I have been reading and am inspired by Dorothy Jacob's *Flowers in the Garden*, and recently I have finally gotten outside for work in the garden on a fairly mild day, fifties and sunny. I cut down all the debris in the porch bed, weeded it down to the grass blade, and manured half of it before quitting for the day. How fine a bed looks that way, all cleaned up and manured and dressed for the balance of winter, the dark, rich brown earth contrasted against the sharp and spare green of the grass, the ivy, and the pachysandra, and soon, the bright verdure of new growth. If one were rich and employed a garden staff, the gardens would all look just like this all the time, but alas, we all do the best we can; there is a recession on, in case you haven't heard, or near enough, and the garden staff are nowhere to be found, as usual.

And how one's mind does travel to spring green in the dead of January. "Oh to be in England, now that April's there," said Mr. Browning in what, considering the foul and disgusting weather England has to endure in April in the real world, is surely the outer limit of the poetic license we should allow even our best versifiers. April in England is certainly no idyll and was surely even worse in Browning's time than it is now. Probably he was writing for the bitterly homesick English living in India, who would have given anything to hear the chilly crunch of ice and slush on the garden path and feel the smart stinging of lovely fresh sleet on the back of the neck. Maybe he had in mind the two or perhaps three really fine days in an otherwise rather severe month, meteorologically. I guess I am just saying that I can't really relate to that particular poem.

But one fine April day a few years ago is fixed in my memory. My son and I had flown to London the day before and gone up to Blenheim by train and bus for the day, overnighting sumptuously at the Randolph Hotel in Oxford, as I had always wanted to do. On the Saturday, I showed him around Magdalen College, where I lived and studied for three years. Well, lived anyway, not studied so much. We walked over the same paving stones trodden by Cardinal Wolsey, C.S. Lewis and Oscar Wilde, to name three Magdalen luminaries that come quickly to mind and who probably would be disconcerted to find themselves conjoined in the same sentence. He was amazed by Oxford and I could see him finally grasping that perhaps his father was not the dear old buffer he had always taken him for, but might perhaps be a bit more interesting than he had thought. I could tell he was impressed as I led him around, reminiscing as we went. His comment was: "Wow, this is really cool, Dad." Every parent of teenagers will understand what a hard-won compliment this was; it was what we call "A Great Moment in Parenting."

As we walked past the President's Lodgings on the other side of the Porter's Lodge, my mind flew back thirty years to my first days there as a very nervous freshman. Terrified, more like. I remembered that, as soon as I started at Magdalen, we had to go one by one and meet the very formidable old President Griffiths for an excruciatingly painful interview. He was on the team that invented radar during the War and allowed Britain to win the Battle of Britain, so was a very serious brainiac, but was terribly shy and I am sure these interviews were excruciating for him as well.

"Ah, what sort of activities are you thinking of, Jensen?" he growled, insinuatingly. "Activities, President?" I said innocently. "What do you mean by activities?"

"What are you going to do beside study?" he thundered. "You can't just study all day, you know; you'll go mad, man!"

"Um, I hadn't really thought about it, President. I just got here," I said lamely.

"Well, my strong advice is, stay well away from the Union, don't row, and don't under any circumstances have anything to do with the OUDS (the Oxford University Dramatic Society). Any one of them will quite ruin your Oxford career. There. You can go now, I guess, and send in the next chap."

And so I was dismissed. Of course, I immediately went out and joined all three and my Oxford career was, in time, completely ruined, just as he foretold. Oxford certainly did its best for me, I know; I doubt very much I did anything for Oxford.

But returning to the father-son trip, we then made our way along the nostalgic beauty of Addison's Walk to the University Parks, which were ablaze that week with acres and acres of daffodils in the bright (and deliciously rare) April sunshine. It was a truly glorious day, and I took a picture of my son that I treasure, of him standing in vast drifts of tens of thousands of daffodils, with shafts of spring sunlight falling all about him. He is smiling in a funny way that suggests that, although his father is clearly insane, he is rather fond of him all the same. Which is nice. Thinking of that, this morning I took Cosimo outside to check our own daffodils in the side yard and, sure enough, they were three to five inches out of the ground already, though it is hard to find them in the fallen leaves and the wintry dark, helped only by the dim light from our security lamp. It is lovely to see the first new growth so early in the New Year.

How typical of the gardener's mind that he scrounges in the pre-dawn dark to find some green shoots to look at, and in his mind, he is immediately transported three thousand miles to myriads of yellow blooms on a bright sunny day in a land far away.

Back on this continent, the gardener in winter stays connected to the garden by over-wintering indoors some plants he particularly cares for. Two of our favorites are small pots of chives and rosemary that normally live outdoors but, for four months of the year, must live inside, in a window in the mudroom. There, they can be useful still, and we clip them for herbs to put into hearty winter cooking. There is nothing better for the cold and dark days, we know, than comfort food: hot, hearty, and old-fashioned. So picture this: you are grilling some steaks on the patio as a light snow is falling, and inside, there is a fire in the hearth and a bottle of robust red wine is open, breathing. Say it's a Napa Valley merlot. No, make that a big cabernet. And you happen to know how to make a foolproof, fantastic mushroom sauce to go with the steaks that are sizzling. Uh-oh, there I go being transported again. Well, here's a recipe that should be in everyone's repertoire for hearty winter meals:

Mushroom Sauce

2 Tbsp. butter, divided
4 cups sliced mushrooms
Salt and pepper
3 cups chicken stock (preferably homemade)
1 tsp. red wine vinegar
¼ cup flour
2 Tbsp. chopped fresh chives (or rosemary, if you prefer)

Any mushrooms will do for the purposes of this recipe. You can go with common, inexpensive mushrooms, or fancy exotics, if you feel like showing off a bit. You can also mix and match, and we recommend using more than one kind; it makes the sauce more interesting. Melt 1 Tbsp. of the butter in a skillet over medium-high heat. Add the mushrooms and cook for about 5 minutes. Add salt and pepper to taste. Add broth and vinegar, then simmer until the liquid is reduced, 12-15 minutes. Yes, the 1 tsp. of vinegar will seem like too little, but it isn't; it gives just the right amount of acid to balance this rich sauce.

Reduce the heat to low, then add the flour and stir briskly; the sauce should instantly thicken into a nice, rich gravy. Add the second Tbsp. butter and the chives (or rosemary), and remove from the stovetop. For classic uses, such as over steaks and other cooked meats, use this sauce just like this. For more subtle uses, for example as the base for a mushroom risotto, it can be puréed in a blender. And try it puréed as a mushroom pesto with pasta. You can also use vegetable stock for a vegetarian version of this, then sauté some exotic mushrooms and use the mushrooms and the mushroom sauce for an intense mushroom pasta that is out of this world.

Jasmine, Camellia, and Cherry Pits

One of the indispensable things every gardener needs is a keen and obliging gardening assistant. I have one of these, and he is of the canine variety. I tried to go out with him on Saturday to clean up the crescent bed's weeds in the weak mid-afternoon sunshine during that one hour when it is just not quite bitter, and we were both so looking forward to a bit of mucking-out time together. He is not much help with the weeding, confidentially, but he is indefatigable and rather a terror with the squirrels and robins, the poor things, and God forbid a *rabbit* should ever appear on our property—that makes him furious. We didn't get very far on the mucking out project, however, finding the ground frozen solid and all the debris pasted down to the frozen earth with ice. I chopped at this mess a few times, just to be sure it was hopeless, before giving up and going on a long winter ramble instead, and that suited Cosimo just fine.

Besides the frozen ground, there are other obstacles to progress in the garden. A friend of mine has invented a garden stake that holds her wineglass while she weeds, and I was amazed at the revelation that you could drink wine while gardening. Wine-gardening, what a concept! I never knew. And just think of all the other accoutrements that could be added to make wine-gardening even more pleasurable. The result would be that more and more hours would be spent everywhere in gardens, but less and less productively, I would imagine.

You know how sometimes—after a glass of wine, perhaps, or from some other source of inspiration—you get a gardening idea into your head, and then you turn it over, examining it from every angle for, oh, about five years before doing anything about it? I have been doing that with jasmine, of all things, and my thoughts would run in these grooves: What is jasmine exactly? Is it hearty enough for New Jersey? Could its perfume really be as intoxicating as garden writers rhapsodize it to be? There must be something to it; they can't all be mad. Most of them are, of course, quite mad.

Where would I put it? What colors does it come in, and what color would I want to have if I had a choice? I wonder if it is expensive. How come I never see it at the garden centers I visit? That probably means it can't be grown here, except in greenhouses. Wouldn't it be lovely to have a nice greenhouse? Of course, heating it would be insanely expensive, and my wife would certainly leave me at last; that would be the final straw for her. And that would be bad, but she has put up with so much, and who could blame her, really? Not me, at any rate. The kids could come visit me in my greenhouse, however, and that would be jolly. I could even move into it if I had to and rent the house out; it would be like living in Key West! Except that the people who rented our house would doubtless be reasonably creeped out that there was a crazy old man living in the greenhouse out back. And so on.

And then, just as I was resolving that this spring I would finally get myself a jasmine vine, along came a neighbor out of the blue, a sort of *deus ex machina* rather, who gave me a jasmine plant as a gift. Just like that, beauty enters! The jasmine plant, I mean, not the neighbor, though she is fine in her way too and no offense. Eerily, she is the same person who gave us a camellia just as I was coming to the end of five years of deliberation—mustn't rush these things after all—and about to resolve to buy a camellia. Could she be somehow perceiving my innermost thoughts? That is a worry. One has to assume that she can, and just think what *that* entails. One hopes that her gift of clairvoyance is limited to horticultural matters. Or could it be an uncanny working of Herr Jung's principle of synchronicity? Anyway, you could have knocked me over with a feather; I had never mentioned this obsessive wish to anyone before.

And thinking of camellias, I am just embarked upon the enormous new collection of letters by the fabulous Mitford sisters. I am currently in the pre-war years. There are lots of letters about jolly visits to Berlin and Munich and what a peach that dear Adolph Hitler was really, and the silly thing he said to us the other day; how we all laughed, my dear, it was too wonderful, do admit. It is all very sickening, knowing as we do and they of course do not, what comes next.

But anyway, one of the letters digresses and tells the story of an extremely magnificent family friend who imperiously accosts a humble gardener at the fabulous Kew Gardens in London, demanding advice about blight, as follows: "Good afternoon. Camellias, dropping of flower buds, please?" The gardener simply grunts and dismissively replies with a single scornful word: "Overfeeding," and scuttles off in the undergrowth about his work, no doubt having already answered the same question a hundred times. And that is why, in case you were wondering, lately I find myself creeping through my own frozen gardens, crazily muttering the word "Overfeeding!" every so often, and laughing crazily too, no doubt adding somewhat to my local reputation for eccentricity.

And thinking of Hitler, recently I re-read the magisterial history of Hitler's demise written by Hugh Trevor-Roper, *The Last Days of Hitler*. What a wonderful work of scholarship this is and what a gripping story it tells of those dramatic final days of the war in Europe. And it reminded me of the time when he was the Regius Professor of History at Oxford, but not yet Lord Dacre. I would see him just walking around the streets of Oxford like an ordinary human, and I would watch him in awe. Once, he came to Magdalen to dine with the dons at our High Table. We had stewed cherries for dessert and we lowly undergraduates pelted him with cherry pits while he ate. I don't know why, really. Apparently it's been done by undergraduates for years and was just one of those Oxford things. But he seemed to find it highly amusing and so, of course, did we. He just sat there hunched over his bowl of soup, spooning up his dinner and chuckling silently to himself, receiving the friendly compliment of a steady tattoo of cherry pits from his student admirers.

February

The Garden Is Bilingual

The garden speaks to us in two languages: beauty and silence. One of the differences between an ordinary gardener and a great gardener is that the great gardener learns, usually over a long life of hard work and respectful study, to speak at least one of these languages. And it is a rare gardener indeed who can learn to speak both, for both languages are very difficult in their own ways.

The easier of the two is the language of silence. I do not here mean that there is no noise in the garden, although in general they are not very noisy places. We love the garden for the sounds of birds and other wildlife that enliven the scene year-round. The sound of the wind in the leaves in summer and whistling through the bare trees in winter is distinctive, symphonic, and greatly varied; the blowing of leaves in autumn can be downright soothing. And what could be better than the sound of living, active water in a garden, whether natural or artificial, for irrigation or contemplation or ornament?

A gardener knows that beauty is everywhere, but sometimes it is quietly subtle and not obvious. Once, on a late autumn walk in some nearby woods, we came upon some common weeds growing in a shallow stream or rill, with half a dozen autumn leaves sprinkled round. Pebbles, weeds, and water; silence and fluid movement; the spangle of a handful of fallen leaves. Sometimes, we find beauty where we were not expecting it.

When the garden is speaking to you of beauty, it is a silent speech, and it is as eloquent in its way as the loving look you get from a spouse when you realize you have been quietly being observed, or the look you get from your difficult teenagers when they realize how much you love them but don't want to acknowledge it. The way your dog looks up at you with his eyes brimming with admiration for the brilliant and omnipotent friend he considers you to be, and you shrink a bit inside yourself, because you know you are not really worthy of such great esteem. These are the looks that speak volumes, and our gardens communicate to us interiorly in exactly the same way. The difficulty is to hear it. We need to be guided in this by William Shakespeare, who advised us to find "Tongues in trees, books in running brooks, sermons in stones, and good in everything."

Go outside in the garden when you can have a quiet hour there and walk slowly through it. Stop to rest and look around in several places, study the garden intensely, and listen to what it is telling you. The chores it wants you to do, the changes it wants you to make, the way that things should be, and the things that are just not right. That plant struggling hopelessly in the wrong sort of environment. That path that needs to be moved or straightened. That beloved plant that just doesn't look right anymore and needs to be brutally cut back or removed altogether. And so on. But not just the wished-for emendations and the faults; look at the great things and the good things as well as all the successes planned and unplanned, and for the most part undeserved. The things that had the heart and character to grow back to strength when you had given up on them. The surprises that ended up looking just right. The dozens of creatures you are so fond of and whose every look and need and habit you know intimately. You love them all, with all their faults, like family and old friends.

This special communion between the garden and the gardener, this sort of horticultural sympathy or telepathy, has long been noticed and commented upon. The formidable English garden writer E.A. Bowles, for example, in his classic book *My Garden in Spring* (1914), wrote of great gardeners who possess "an inexplicable knowledge and feeling [enabling them to receive] a sort of wireless message from the plant to the invisible antennae of the gardener…"

Or listen to the way the great garden designer Russell Page articulates his special gift for *seeing* the constituent parts of the garden design: "My understanding is that every object emanates—sends out vibrations beyond its physical body which are specific to itself. These vibrations vary with the nature of the object, the materials it is made of, its colour, its texture, and its form." Compose the elements correctly, so the emanations and vibrations are right, and it just feels right; the gardener/artist can see that it is so. Change them slightly and the design is simply all wrong.

A great help in learning the language of silence is to practice it yourself. I know this because it is a particular failing of mine, though I work hard to do better at it. It kills me to be still in the garden; usually, I am rushing here and there, weeding, watering, deadheading, digging and so on, with my brain teeming with ideas and judgments and plans and correctives. We all need to stop every now and then and just let the garden speak to us. And that means being physically still ourselves and adding no noise to the scene. Mr. Thoreau was an advocate of sitting perfectly still at the side of his pond and watching the amazing scene of wildlife and insect life that would come around to interest him. It is an esthetic discipline to be followed broadly. It repays study. We are not slaves in our gardens, after all; that they are for pleasure, we (I, certainly) sometimes forget. Too, we must practice stilling our minds, that incessant prattle and gibbering that goes on between our ears (I am talking to myself here, you understand, but if you feel it applies also to yourself, please by all means feel free to take it to heart).

When you do this, you can begin to understand what your own garden is trying to tell you. And what a good discipline it is for the gardener to listen hard to what the garden is saying. Too often, the gardener is out in the garden as the one imposing his divine order on a chaotic corner of the world. His is the power of creation and destruction, life and death, flourishing and perishing, and so on. I saw myself that way as a young gardener, in my juvenile folly. As I have grown more mellow and more experienced, I have learned the reality that, at most, we are a partner in the garden and, I increasingly suspect, the junior partner of the enterprise. Sometimes I wonder if we gardeners are strictly necessary at all. Of this I am sure: a really great gardener has gotten most of the ego sandpapered off him over time, and he listens to what the garden is trying to tell him in the language of silence. He knows in his heart that his place is not so much to order the garden to his liking as it is to cooperate with the garden in fulfilling its own beautifully unfolding potential.

This brings me to the language of beauty that the garden also speaks. In one sense, this is a very easy language to understand. Most gardeners are drawn to gardening for strong esthetic reasons: gardens are inherently *about* beauty. Other things too, of course: food, medicine, philosophy, tradition, life. But beauty is right up there, and most gardeners have a strong sense of what is beautiful. I don't hold much with theories of beauty that say all beauty is in the eye of the beholder. I think gardeners allow each other wide room to like and dislike all the plants we have feelings about, and that is certainly a different list with each gardener. That diversity of view is a great thing. But at the same time, gardeners know that beauty is not entirely relative and subjective, in just the same way that truth is not. Some things are true and others are not. Some things are more beautiful than others and that is just the way it is. Please don't complain to me about that; I was not consulted when these laws of beauty were laid down. And neither was Aristotle, although certainly he understood them better than most of us.

To speak the language of beauty that the garden speaks, you have to *see* the garden clearly. Have you ever really contemplated your garden in long and perceptive detail, with a clear eye, not for what needs to be done, but just for what you see before you? Have you gone to the back of a flower bed and looked at it from the back toward the front? Have you looked down on the garden from a high window or from across the street? Have you gotten down on your hands and knees and looked into the tiny immaculate bell of a lily of the valley, or crawled inside that lilac bush or Japanese maple you love and looked at the world from the interior of a plant?

Try lying down beneath your rhododendron and watching the fleecy clouds pass by above, filtered by their gnarled and twisted branches. Or stare into that lily pond until you grow dizzy with the hypnotic effect of sunlight, water, dragon flies, and goldfish. There are miracles all around us, but too often we forget we have the gift of a kind of second sight that lets us *see* them. Albert Einstein famously said, "There are only two ways to live your life. One is as though nothing is a miracle. The other is as if everything is." Each of us needs to ask: Which way am I living my life, and am I happy about that?

My mind is running along this groove of beauty because I am remembering a funny thing that happened on a late fall afternoon a few months ago. I was suddenly struck by how over-the-top gorgeous our solitary, tall pink rose was as it stood with its dark green leaves in a shaft of sunshine that seemed to light it up like a spotlight. At the top was one last rose of the season, looking rather blown but still magnificent. And as I stood still and silently admired it, at an unseen and unheard cue, the pink petals suddenly dropped, creating a shower of brilliantly lit pink spangles, floating silently down through the golden shaft of crystalline autumn sunlight. And to think I might have missed it had I not been right there just at that moment. Yep, another miracle, all right.

There is more a gardener can do, other than just being conscious of looking at the garden more intently and with quiet study, to see the garden more clearly. Two unobvious tools that should be part of every gardener's equipment and should always be close to hand, if not actually in your pocket, are a small camera and a note pad. The camera allows you to capture the beauty that you see, and just having it in your pocket makes you look for beauty more consciously as you go about your garden rounds. You tend to notice things more. In the same way, carrying a notepad to jot down some observations about what you are seeing makes you a more diligent observer. They are small things, but they sharpen your sight in surprising ways.

Reading about the garden is as important as writing about it, and every serious gardener should be a serious garden reader. For beginning gardeners or beginning garden readers, I usually recommend Henry Mitchell's three great gardening books. He has a lovely mellow gardening sensibility and is serious about gardening without being in any way doctrinaire about it; he has a wonderfully sly sense of humor, and his books are crammed with information and wise experience. Plus, these charming books will lead you on to other great writers.

One last thing. It was Elizabeth Lawrence who said, in *The Little Bulbs* (1957), "From putting together the experiences of gardeners in different places, a conception of plants begins to form. Gardening, reading about gardening, and writing about gardening are all one; no one can garden alone." No one can garden alone; what a wonderful thought. In really seeing our gardens, in reading and writing about them and photographing them, we are connected directly to the beauty strewn around us and to the great society of fellow gardeners who are steeped in it too and who, like us, speak the garden's two languages of silence and beauty.

On the Town Sledding Hill

Morning sunlight is pouring in the kitchen windows, dazzlingly illuminating possibly the best dish of paperwhites we've ever grown; they are magnificent. I was sitting in the reading room, turning a garden problem over in my mind, when I distinctly heard three steady coos of a mourning dove; it made me think that I haven't heard them in a long time and I wondered if they migrate or are resident year-round. I suppose they do migrate, but if so, I don't know what they would be doing back here today, with winter just half over to the day. A mystery, so I looked it up and it turns out that they are migratory, but the availability of ample birdseed in bird feeders entices some individuals not to migrate (even in Canada, it seems). So probably this fellow is one of that lazy sort, but we do not have bird feeders in our garden, as we don't want to attract squirrels and mice. Did you know that twenty million mourning doves are killed each year in the U.S. alone, for sport and meat? It does seem a bit excessive…

The garden problem I am thinking about is what to do with the very dry northern edge of our front grass, where even the grass itself does not do well. My thought is to put half a dozen Russian sages along that length to define a line where they will do fairly well in that sunny but very dry site. So would lysimachia and they would look great together—the pale purple and gray-green foliage of the sage against the white wands of the lysimachia in midsummer—and both have a long flowering season. Plus, the rest of the long runs would be perfect for irises, and I will soon need a place to move them to, as I have been rather lazy and have not divided many of them in five years, shamefully.

They can wait until August, however, when the garden and the gardener will be fairly exhausted and I won't be able to think what to do next and will need a pick-me-up design project. August is the right month to be moving irises, but I confess I have moved them every month of the year, sometimes (under duress) even in winter. Also, sedums would look well there, and some of them will need to be divided in spring, when the sage and lysimachia go in, so timing all this will be difficult. Not to mention the obvious and tricky problem of how to effect a major garden expansion under the disapproving notice of the ever vigilant War Department (also known on the premises as She Who Must Be Obeyed), especially a scheme involving Russian sage, which she and two other residents of this household are prejudiced against for the very reason I like it, namely that it attracts bees. Yes, it all might be a bit tricky, but we shall see.

Just in the few minutes I took to write this, the sun has been overtaken by clouds, the bright ambient light has gone dull and gray, and the sweet wrens in the pyracantha are trying to get up the courage to go eat the bread I put on the patio table before the greedy and starving squirrels find it. The weather continued to worsen, and then snow started falling in earnest this afternoon. I almost forgot to tie up the skyrocket junipers, which otherwise would have been crushed flat under the heavy wet snow, but I remembered them just in time. When the snow finally stopped, we had two feet of the stuff, a bit too much to call beautiful when I think of all the work it will be to clear it. Afterwards, I beat the trees to free them from their heavy burden of snow and all was well, except that a huge branch was broken out of the crown of our beautiful dogwood in the center of our patio, and the slim and willowy thirty-foot birch in the hedgerow was bent almost double, so that I doubt it will ever be the same again.

Our town actually has a town sledding hill, which descends rather steeply for perhaps 150 yards off of Main Street and is, appropriately, right across the street from the mansion formerly owned by the man who invented the famous Flexible Flyer sled that every American child of my vintage had growing up. When there is a big snow like this one, the whole town turns out on Stokes Hill to go sledding, and the scene is right out of a Norman Rockwell painting. After a day of sledding, we then had a lovely impromptu dinner party at a neighbor's. All very festive, with every house in this historic old town covered in the deep snow and looking like an absurdly romantic, old-fashioned picture postcard.

Switching to the kitchen, I wanted to mention one simple but really nifty thing you can do in winter while waiting patiently for better gardening weather. Recently, we were staying at a high-end resort in Mexico, and at dinner one night, we had garlic mashed potatoes with partially dried cilantro on top of it. The flavor was deliciously intense and so, when we got home, I experimented with it, and here is how you make it.

Dried Cilantro

1 rimmed baking sheet
Baking oil spray
One large bunch of very fresh cilantro, washed and spun or
    patted dry

Pre-heat the oven to 150. Spray a cooking sheet with a very light coat of cooking oil. Arrange the best stems of fresh cilantro on the sheet and dry in the oven for about 30 minutes. You will know when they are done, because the leaves wilt flat against the warm pan and begin to turn a little bit brown. Make several batches. The idea here is to wither the leaves, but not to dry them out entirely. We are trying to intensify the cilantro flavor, not make the rather tasteless dried cilantro you can buy in the spice section of the grocery store. Then you can chop the semi-dried cilantro and store it in the freezer in a plastic bag, to be added later to soups, pastas, and roasted meats. And you can save some nice fans of partially dried cilantro for your own garlic mashed potatoes.

The other thing that was remarkable about this resort is what happened poolside one placid, tropical afternoon in the middle of our visit. The lady four lounge chairs down from me was dozing in the sun during her post-lunchtime siesta when a large, scaly and nasty-looking iguana, probably three feet long from head to tail, crawled up onto her lounge chair, stretched out comfortably along her bare leg, and calmly began eating the remains of her lunch with the air of a practiced connoisseur, while enjoying the warm sunshine, as we all were.

The woman felt something strange brush her leg and woke up to find this giant reptile sharing her lounge chair and…well, let's just say she screamed quite a lot. Several attendants came rushing with towels to capture the iguana, while the lady kept screaming and clambered onto the chaise next to her. Seeing the attendants coming for him with the towels, the iguana went the same direction as the woman and scrambled onto the same chair, giving the poor lady the strong impression she was being pursued by the ruthless iguana. It was all just an inter-species misunderstanding, really, but it caused quite a stir in an otherwise perfectly tranquil afternoon. It was awful; we all had to have several more umbrella drinks before we were able to calm ourselves down again. Still, it was a nice respite from late winter in the Mid-Atlantic States!

Gardening without Chemicals

The American writer Henry Brooks Adams issued the famous dictum: "Chaos was the law of nature; order was the dream of man." And it was the chaos part that we had yesterday, as I awoke to hurricane-force winds in the dark ayem. They blew so ferociously that, after each blast, I would actually cringe with my head under my pillow, waiting for the crash of a towering tree on our roof, and reflect on how nice it is to live in a house made of two-foot-thick granite walls and ribbed with foot-thick New Jersey cedar beams. Then the great winds finally eased up and I ventured timidly outside and it was actually *hot* and humid, which was very disorienting, but I guess accounted for the fierce winds. It was sixty degrees at 8:00 a.m., a temperature that was so shocking that I had to look up the temperature in LA, which was a paltry forty-seven degrees, so sad for them. Then torrential rains commenced, on the cresting waves of which I floated into the city, and it rained furiously all day.

Today, more chaos: we are afflicted by an ice storm. It was cold and raining this morning, on top of last night's light snowfall and last week's more serious leave-behind. It was quite a mess, and the morning commute was atrocious, but the world was beautifully transformed, in that way it is only once or twice every year or two, by a serious ice storm that glosses every twig and bud and branch in creation with an icy lacquer and turns the snow on the ground into a hard coating of frozen marzipan.

It gives the garden an otherworldly shimmer and sheen and picks out every single complex detail in strikingly brilliant relief. It really is quite a new way of seeing altogether. Extreme cold and snow and ice are healthful and useful in the garden, and many bulbs and flowering plants cannot flower and fruit without a requisite number of cold days, so the gardener should glory in the bitter weather, as much as he can bear to, really. It is difficult in life to remember to be thankful for everything you are given, not just the things you want or were hoping for or think you need, and the garden helps us to remember this. Someone once told me that you should live your life as if, when you wake up each morning, all you will have in the world is what you remembered to be thankful for yesterday.

We know that a good hard coat of ice or snow actually protects, rather than hurts, the plants it covers, holding their temperature just at the freezing point and protecting them from the much colder temperatures they might otherwise be killingly exposed to. And yet, the gardener frets and worries and wishes the cold weather away, so perverse are we in our wish to control the elements and have the garden our way, not nature's way.

I once, as a much younger man, thought of having the Adams quote about chaos and order inscribed in stone and placed at the entrance to our garden. It perfectly captured what I then thought of as the way the gardener tries to change, discipline, and improve chaotic nature and wrest from it the orderly, beautiful, and disciplined garden he had in his mind. Which would only ever exist in his orderly mind. I now consider this an absurd and actually rather immature point of view. One of the things I wish someone had told me long ago in my gardening life, and told me in a way that I would believe it despite my pig-headedness and unguided zeal (crosses I continue to bear), is that gardening is not about subduing or even changing nature; it is more about *cooperating* with nature.

If it is not in the nature of a forsythia bush to grow where the gardener would dearly love to have one growing—for example, blazing away in spring in a sulfurous flare of acid yellow to brighten up a dark and shady corner of the garden—then he would be well advised to find another place to put it, where it can flourish in its own way and as nature intended, in sunshine. If the gardener thinks delphiniums are gorgeous but has demonstrated no success with them whatever, which is the case with me, then he should accept the fact that delphiniums are probably not going to be in his life much, and the sooner he accepts that and learns to love foxgloves, which are about the same height, same color range and nearly as gorgeous, the better for all concerned, especially the poor delphiniums.

If I were to carve a motto in stone and put it at the entrance to my garden today, I think it would be a far more simple and modest one: "*Qui plantavit florebit.*" He who has planted will flourish. Especially if he has planted in a way that cooperates with nature rather than seeking to impose his order on the natural world around him.

I cringe now in shame when I think about how enthusiastically my young self tried to change nature and poured out poisons and chemicals on the garden: fertilizers, herbicides, insecticides. I had a curious and inexperienced faith in their efficacy, and a zeal to remake the garden into a sort of chemical perfection. In mitigation of these atrocities, I can only say that at least I only did them when I was very young and foolish. I did many stupid things when I was young and foolish, as who has not, for it is an excellent time to do them.

But I realized fairly soon to be skeptical of the powers of all these chemicals because I could see with my own eyes that they don't work very well. And soon I could see, again just by direct observation, that what in fact does work well is healthy plants growing where and how they ought, in congenial conditions and a healthy rich soil with the right amount of sunlight and water. And gradually I came to be more in tune with the garden and to cooperate more with nature. I learned that the better thing is not to think about what the gardener wants and desires and needs of the garden, but to perceive what the garden wants and needs and desires of the gardener. That is a very different thing altogether. The garden is always teaching; the great thing is for the gardener to begin to learn.

If healthy and holistic gardening is not enough to win you over, perhaps you might consider this: recent research demonstrates that your chances of having Parkinson's disease rise by 47% if you are a frequent user of pesticides. Information like this, plus my growing seriousness about the responsibility of my stewardship for this little plot of ground, changed my view entirely. Now I use no chemicals in the yard (except a bit of fertilizer on the grass out of laziness) and work instead to make sure the soil is healthy and full of natural nutrients. This garden, in a sunny spot in the Mid-Atlantic region with a relatively benign climate for gardening—like England but sunnier—has now been chemical free for over eight years (ever since we came here) and it has been amazing to watch how fast nature heals. Birds flock here in huge numbers and do more to keep the insect pests down than any amount of pesticides. Bees and humming birds, fireflies and butterflies, all particularly sensitive to and repelled by garden chemicals, are in this garden all the time now, and I have often seen nearly a hundred butterflies at a time here: clouds of them in the strong midday sun; they are fantastic. I am thinking of opening a town "butterfly pavilion."

I never have problems any more with common pests like aphids, which are eaten by our luckily numerous ladybugs. I used to be plagued by Japanese beetles, which shredded the canna lilies; now I never see them. The grass is positively lumpy with all the earthworm activity, and if you dig a spadeful of grass up, it is amazing how it teems with worms. Yes, our lawn looks rather seedy and tired in midsummer (we also do not have a sprinkler system, relying on rain and sometimes hoses), and the lawn weeds are extremely tiresome to remove by hand, but I consider it a small price to pay for the glories of yearlong birdsong and the sublime gift of seeing a hundred butterflies at a time in one's garden, or the joy of sitting in the dark on a warm summer night and seeing the charming, magical flicker of fireflies alight all over the garden while the orchestra of cicadas throbs and buzzes.

More important, perhaps, are the interior changes that come over the gardener when he is truly in tune with the garden and is cooperating with it intuitively and holistically. It is the same with faith and grace in the spiritual sphere; these are not two distinct ideas, but the same idea operating the same way and only seeming to be different. But this idea of a spiritual gardener is a truly large idea and something that a stronger mind than mine will need to parse.

The Gardener in Winter

Travel can be treacherous at this time of year, and airport closings and road delays maddening. Even so, since I can't really get my hands dirty in the garden, I don't mind a bit of business travel, especially if it lends itself to a stopover in the west. Last week, I traveled to Seattle, Portland, and Denver on business. In Portland, I woke up on East Coast time, much too early, so I made some strong coffee in my room and quietly sketched out a design for a patio extension we have been thinking about. It's funny how the mind of the gardener can pore over every inch of the garden and its distinctive features, even when three thousand miles away.

Then on to Colorado, where, after my business meetings were over, I went skiing for a day and then took an extra day to drive to Moab, Utah, for some redrock hiking and climbing. I badly needed to get some western topography imprinted on my retinas. In Western Colorado, the peach orchards were all blushing furiously with the rising sap of late February and were getting their winter pruning. My Colorado wildlife sightings included three small herds of white tail deer, a big glossy coyote, a Colorado bighorn sheep (near Georgetown, of course), and two spectacular bald eagles wintering over in De Becque Canyon.

Returning home, I find that the absurd and excessive winter cold persists. We had an icicle hanging off an eave on the north side of the house; it was about eight feet long, and hung all the way down to the ground-floor kitchen window, which was quite amazing. Icicles are a very beautiful aspect of winter, but of course, the reason they are hanging on your house is that you are leaking heat like mad from a poorly insulated house and probably also have roof and gutter drainage problems that you should take care of, so they are not exactly something a fastidious homeowner should be happy to see. But there you are; they are beautiful all the same. Beauty is often associated with trouble, as countless people have noticed to their chagrin through the ages, but I can't really tell you more about that than the troubadour Ricky Martin already did in "Livin' La Vida Loca." And speaking of troubadours, last night, it snowed heavily again and our son and his friend built a huge fire in the fire pit at the foot of the garden, then got their guitars out and played and sang in the blizzard by the blazing fire. Boys are so wonderfully odd.

Inside, by a warm fire of our own, I am reading Penelope Hobhouse's superbly photographed book, *Flower Gardens*; the pages fairly explode with color and Hobhouse's prose is informative, lively, and refreshingly no-nonsense. The book fills my head so full of plans for my own garden that I have had to make a long list of ambitious projects I want to undertake. Most gardeners are prone to these winter fireside reveries and plans. Each fall, I find my list of spring and summer projects, made the previous winter, and am amazed at how much I actually manage to get done in the way of substantial improvements around the place, which all have to happen in addition to all the general run-of-the-mill upkeep and maintenance, indoors and out. We have now lived long enough in this garden that I finally feel I have accomplished a lot—though of course it never ends—and I am starting to see some maturity and execution in my plans. Satisfying, that.

And so, inspired to bestir myself and get some garden projects under way, I put my spring foxglove seeds (the flowers will be pale pink) in the fridge today for five weeks of chilling before I plant them indoors on windowsills on April 1st. We are finally having a sunny and rather mild day every so often, which should melt quite a lot of our remaining snow, this mini ice age now looking like thick and rather dirty marzipan encrusting everything. I cut the buddleia way back and cut down the few remaining phloxes and the raspberry canes and then got a little aggressive with the very overgrown honeysuckle in the back corner of the yard behind the footbridge. It had been bowed down over the sidewalk by heavy snow, and when I started cutting it back, I noticed it had invaded and was smothering a big and very ancient box tree, so I cut it out of that, and how magnificent that old box now looks. By its size, it is very venerable and must have been here ages.

I was at the hardware store last weekend and saw they had beautiful white lilies ('Casa Blanca') for sale, so despite my decided lack of success with lilies, I decided to try again. The only really successful ones I have ever had were here before we bought the place and I am pretty sure our highly efficient rabbits finally got them last year. I bought the 'Casa

Blancas' and am raising them first in pots this spring, at least until they get far enough along to be put out in the cruel garden to try their luck in life. Parenting runs on very similar principles, and it is never easy either. As for the white lilies, how great it would be to have armfuls of these stunning creatures, as in my imagination, of course, I already do.

In birding news, while walking Cosimo around the golf course, I heard an owl hoot in a neighbor's yard, at 3:00 p.m. surprisingly, and saw the first blue jay of the year. And during the heavy snowfall last week, I watched hundreds of robins feasting in the holly tree and flying to the gutter for sips of water, each one leaving a tiny puff of snow as it exploded out of the holly. What a show; I watched for ages! These robins continue to feast on the rapidly dwindling bounty of holly berries, trying to eke out a living in winter until the proteinaceous earthworms are available again, which they soon will be. One of the joys of not using chemicals in the garden is that earthworm populations rapidly explode, doing many good things for the garden and rejoicing the local bird population. It's all good.

Indoors, we are making brunch more interesting, and after lots of experimentation with adapting pasta for the breakfast table, we have come up with this easy and delicious dish that we call simply Bacon and Egg Pasta. Add a peach Bellini and it's a party!

Bacon and Egg Pasta

16 strips good quality bacon
½ medium onion, diced
2 garlic cloves, peeled and finely minced
30-40 cherry or grape tomatoes
¾ cup heavy cream
1/3 cup grated *parmigiano reggiano*
Salt and pepper

16 oz. spaghetti pasta

2 Tbsp. chopped fresh chives for garnish

8 whole eggs

1 Tbsp. vinegar

1 tsp. salt

Fry the bacon until it is slightly crispy, but still juicy. Transfer to drain on paper towel. When cool, chop 8 strips bacon into a quarter inch dice and set aside. Leave the other 8 slices whole. Reserve 2 Tbsp. bacon grease. Brown the onion and garlic in the bacon grease. When they are golden, add the tomatoes and continue cooking until about one third of the tomatoes burst. Turn heat to very low, add the cream and the cheese, and stir until the cheese melts. Add the diced bacon. Season to taste with salt and pepper. Turn heat off and leave pan on the warm stovetop.

Put eight whole eggs in a saucepan, cover with at least one inch of cold water; add the vinegar and the salt (they prevent cracking, make the eggs easier to peel, and prevent the white from leaking if the eggs do crack). Bring to a boil, watched closely. The second the water begins to boil, turn the heat down, so the water boils gently for a steady count of exactly 180. To get the slightly runny egg you want for the finished product, it is important to start with a precisely three-minute boiled egg. With a slotted spoon, transfer the eggs to a bowl of cool water; run cool tap water over them, the idea being to stop the cooking process. Then very gently peel them, taking care to keep the eggs as whole as possible. Make a few extra the first time, until you get the hang of handling them, as they are wobbly and break easily.

Cook the pasta *al dente*. Toss the pasta with the cream sauce. Divide the pasta into four pasta bowls. Put two strips of bacon and two soft-boiled eggs on top of each dish of pasta, then garnish with the chives. Serves 4. We never said this was healthy, merely that it is delicious. We can't be angels every day, after all.

March

Rêve du Jardin Bleu

Our world is far from perfect, in case you haven't already noticed this. One of its most lamentable shortcomings, for example, is the lack of the color blue in our gardens. It does not seem to have been a color greatly favored by evolution, possibly because louder colors are more stimulating to pollinators: bats, birds, bees, moths, and so on. But I have not gone into the science of the matter deeply, as I have troubles enough of my own to contend with.

Where we do manage to have blue in our gardens, its pale, cool elegance tends to get lost in competition with the more intense hues of yellows and reds and whites, and in the general greenness of the garden landscape. How lovely it would be to have a garden all in blue, the way some gardeners manage a garden all in white. Well, not all in blue, exactly, as the original Garden Designer chose green to be the color of chlorophyll and we are more or less stuck with that as the background color of foliage, but how lovely it would be to have a garden where all, or most of, the flowers are blue and where they bloom strongly throughout the growing months.

In this dream of the blue garden, we might have to admit a very little bit of violet into our blues to increase the plant choices we can work with, because there is very little in the garden palette that is truly and purely blue. So we would not want to be absolutists about it. Most serious, steady gardeners are not absolutists about much of anything, because one thing gardening quickly teaches you is that absolutism and gardening do not really go very well together. Try it for yourself if you doubt the wisdom of this; you will soon be converted to a more sensible way of proceeding. Rules about planting and tending gardens are heavily qualified with "it depends" clauses, as every gardener knows, and rules must give way to the tastes and habits (good and bad, often very bad indeed) of individual gardeners.

I find it nearly impossible, inexplicably, to transplant poppies, but perhaps these are the easiest things in the world for you. I grow a happy little fig tree in a climate zone where that is supposed to be completely impossible and I don't know why I succeed with it, but I do. And sometimes the reverse corollary is also true. And then there is the notion, widely accepted as dogma by the ignorant, that beauty is in the eye of the beholder. What perfect nonsense. While allowing for differences in taste—I may prefer dahlias while you perhaps prefer chrysanthemums—every gardener knows that a rose is just inherently more beautiful than a marigold and that is never going to change. So you can put that in your pipe and smoke it, if you have nothing better.

Anyway, as I was saying, we would much better admit a little bit of violet in our blue dream in exchange for a broader palette of plants to work with. But we must be a *little* strict here; there is no need to go hog-wild for purple, nor would that work well. So let's admit some violet in the bluish form of, say, a clematis or a buddleia, but exclude the more purple shades of blue in a crocus or a lilac. We will still have plenty to work with and it will be much more, well, *blue*. And I also think this a good place to say that we should think about some other exceptions to the blue rule to enhance its overall blue-ness. For example, a pure white iris here and there and a 'Blanc Double de Coubert' rose or two would greatly intensify the overall effect of the bloom of the blue irises, and a bit of pale yellow would do the same, and a little of both would be best of all. No less a color authority than Vincent van Gogh laid down this dictum: "There is no blue without yellow and without orange." I do not think I can go as far with him as orange, but yellow certainly. Just a very little bit is all we will need, but the overall effect will be so much more satisfying than all blues, which would otherwise run the rather obvious risk of monomania. Or boredom.

So let us begin with carpets of the true blue pansies and muscari in March. They should smother a lot of bare ground with a blue coverlet to rejoice the eye as winter gives way reluctantly to spring. This is the great month also for chionodoxa, whose hues of blues are very refreshing and true. A neighbor of ours has a large bed of brilliant white daffodils thickly under-planted with chionodoxa, and what a great and successful pairing this is. Spanish bluebells should ring throughout the blue garden in April, likewise the much tinier bells and very intense blue of hyacinths.

April would be a great time to try to arrange two things to bloom together—jacarandas and agapanthus—if you are lucky enough to live in a suitably mild climate where both can grow and you are skilled enough to bring them into bloom at the same time. I once saw a venerable old jacaranda growing on one of Buenos Aires' broad, handsome boulevards and in brilliant blue bloom (well okay, blue-violet really) on a sunny spring day. It was heavily under-planted with simultaneously blooming agapanthus, the lovely creature also called the lily of the Nile, in exactly the same shade of blue-violet, and what a stunning effect it was. I was terribly late for a business meeting from having stopped too long to admire this vision, and had to make up some lame story about having lost my way. It's just not very businesslike, you see, to say you were late because you were admiring the jacarandas. The jacarandas of Los Angeles and Mexico City and elsewhere enlighten a spring visit with their other-worldly violet bloom, like a fantastic tree growing on Venus. They look gorgeous standing alone, even at the side of a busy highway. And the agapanthus will go on jetting its blue fountains in our dream garden for much of the summer, long after the jacaranda's display is finished and it subsides into arboreal ordinariness.

May would be the time to concentrate on irises, a plant that comes in almost all imaginable colors, but whose specialty is surely the blue and purple tones; so recruit heavily from the blue registers here, and pair it with the more blue forms of salvia, which will go on faithfully blooming for much of the summer. Columbines too will be at their best at this time, and some of the most fresh and vigorous of them are the blues. At the end of the iris season, the *Iris pallida variegata* will be in fine form, with its handsome pale and pure blue flowers borne on tall stalks and set off by its distinctive cream and light-green sword leaves.

As the irises begin to slow down in June, other gardeners will have surfeited themselves with peonies and will now be glorying in their roses, but none of them for us (except perhaps the white and pale yellow accents mentioned already). But we will have our blue compensations. This is a great time for delphiniums, and their classic colors are the intense blue ones, both dark and light. I have already confessed my lifetime of failure with this plant, so I cannot have them even in a dream garden (he says with some bitterness), but you, of course, are not limited in this way, and are probably a better person too, so knock yourself out.

The rare and famously difficult Himalayan blue poppy would be in its glory now too, so feel free to include that in your dream, but I do not recommend trying to grow them in reality. They've rightly earned their reputation for being difficult to grow, but you can try it if you like, or dare. Gardeners will always rise to foolish challenges like this, of course, but you will very likely find, like the rest of us, that it was a waste of time, money, and garden space after all. Much easier would be the *Baptisia australis*, which grows like the weed it is and flowers like mad in June, and it is a very true blue. When I was a boy, living in Australia for a while, I used to be enchanted by these wild weeds. They covered great swaths of paddock and pasturage in the countryside with vivid blue and were extremely picturesque, though of course a great burden and curse for the poor farmer. In our dream garden, they can take the place of phlox, and supply blue instead of the phlox's purple and pink.

Then, as summer kicks into high gear, the blue garden comes into its own in very interesting ways and can even out-perform a less restricted garden, with so many blue-flowering plants that can sustain their blooms through most of the long months of midsummer. Imagine dark blue clematis climbing in the garden trees, and a sky-blue morning glory on a tall tuteur in full sun. At the back of the garden, the lighter blue varieties of buddleia may be grown, with the long-blooming blue forms of Russian sage in the middle, along with great blobs of blue from hydrangeas and spires of a variety of blues from lupines. In front would be scabiosa, simple cornflowers, and nigella, with lots of petunias in multiple blue shades. All this at once would verge on the tedious, so you see the virtue of allowing a bit of pure white and pale yellow here and there, to relieve the eye and intensify the blue effect.

In late summer, the palette thins out a bit, and you are going to have to fall back on things like cardoons and lots and lots of asters crammed in everywhere, with long-blooming hydrangeas to fill in the gaps. Also, in late summer, the blue focus can shift more to foliage. We can't really achieve blue foliage, of course, but we can suggest that effect with glaucous, gray-blue foliage. This blue garden of ours should have blue spruces, for example, the tall forms in back and the dwarf forms in the middle. Think how well a Russian olive would look in the overall blue haze, and the columnar forms of blue junipers would provide the right structural notes of uprightness, elegance, and solidity. In the foreground, the very beautiful, soft gray leaves of stachys would look well, and so would the blue-leaved members of the hosta family. You could allow or disallow the hostas' white or purple flowers as you like; for myself, I would allow them, as I am a fairly indulgent and grateful gardener and cutting off flowers because of a fantasy color scheme is not in my nature.

And having gone this far, we might as well go whole hog and build a small water feature in the sunny center of this blue garden, planting it of course with pale blue water lilies. At each of the four corners, we would have to have statuesque, sculptural blue agaves for accents. We would keep the pond clean and carefully heated to a delightful temperature, and stock it with vivid blue Siamese fighting fish. They would not of course have to fight, the poor dears. Remember, this is a fantasy, not a practical garden plan. And on really special days, when guests came over to tour this marvel of blue, we would bring our spectacular blue Brazilian macaw outside into the garden on his tall wooden perch to complete the picture. Okay, perhaps the macaw and the blue fish are a bit much, but the point of the exercise is to go deep into a color within your mind and to try to aim for a more profound color instinct when planning a garden or part of a garden.

"A color of blue reigns here that elsewhere is but a dream."
—Colette

Returning to reality from this gorgeous dream of a blue garden, I find the real garden quite boringly different. We have only a fortnight of winter left and already poor old winter seems to have given up the ghost. It is going to be nearly seventy and sunny today and tomorrow. I notice that the few daffodils already open in our garden, in pure chromatic yellow with big flowers and sturdy trumpets, have a faint, sweet scent, exactly like what a newly-opened jar of honey smells like. As I leave for work each morning, the yard is teeming with birdlife, and I see several pairs of wrens busily checking out the small birdhouses we have put about the place. For a few years, I have been buying four or five of them each year and placing them high up in our many trees, so now we have something like twenty of them and most are used once or even twice a year.

Today, I am in Washington for business and, from the hotel where I am staying, you can just make out a cherry tree blooming inside the palings of the White House fence under the stern gaze of Mr. Hamilton's statue on the south piazza of the Treasury, and it is at least three weeks early. On the north piazza, there are two large *Magnolia soulangeanas* in full bloom, so *that* makes me feel spring is really here.

Unseen Sunrise, Physic Garden

Sometimes, I find, dreams really do come true. We have just returned from a short spring break in Colorado to find spring here surprisingly and agreeably far along. A solid week of very mild, even warm, weather has caused the flowering trees to explode all at once into color, and whole trees have hung out their unfurled leaves by the millions around our town. It is a dream of spring, a fantasy of verdure. It was no less an authority than Jane Austen who opined: "To sit in the shade on a fine day and look upon verdure is the most perfect refreshment." It is hard to improve upon that, insofar as an appreciation of verdure is concerned. The hostas on the patio are not only up but are also unfurled, in their clean light green, and the tulips are blooming suddenly with the daffodils in cheerful confusion. How I love this time of year, when every day brings to the eye new delights of color, beauty, and renewed life.

One of the first things I did upon our return was to take Cosimo for a long walk around town, just to see what was new. The most remarkable thing I saw was in the front yard of a very unprepossessing house a few blocks from us, with nothing much to distinguish itself except this: a two-story-tall, ten-foot-wide camellia, by far the largest I have ever seen, completely smothered in huge, fist-sized, clear pink flowers, all at the height of perfection. It stopped me in my tracks, and I had to just stand there and marvel at it. We need M. Renoir at a time like this, to paint such a glorious specimen. If I had seen the proud homeowner, I would have suggested they sell tickets for people to come and look at it. It was a stupendous sight and, though we have lived here a long time, I had never noticed it before; I suppose because I had never happened to walk down this street at just this time of year, when its beauty was pitched at its greatest height. And it got me to thinking about perfection in the garden; how constantly we gardeners aim for it and how consistently our efforts fall short of the mark. But it is the aiming that is important, and sometimes a beauty of this kind of perfection graces a simple home with all its effortless bliss to make us realize that perfection, whether planned or not (usually not, in my experience), can sometimes even happen in earthly gardens. Though briefly.

While in Colorado, we stayed at the grand old resort of The Broadmoor. Up very early one mild morning, I slipped outside and found a quiet seat in the manicured grounds of this gorgeous old property, perfect in their own stately and rather mannered way, where I could read my book. I was so absorbed in it that I did not hear a beautiful doe step quietly through the shrubbery at my elbow on a morning quest for tender shoots to nibble. And she did not see me until the same moment I saw her. She stepped silently through the shrubbery not ten feet from me. We made eye contact and her initial alarm changed slowly to composure, and she went on about her browsing errand. I watched her, enchanted, and she kept an eye warily on me.

The resort is situated in the foothills behind Colorado Springs, and I knew the sun would rise on the eastern plains below just at 6:57 a.m., because I had seen it do so the day before. Perhaps two minutes before that sunrise, you could see the rosy glow of the sunrise already illuminating the top of Pike's Peak, the 14,000 peak atop which "America, the Beautiful" was composed, though the sun had not yet come up enough to be seen at the elevation I was standing at (perhaps 6,000 feet). It was a sort of pre-sunrise, or as I named it to myself, The Unseen Sunrise. But then, in just a minute or two, the sun rose fully out on the eastern plains and its rays lit up the whole world that I could see, uniting its light and dark portions into one lit entirety. Things like this are what you get to see if you are lucky enough to get up early, when the day is still quietly gathering its resources and is just beginning. Just like spring itself, this time of day fills you with wonder at the unraveling freshness and potential of it all.

The Unseen Sunrise has been a peaceful interior memory, and one I have needed for my peace of mind lately. Recently, I visited a friend who had the misfortune to be laid up in the intensive care unit of a large local hospital, not the sort of place you want to be in for very long. Certainly not as a patient, and not so much as a visitor either. Anyone who has spent days in a hospital worrying about a loved one, as most of us will do sooner or later, knows the great sorrow of this vigil and how worrying and wearing it is. Of course, it is even harder for the main sufferer, who is there as the patient.

But I was intrigued by this hospital because it was innovatively built around a large, glassed-in rooftop garden visible from many vantage points inside the hospital and accessible through large glass doors on all four sides. It was called "The Healing Garden" and was reminiscent of a time long ago, when the only medicine that was available came from the family garden in the form of herbal remedies and folk medicines. Then, such gardens were called physic gardens.

Humans have always known that plants have the power to heal the body, mind, and spirit. Long before modern medicines were invented, we had only plants to help us through the great adversities of life – childbirth, all the aches and pains and the thousand tribulations that flesh is heir to, and finally disease and death. In most cultures, it was the womenfolk who raised the plants and studied the herbs that were their families' only medicine. Only our wives and our mothers, with their folk medicine and healing plants, were there for us in the dark watches of the night. Many were the folklore medications that were inefficacious; they were only balms to the troubled and fearful spirit, but still, they were a comfort in a world that held no other.

But there were also real medical marvels that are with us still. The quinine tree (*cinchona*) of the tropical Andes gave us a cure for malaria. Acetylsalicylic acid, commonly called aspirin, comes from the bark of the common willow. The miracle cancer cure Taxol comes from the yew tree (*taxus*). Echinacea, the humble coneflower, gives us a powerful herbal antibiotic and immune booster, and so does the herb goldenseal. Digitalis to cure many heart ailments comes from ordinary foxgloves. Many soothing herbs provide wonderful teas and infusions: valerian, lemon verbena, mint, and chamomile. Red yeast rice is a natural statin. Humble turmeric eases depression. Tea, tobacco, and coffee provide wonderful stimulants, while opium poppies, hemp and marijuana provide psychotropic effects, intoxicants and critical palliative care for serious pain, and I could go on and on. Modern scientists are exploring ever more exotic plants in the search for new compounds to help bolster the storehouse of modern medicine, ensuring that this list will only grow longer.

Plants have intertwined their evolutionary history with our own, randomly producing miraculous chemical compounds that we have found and adapted to our own uses and needs. But who is using whom in this chemical interdependency and mutual manipulation? It is symbiosis on an epochal, global scale.

But back to the hospital garden I was talking about. It also grew healing herbs, each with its own small placard explaining its use and efficacy in early medicine. In the center of the garden was a large and splashy water feature, where the sound of running water and the beauty of darting goldfish could soothe the frazzled nerves and harried minds of worried and distressed family members. This pleasant garden teemed with flowers as well, and their scents and fresh colors rejoiced the eye and reminded the anxious visitor that life is beautiful after all, and full of hopeful possibility.

One of my favorite features of this hospital garden was an area marked off as a "scent garden." In it grew aromatic plants like rosemary, sage, geranium, mint, basil, lemon verbena, lavender, and even a small piñon tree. Visitors were invited and encouraged to pick greenery from this garden and enjoy the soothing scents, and to share them with the patients they were visiting. Everywhere we saw people who, though they were seriously ill, were holding little sprigs of fragrant greenery as they were wheeled about in wheelchairs, or they had these sprigs on their bedside tables or windowsills. It was charming, and I marveled at the humane and loving talent behind this thoughtful design. Each little sprig was a sign of hope, a shoot of faith: that life is good, life is strong, health and vigor will return, life will go on.

Every hospital, every place where people are seriously ill, should be built on this excellent, reassuring, and life-affirming principle. The sound of water splashing, the sight of sunlight flickering on growing and blooming plants, the fragrance of sun-warmed herbs or the Christmas tree memory of a twig from a piñon tree—these all remind us that healing is more complicated and more holistic than mere modern medicine admits.

Intimations of Spring

The flowers will bloom again and there may or may not be bluebirds over the white cliffs of Dover, but there are bluebirds in our reading room, because we found some beautiful and realistic bluebird candles, of all things, at a local store and have them nestled in a pot of orchids.

But flowers do bloom again, in real life and eventually, no matter how harsh the winter, and my eagle eyes were rewarded yesterday when, driving home with my daughter from the farm where her horse boards, I saw a large patch, about the size of our dining room table, of snowdrops blooming on the side of the road out in the country. My heart leapt up, and I guess there is hope in the world after all. My daughter had wanted Cosimo and me to come to her barn and play with Chico, the new horse she is leasing, so we did, and I sat in the strong sunshine on the deck outside the barn, burning my face in the delicious sun while she got him tacked up. Then she and a friend rode their horses, while Cosimo and I walked to the cross-country field, and Cosimo was deliriously happy to be on a walk and off his leash. He chased geese and jumped some of the low jumps, and his eyes were bright with joy, as indeed mine were. It was high fifties Saturday, sixty yesterday, and already forty-eight at 8:30 today, so South Jersey is going fairly nuts with the sun and warmth, literally our first really mild days since October, I believe.

I spent most of Saturday in the yard, and what a treat it was to be out doing things in the garden again. First I picked up quite a lot of storm debris and branches knocked down by our four heavy snowfalls, then I minutely weeded the porch bed, using imaginary tweezers, in fact, where some crafty winter weeds were already flowering. The wicked things. Then I quickly pruned the grapes and roses, and also the cherry, forsythia and peach, bringing two large bunches of cut fruitwood indoors to force them into bloom. How great it is, when you are starved for the sight and smell of blooms, to have a giant spray of forsythia in one room and another giant spray of fragrant peach and cherry blossom in another. The simple joys of the garden, as is true of most things in life, are the best—a lesson we have to learn over and over again in life, until one day, after about five hundred repetitions, it occurs to us that perhaps that is significant in some way. Well duh, as the young people say. The Christmas red camellia, I note, has two flower buds, its first after having been in the ground two years now, and I hope, no doubt unreasonably, to have a camellia bloom for me before I die. Is that too much to ask? Quite likely it is.

One day last week, I showered, shaved and dressed and was ready to go to work, but then realized that my computer was being switched out and I had no appointments at the office, so I stayed home instead. Impromptu vacation! I went to the hardware store and picked up the split, six-paneled door I had ordered for the linen closet and spent most of the day knocking out some of the panels and carefully replacing them with six leaded glass panels I found inexpensively online. I completed one door Friday and the other Saturday, and then painted them Sunday, and they turned out very well. I am not a very brilliant carpenter, but I find I can do pretty good work if I go slowly and think carefully about what I am doing. Which is hard for me, as I am usually in a great hurry; this is another simple lesson I have had to learn over and over again, in my general obtuseness.

While I was working at this carpentry in the garage, I had to chuckle, remembering ruefully a time many years ago when I was doing a similar woodworking job with my son, then only five or so. He was helping me with some interest, and I let him carefully measure out some of the boards we were cutting. He wanted to handle the saw, but I told him I had better do that, as it was a bit dangerous. He was pensive for a while as I continued to work, then he said:

"Dad, when I am a man, I hope I will have a son."

"I hope so too, honey; it is a great thing for a man to have a son."

"And when I do, I hope he will do jobs like this with me, just like we are."

"Yes, I hope so too; that would be very nice. Fathers and sons should work together; it's important."

Then after a pause came the devastating kicker: "And I will let *my* son measure *and* cut."

Well, I had to stop a moment there and think. This was a mild but deserved rebuke. Of course, I let him use the saw from then on and he did fine. We think we are teaching our children, but sometimes our children teach us, as every parent knows.

Back to the quickening garden. I started re-painting the wooden growing frames that give much structure to the crescent bed, and generally I enjoyed pottering about musingly in the freshening garden. Around town, I notice snowdrops everywhere, and now quite a few crocuses as well. At a friend's house this weekend, I saw winter-blooming jasmine and a witch hazel in bloom for the first time. The glories of spring are nearly here, and the hungry heart is so ready.

On Saturday night at 10:00 p.m., we sat out in the crook of the house between the porch and the patio, having a glass of wine under a nearly full moon and imagining what our new patio area there will be like. On a walk this weekend, we saw a neighbor with a dinner plate-sized patch of purple crocuses open. In the house, we have a huge vase of black-green yew branches and redtwig dogwood that has just sprouted its tender, bright green leaves. There is not much going on in the yard yet, though tiny tips are poking up everywhere. I planted fourteen lilies in the side yard. *That* ought to give me enough lilies around the place to keep me from mooing about them so pitifully. There is lots of cutting down and weeding left to do, and only the crescent bed and porch bed look really tidy, but oh well. Life is long, I find.

Daffodil Gluttony

Gluttony, we are warned, is a deadly sin, and yet the gardener proceeds merrily and at his mortal peril to lust for a glut of whatever floral creature has enchanted him for the moment, even at the risk of his everlasting soul, as if going off your head for a flower were a charmingly forgivable eccentricity. It is not, either in heaven or here on earth, and is to be generally discouraged. Unless nothing else works, and it's absolutely necessary!

For me, just now, it is daffodils and tulips and this is, of course, their great time. Last fall, knowing this fever would come upon me (as it does every year, unfailingly), I went to a big-box retailer and bought a huge sack of mixed daffodils, every variety imaginable except for the big bold yellows and whites that I already have plenty of. These I stuck in everywhere I thought they might be able to bloom. And now they are all blooming, and what a joy it is to see the wide range of forms and colors they come in. I was mad not to indulge this mania before. What was I thinking? Yesterday evening, I trotted about the yard with my scissors, happily cutting a huge bouquet of dozens of daffodils, almost every one different from the others. Then I just sat and admired them, like a greedy old Silas Marner, gloating darkly over his miser's hoard of secret gold.

Satiety is sometimes the only cure for gluttony, though to be sure, I speak in a floral and not a theological sense. And daffodil satiety is a wonderful thing. Other than yesterday – when I sat gazing avidly at their diversity, besotted—I have only experienced it a few times in my life. I have often been in London on business in March, when the daffodils are at their height, and remember many long runs in Hyde Park, where the daffodils are strewn about for miles. Another time, I was on the Island of Guernsey in the Channel Islands with a friend at, of course, the same time of year, and we discovered that Guernsey farmers grow millions of daffodil bulbs for the English market, and saw even more acres of them spread out as far as the eye could see. And that finally cured me. But just for that year.

I go nuts for tulips this time of year too, as who does not. They are popping up all over our garden now, and I never get over how greatly they rejoice the eye. My favorites, I guess, are the "broken" Rembrandt tulips, the yellow and red ones especially. Or a large vase crammed with a pairing of greenish-white viridiflora tulips and pale pink tulips is a spectacular combination. I also have a section of the garden where I have planted dark red tulips and tulips of so very dark a purple that they look almost black, for a big dramatic wash of red and black tulip drifts.

I know a farmer in Western Colorado who ingeniously turned his own mania for dahlias into cold, hard cash. He is called The Dahlia Rancher locally because he so loves this flower that he has turned his entire working farm into a dahlia farm. He has acres and acres of them, and they are gorgeous. He grows them in a very specific way: he pinches off all the growing stems but one, forcing the plant to put all its energy into this single stalk, which he supports with a tall stake. Then he pinches off all the flower buds but one, forcing the plant again to channel all its floral energy into a single bloom. The result is a solitary, enormous, dinner-plate-sized flower that is really quite amazing to see. He carefully harvests these in great numbers, and then drives around to all the expensive resorts in Western Colorado—Telluride, Crested Butte, Aspen, Vail, Keystone, Breckenridge, Steamboat Springs, and so on— and sells these astonishing blooms to the resort hotels and restaurants, who will pay any price for them. As I would, if I won the lottery!

One last thing. March is the month we think of leeks in the garden, of course, because March 1st is the feast day of St. David of Wales (the saint whose name I share, which is why I care about this), and March should not be allowed to end without honoring him. On March 1st every year, every proud Welshman and woman goes around with a leek pin on their lapel (actual leeks in the old days), a charming tradition largely not followed now by Welsh Americans. But here, we can at least put the humble but delicious (and remarkably easy to grow) leek to good use in the kitchen, by using it to fortify a really good butternut squash soup.

Butternut Squash Soup

For the croutons:
½ loaf of French bread
4 Tbsp. butter
½ tsp. salt
½ tsp. freshly ground black pepper
½ tsp. cayenne pepper

For the soup:
Olive oil
6 lbs. butternut squash (3 medium gourds)
4 Tbsp. butter
1 carrot, peeled and chopped
2 leeks, split, washed, and chopped
2 stalks of celery, washed and chopped
½ yellow onion, peeled and chopped
2 firm apples (Honey Crisp preferred), peeled, cored, and sliced
1 Tbsp. chopped fresh rosemary leaves
10 cups chicken or vegetable stock

½ cup cream

1 tsp. salt

½ tsp. freshly ground nutmeg

½ tsp. freshly ground black pepper

8 Tbsp. sherry (optional)

Pre-heat oven to 450. Cut or tear the French bread into one-inch cubes, not smaller, and put them in a large bowl. (Tip: double the crouton recipe and freeze half; they are great to have on hand.) Toast the croutons in the hot oven, turning once, until they are toasted and dry. Melt the butter and combine with the salt, pepper, and cayenne; in a medium-sized bowl, toss the spiced butter with the bread and put aside. Oil a baking sheet with olive oil. Peel the squashes and cut them in half lengthwise. Remove the seeds and cut the squashes into one-inch sections, then roast them for 45 minutes or until tender. (Alternative: cut the squashes in half and seed them, then roast them like this, cut sides up; afterwards, cut their peels off. Either way is a bit labor intensive.)

In a large stock pot, add the butter and the next five ingredients and cook them slowly over a medium heat, covered and stirring occasionally, until they are tender, about 15 minutes. Add the squash, rosemary, and stock and bring to a boil. Then turn the heat down and simmer uncovered for 15 minutes. Puree the soup in a food processor in batches, and return it to the stock pot. Add the cream, then season with salt and pepper to taste. After pouring into soup bowls, add a handful of the spicy croutons and pour 1 Tbsp. of sherry into each bowl. Serves 8. And save a bit of the leaf from a leek to pin on your lapel!

$\mathcal{A}pril$

April Tools Day

Now begins the busy season in the garden, when much needs to be done to make the high-season months of May and June the best they can be. Any structural or building work can be done now, while the garden is still partially dormant. It is also a good time to move plants, before the jolt of spring growth begins. For those of us who put the garden to bed last fall in a less than pristine condition (pretty much all of us, I would suppose), now is the time to add a thorough weeding to the general spring cleanup. Or else we will soon come to regret it, as we have all learned from bitter experience. Especially be on the lookout for dandelions and get the crabgrass preventer down in time (when the forsythia is blooming, is the traditional way to remember this).

But it is also the time to think about the condition of the garden tools. Well really, you should have done that (I say you) last fall, or in the garage on a bitter winter day, but better late than never. Probably only Martha Stewart has her garden tools perfect when autumn draws to an end, and she no doubt has a staff of fifty on her wonderful Connecticut estate to help her get all the work done. I only have a dog, and I don't like him to handle sharp implements, so I must do it myself whenever I get the chance. Many of us work for a living outside the garden or have otherwise very complicated lives with little help. I am sure Ms. Stewart goes to her special tool-sharpening shed at the foot of her lovely garden on the first really sharp day of autumn, fires up her antique forge for making replacement spare parts, and has all of her garden tools stripped, cleaned, sharpened, rebuilt and better than new by the end of the day, and long before her hundred guests arrive for a sumptuous autumn celebration and photo shoot for a magazine layout. But we mere mortals have to get these chores done whenever we get a spare moment, and if we get them done at all before the spring is fully afoot, we are feeling pretty much like the cat that got the canary. This is not to run down Ms. Stewart, who is a marvel and an admirable force of nature in the design world, but most of us common folk simply cannot run our lives at that pitch of perfection.

Gardeners, we know, are very particular about their tools; at least the serious ones are. Most of us have lots of garden tools, but only a few that we think of as really essential. You could take away all but two of mine, and I could still be pretty effective in my garden. I would insist on keeping my simple hand shears and my garden trowel, and would be quite lost without either of them. Some people prefer a long hoe, so they can work upright in the garden, but I find I have to creep through the garden on all fours and really get right down in amongst it to see what is going on and to be thoroughly effective. I have sliced off far too many peony shoots, up-coming tulips, lilies, and the like with a hoe to want to work upright.

I would recommend buying the stoutest garden trowel and the most durable (that does not mean fancy or complicated, but rather solid and functional) hand shears you can find, as one uses them incessantly. Yes, these can be expensive, but money spent here is well worth it, else you will be replacing them over and over again during a long life in the garden. The shears need to be kept clean and oiled, and it is wise to take them apart and sharpen them as well a couple of times during the summer. A rainy day when you can't get outside anyway is the best time to do this, and provides an excellent defense against the possibility of being dragooned into unwelcome household chores. Such domestic obligations, imposed by members of the household always on high alert for signs of a gardener's availability, can detract shockingly from the time that would be better spent in the garden. The same can be said about daytime jobs in town, of course.

In addition to these two essentials, the trowel and the shears, I go about everywhere with a bucket, for hauling water, manure, and compost and for moving plants, filling with weeds, etc. Isn't it amazing how much utility you can get from the couple of bucks a good bucket costs? Very few things (cement, bricks, and good twine are other wonderful examples) give as much value or satisfaction for the price. I am easily pleased—a very winning characteristic overall, I think—and I love my bucket with a devotion and simple-mindedness that is quite idiotic. Indeed, it is the subject of much drollery and facetious comment in my household and among my extended family, but my bucket and I pay it no mind. Another hand tool I like is an Asian hand hoe, which is sort of a trowel, hoe, and rake all in one, depending on how you use it. I also love a hand tool that has a hatchet-like blade on one end and a three-tine rake or fork on the other; this is good for breaking up harder soil and cultivating around plants.

I keep a stout old steak knife in the tool shed, very dull now, which I use for excising difficult weeds; it is perfect for stabbing underground to get below the growth node on dandelions, for example. It does give innocent passersby a bit of a fright to see me all muddy and crazed looking, creeping about the shrubbery with a bloody great steak knife, but there you are. Serves them right for peeping in my garden. I use the old-fashioned grass clippers to trim grass around plants when getting really close with a power trimmer is simply too dangerous, and nothing gives the lawn a crisply barbered edge like this tool, though of course it is tedious work. It would be nice to get some of the teenagers about the place to take this chore over, but there is only so much teenage brow-beating a parent can stand; after a while, it is a bit like throwing pebbles at Mt. Rushmore and you just give up. Discretion being the better part of valor, and all that. I like a nice square shovel for edging lawns, but for most serious digging, I prefer a regular old spade. Spend some money here and get one with a good solid shaft of hardened ash, or you will just be replacing it every year as you snap them in your excavating zeal. You can guess how I know this.

Some tools just resonate more with gardeners than others, and I think this is true of male gardeners in particular. One of my prize possessions, for example, is a very old adjustable wrench that my father's father worked with in his job in an automobile factory nearly a century ago. The Japanese used to believe, perhaps they still do, that tools take on an animating spirit after they have been lovingly used for about a hundred years. This wrench is very solid and well made, still in perfect condition, and I love the fact that my grandfather long ago scratched his name on it, so no fellow worker would make off with it. I have a memory of him, when he must have been near seventy and I was just a boy, working with me and my dad, digging fence holes on a hot summer day in Colorado. He explained to me that the secret to being productive at physical labor was setting a pace you could sustain all day, and then working steadily at that pace. And I watched this old man work all day in the blazing sun, digging fence holes and stopping only for hot coffee; it was the way the old Danes used to do it, he said, on the theory that the hot coffee made them feel cooler.

I have a picture from years later of my father, old then too but before his health began to fail him. That day, he was helping me move a huge pile of dirt in one of my former gardens and explaining to my own son, who would have been about four then and who adored him, how to rest on your shovel the way real-life ditch diggers do it. He crossed his wrists over the top of the shovel's shaft, put his chin down on his crossed hands, and lifted one booted foot onto the top of the spade-head as if it were the foot-rail in a bar. My son copied him with his boy's shovel, and the picture I have is of the two of them standing there, resting from their labors.

Good tools are extensions of ourselves; they are the way we touch and shape and change the garden, and care for it throughout the year. It is all right to have a bit of a worshipful cult about your garden tools. They are interpretive and expressive of the special relationship that exists between you and the garden. Also, they have magic and spirit in them; you can just feel it.

Drunk with Color

I am sometimes called The Treasury Department by members of my family, usually when they are hoping I will print some money for them; and sometimes, more regrettably, I am called The War Department behind my back. That is usually when I am being found difficult, uncooperative and bellicose, which of course hardly ever happens.

But today, I was in a good mood and intended to spend money like a drunken central banker, as I went to the garden center with lust in my heart and a long (mostly spouse-approved) shopping list in my hand. At the top of that list was a very fat and healthy looking rhododendron to replace the old and attractively gnarled specimen by the entrance to our drive that we lost this winter. When I returned from the garden center, I immediately set about planting it. Then, with rhododendrons on my mind (it is funny how the gardener's mind runs in grooves like this), I trimmed back all the ones on the patio that were gradually leaning out to shade the hostas there and pluck the sleeves of human passersby.

At the garden center, I also found a gorgeous oriental poppy of goodly size, which is to be planted by the buddleia; it is bright pink with a bold black eye, the kind I have always wanted. Poppies in general do not seem to be as fond of me as I am of them, which is hardly fair, but I persist in trying to grow them. They are mysterious, are they not? They grow where they want to and not where we want them to, as a rule. They tend to drift around rather vaguely and show up in surprising places, where they do not belong. They come and go in unfathomable rhythms of their own, and for purposes we know not of. Like teenagers. They arrive in colors we may not favor, and the ones we plant in colors we *do* like do not thrive. At least, that is what they do for me. Over the years, I have learned that, if you are lucky enough to have poppies in your garden, or teenagers in your house, it's best to just be thankful, pretend to ignore them, and never mind that they are not just where you want them when you want them. They will be gone soon enough. Dogs are exactly the same, of course, and our time with them is also precious.

I also found and brought home two new pink clematises called, I think, something vaguely Asian-sounding, like 'Asao'; one will go at the base of a wisteria vine and one at the base of a climbing rose on the front of the house. The idea is to spangle the pink stars of the clematis among the louche racemes of the wisteria in a promiscuous sort of way, and to let the other dark pink clematis mingle with the very pale pink of the climbing rose—pink on pink, you see. In my mind's eye, the scheme is very sound; in reality, well, who knows. One has been disappointed so often. I filled two rectangular planters on the patio with dark blue petunias and spiky dracaenas, then put two large pink geraniums in each of the big pots atop the patio columns, together with four of the amaryllises from inside (three are still flowering inside, absurdly late; I have mismanaged them once again this year, true to form).

A word about nomenclature here. When I say "amaryllis," I mean, like most people, the florid South American bulb we all know and love and force to bloom indoors in winter. This is properly called a hippeastrum (not that anyone does), and the true amaryllis is a South African bulb that looks a little like the hippeastrum, which is why, I suppose, they are confused. There, is that all clear? They are distant relatives, but nothing more; probably they had a common ancestor long ago, when the continents we now know as Africa, North and South America, Australia, and Antarctica were all one giant land mass. Things have gotten very confused, in so many ways, since that simpler, happier time.

At any rate, the bright pink geraniums will pair well with the creamy pink 'Eden' roses and will, I hope, clash interestingly with the bright, orange-red canna lilies. Pink and orange-red is a garden combination I would not have had the nerve to try, but for having seen it in a gardening book that included a segment on Christopher Lloyd and his superb garden at Great Dixter in England. He daringly throws in a bit of pale yellow as well, and it looks fantastic, but I cannot go that far, at least for now. Perhaps this whole garden scheme is garishly mistaken (mine, that is, not Lloyd's), as bold garden schemes so often are. We shall see. But at least I am trying to overcome my color timidity and be a bit bolder than my normally safe self.

I have bought two tomatoes and put them in a raised pot in full sun, in front of where I park my car. I am seeking to baffle the squirrels and chipmunks this year by planting them more than four feet off the ground in a pot that is balanced on two other upside-down pots. Think crude totem pole, without any beautiful carvings or drawings. I must admit it looks a bit trashy. She Who Must Be Obeyed thinks I should spring for a proper raised bed for the tomatoes, with perhaps a bit of fencing around it, but she is not being obeyed in this, as I am reluctant to part with either the money or the space. Why should I, when I can stack tomato pots by my car? It's all probably hopeless, though, and certainly it all looks very odd, and if this does not work, as seems quite likely, I think I will just have to give up on tomatoes. A wise gardener has to know when to accept utter defeat and abject humiliation, such abundant commodities in the garden and such good training for parenting, after all.

My final purchases were a pot of chives and one of rosemary for the patio, ten hollyhocks for the crescent bed (ten!), and six yard-tall lilies for the porch bed. These last sixteen beasts had to be left inside until I could get to them; they rather took over the pantry, and certain people in our household were heard to grumble ominously about them in a way that I did not quite like. They are already, in fact, driving us all mad, so it will be nice to get them out of the house and into the ground at last. All of us, certainly the lilies included, will be much happier as a result, and peace will reign within once again. A half-acre greenhouse would be so lovely for problems like this, provided it came with a substantial trust fund to pay for its heating and upkeep. You could have a charming little tropical zone at the end furthest from the door, and in winter, you could sit there and read the morning paper with your coffee and toss bits of fish food to the magnificent ornamental koi.

Back in the real world and driving around town, I see wisteria and lilacs in bloom everywhere, and at home, our small crab apple in the oval bed is blooming beautifully too, I think for the first time. How I love the bright pink of the Sargent crab, with its tightly shaped flowers. Also, the large, deep-red azaleas are opening up and, amazingly early, the dark purple irises on the corner already have their bloom stalks up, with two of them coloring up and ready to open, perhaps when I get home this evening. Ah, I am fairly drunk with color.

Sobering up a bit, I went to the grocery store to get supplies for a family patio party: boiled Belize shrimp, artichokes and dip, chips and salsa, and sushi. All very fun. For dessert, we had Key lime pie, which my daughter is nuts for. In fact, she is an expert on the subject, as it is about the only desert she will eat, and she would contentedly have it at every meal, if life could be so agreeably arranged to her liking. Below is the recipe she likes best, perfect for a fresh spring evening. But first, two further thoughts. We have occasionally been criticized for using alcohol in too many of our recipes, a criticism that we intend to face head-on, just after I go make myself a martini. There, that's better, now where was I? Oh, yes, the Girl Scouts. This recipe is made with their "Thin Mint" cookies, which are better than crack cocaine, I have been reliably informed by members of the crack cocaine community. If those darn Girl Scouts ever turn their hand to cooking meth, this country is doomed.

Key Lime Pie

1 vanilla bean (or 1 tsp. vanilla extract)

1/3 cup light rum

1 pkg. Girl Scout "Thin Mint" cookies (32 cookies)

5 Tbsp. unsalted butter, barely melted

2 14-oz. cans of sweetened condensed milk

1 cup key lime juice

2 large eggs

1½ Tbsp. grated lime zest

One week before making the pie, split the vanilla bean and scrape out the pulp and seeds. You can use vanilla extract if you can't find a bean, but as always, the real thing is much better. Add the vanilla pulp and the skins to the rum in an airtight container and allow to infuse for a week.

Pre-heat oven to 375. Crush the cookies with a rolling pin and put them in a mixing bowl with the butter. (You can use 1¾ cups of crushed graham crackers if you can't get the Girl Scout cookies, plus ¼ cup sugar, but that is not nearly as good.) Press the mixture into a 9-inch pie pan to form the crust and bake for 20 minutes.

Reduce oven temperature to 325. In a bowl, combine the infused rum, condensed milk, lime juice, and eggs. Whisk well and pour into pie shell. Bake for 20-25 minutes and then chill in the fridge for at least 2 hours. Garnish with grated lime zest, and serve very cold, with either mint chocolate chip ice cream or lemon sorbet, if you like. This recipe is best made a day ahead.

Garden Structures

We had a torrential cloudburst this morning; it was positively monsoonal. Yesterday's very warm weather advanced the herbal clock of spring quite a lot. We sat out on the patio for only the second time this year, and I noticed the hostas have moved in one day from asparagus spears to unfurled leaves, very beautiful in the variegated form in particular. We love their white flowers and heady perfume later in midsummer at the edge of the patio. While we were sitting there, our huge neighborhood hawk swooped down into the high branches of a very tall tree near the street, in the limbs of which a squirrel was running around. The squirrel immediately perceived his peril, froze, and we watched, fascinated, as he then tried inconspicuously to descend the tree and get out of harm's way. A squirrel trying to be inconspicuous is inherently a very comic proposition. The hawk watched him intently too, possibly not without a sense of humor, but let him go without incident, either because he was not hungry enough to care or he calculated that a close-quarters attack was unlikely to be successful in the thick branches of the tree. And so the tense moment passed without bloodshed.

And too, I notice the flowering trees have sprung open in rapidly increasing numbers. The large *Magnolia soulangeanas* that I see on my way into the metropolis and that stand in full sun are fully open already. Likewise cherries, and even a few plums, are opening their blossoms. Our hyacinths have just opened fully and their heavy perfume is enough to make you swoon when you pass them on the way around the house to the side yard. One cut bloom is all it takes to perfume a room in the house, but the perfume tends to turn a bit sickly as the flower fades. Everywhere you look, trees are covered in a bright green fuzz as leaf buds swell or start to open or, in some early cases, are actually open and have already shaken out their mint-new solar panels.

Early April is a great time to think about moving and dividing plants. The extremely busy season in the garden has not quite begun and it is an opportunity to run over the garden in your mind and think about each citizen of the garden ecosystem. Is it happy where it is? Would it flourish more or look better in another situation or paired with another plant or plants? Does it need dividing? If so, it is well to do it now, when most plants are fully charged for robust growth but have not begun their growth spurt. Moving and dividing plants is a hard job, but if, like most gardeners, you have spent a fortune at garden centers and nurseries over the years, the idea of having the right plant in just the right place is an appealing one, and so especially is the idea of the free plant stock that comes from conscientious divisions, especially assuming you are growing plants you like in the first place. If you are not, perhaps this is as good a time as any to re-think that approach.

Left to my own devices and unchecked by my ever-vigilant wife, for example, I would divide and re-divide my irises every year (or more than once a year, if I could), instead of every four years or so, until I had, oh, about 30,000 of them covering every inch of ground at our place. And then, during the height of their blooming season in late May and early June, I would take at least two weeks off from my day job to take a lawn chair outside and live among them in their orchidaceous (yes, it's a real word; you can look it up if you doubt me) glory from dawn to dusk. Actually, it would be lovely to sleep outside among them too, and fall off to sleep in an ecstatic stupor induced by their spicy, exotic perfume. The neighbors would talk, but that can't be helped. We must suffer for our art in a world that does not understand us, I suppose.

But where was I? Oh yes, dividing plants. I strongly recommend that you do this – promptly, routinely, and in a businesslike way. Not that I do it that way, you understand, but I feel fairly strongly that you should. I tend to divide plants when I damn well feel like it and when the spirit moves me, or when I need some more plant material and cannot wring any more cash out of the family treasury. My irises are in pretty good shape, as I tend to be just a tiny bit greedy in that area as I have hinted, but I have hostas, Shasta daisies, chrysanthemums, phlox, daylilies, and even peonies (the shame of it!) in an overgrown state, all of which badly need to be divided. And of course, each year I think, well, perhaps I can leave them alone just one more year. This is just the kind of laziness that, while I understand it and tolerate it in myself, I emphatically deplore in others.

Another thing I strongly recommend in others, and here I am somewhat better in doing this myself, is that you be a bit ambitious and adventurous in designing and building structures for the garden. Using bricks or pavers to line a garden bed or a path is easy and gives a garden area a lovely, well-cared-for look. Walks, patios, and stone walls are surprisingly easy to build, with or without mortar, and this hardscape gives form and great gravitas and dignity to the garden. Solidity and substance make a wonderful backdrop for the lush and floppy growth habits of many plants, a foundational axiom of good garden design.

Pillars are a lot of fun and give you the chance to create garden exclamation points or points of visual interest. I used a simple form made out of two-by-fours to shape a foundation that was eighteen inches square and about six inches deep, then poured a small foundation using premixed concrete in a bag from the hardware store. While this dried, I got on the internet and watched simple instructional videos on how to lay bricks. Then I built a series of pedestals or pillars, plinths I think is the actual term, about two and a half feet high, and capped each one with a two-foot-square concrete stone that looks like natural slate. I ordered a load of rock delivered and dry-stacked this between the pillars to create a low fence or dry stone wall, and the whole defines a new patio area that looks as if it has been there a hundred years. Instant old. Though I am not very fast at this kind of work, it is very satisfying. Gardens need definition and structure, like teenagers, or else they just become messy and incomprehensible. Said another way, the wild abandon of the growing plants needs structure and form to show itself to the best advantage, and vice versa. There is real beauty that comes from the creative tension of this combination.

On the three pillars, I placed large pots planted with the 'Eden' roses I was talking about earlier, for a very formal but graceful air. It sounds difficult, but was actually surprisingly easy and cost very little. The hardest part was laying the bricks, which, if you have not done this much, is hard to get the hang of, but I found it turns out fine, though I was certainly a bit clumsy at first. Building small ponds or water features is similarly easy, and I would gladly do that if I could get permission from others in the family (of a sometimes tyrannical nature) to do that, but alas, I cannot. Not yet, anyway, and I have not entirely given up hope.

Another thing that is easy to do is to build structures in the garden for leaning plants. Tall roses, for example, look better if given some support. I dig small cylindrical holes in the ground with a fencepost shovel and stick an eight-foot one-by-two of treated wood in that, then pour dry, pre-mixed concrete from a bag to fill the hole; the dry concrete wicks the moisture it needs to harden from the surrounding soil, and this is a no-mess way of building some solid supports. For a very large rose, I use three of these posts. I paint them a flat black, finding this looks handsome when the garden is bare and disappears visually when the garden is green. I don't know why this is so, but it is; try it yourself and you will like the result.

A variant of this is what, in formal gardens, they call a "tuteur," which is a sort of frame that supports a climbing or leaning plant. Classically (and durably), these are made of metal, but few of us can support this kind of expense for our lazy, floppy plant friends. An inexpensive version is to purchase treated one-by-ones in eight-foot lengths. Visualize four eight-foot lengths forming a square two feet wide by two feet deep and eight feet high; then, at four feet high and at the top or eight-foot level, you screw in four cross pieces. I also build a version of these that is half as tall to provide a frame for our helianthus to grow in, as they are notoriously floppy in midsummer and tend to oppress their neighbors. At the top, you screw on four decorative finials, which are available at any large hardware store, one at each corner. You paint the whole thing flat black and it looks like an elegant iron structure that cost you hundreds of dollars.

Walkways or small terraces are easy to do, too. You use treated one-by-twos to frame the area, then use bricks or pavers set in sand to fill it in. I like to use flat fieldstones for walks, and when they are fairly level, I pour dry concrete mix around them and leave it to harden as it wicks moisture out of the ground. All good harmless fun, and far less expensive than golf or boating, not to mention maintaining a drug habit or conducting romantic affairs, or other popular contemporary pursuits, such as robbing convenience stores or, worse, going into politics.

In another garden, I built a beautiful screen by placing four eight-foot tall redwood two-by-fours in a series: the first two were four feet apart, the second and third were about thirty inches apart, and the third and fourth were four feet apart again. The middle two formed a doorway and the outer pairs were frames. To each of the frames, I attached an upright four-by-eight sheet of crisscross redwood trellis screening using one-by-two redwood strips. I then trained some honeysuckle to grow up the screens, which was easy, as honeysuckle needs very little encouragement. Another two-by-four was placed to run across all four posts to complete the frame, and above the doorway, I installed a wrought iron screen that was actually an antique fireplace screen I once bought inexpensively in Santa Fe. The result looked like a very formal and gracious entry into a new part of the garden, a kind of rough-grass area with wild flowers, but was very inexpensive, easy, and satisfying to build. In the same garden, I built a horizontal version of the eight-by-four screen, and trained sweet peas to grow on this.

Sometimes it is not the things we planted and made in a former garden that we most miss, but rather the things we meant to do but never did, the things we wanted to build but never got around to. I have just such a regret about our former garden. We had more formal plantings nearer the house, as is common, but further from the house, the garden transitioned to a more casual and rustic look. The garden was located in rather rugged country, above 6,000 feet in altitude, and the main vegetation that naturally occurred there was Ponderosas and shrub oak. We marked the transition from the more formal part of the garden to the rustic part with a sort of rough stone path that proceeded under the arched gateway I was talking about above. The rustic area had rough boulders and native shrubs that we planted, together with some native grasses and wildflowers. We planted a tiny orchard of fruit trees there – two each of cherries, peaches, plums, and apricots – to make a little alley of flowering and fruiting trees that you could walk through, very pleasant when in blossom.

This alley was to lead to a small clearing where a rough-hewn picnic table stood, where we would have casual dinners or dessert parties under the pines in the cool of the evening. I always intended to define the area around this picnic table a bit better. It rather bothered me that the table was just stuck out there in the bushes, like something that fell off a wagon on the Oregon Trail. It needed some design *reason* to be where it was, some structure that defined its presence better and created a sense of drama around it, without being at all pretentious and remembering that rustic was the overall feel we were going for there.

What I had in mind was to dig four big postholes outside the four corners of the table area, not so close to the table as to be claustrophobic. Then I was going to stick a ten-foot redwood 4 x 4 in each posthole and fill the holes with concrete, using a level to make sure the posts were perfectly straight and vertical. Then my plan was to attach heavy chains from the top of each post to define the perimeter (and possibly crisscross over the table, but I hadn't made up my mind about that), and then to plant a grape on each post, to scramble up the post and across the chains. I was thinking of grapes because I wanted this to have a Napa Valley kind of feel to it, unpretentious but still stylish. In a different setting, closer to the house or in a more formal area, clematis, wisteria, climbing roses or honeysuckle would work well too, as would many other climbers.

Anyway, the point is, the whole structure would cost next to nothing, would look fantastic while still giving off a rustic feel, but would define any space beautifully and authoritatively. You could weave a string of lights among the grapes, if you chose. I still think that is a great idea, and would work in many different places – anywhere you had an open space where you wanted to use a simple structure to define the space and give it cohesion and integrity. You could pave it with rough stones or rustic pavers. Some people like a nice formal look to their masonry, but I am not a good enough mason to achieve that and, happily, I like a more rustic look anyway, so that all works out okay.

Structure and definition, as I say, are important in a garden, and unless one's funds are unlimited (and whose are), it is handy to find ways to provide this structure without breaking the bank. Plus, it is fun and satisfying to do this, if you have any aptitude for it at all (it does not take much, believe me, if I can do it); and if you have any children about the place, you will find they love building things like this and can often be co-opted to help you.

Waiting for the Orange Peony

Money is annoyingly finite and one can't have everything—these are two things that every gardener bitterly knows. However, we did finally cough up some dough for professionals to come in and finish up the dratted window-painting project. A team of experts painted all the higher windows this week, She Who Must Be Obeyed having forbidden me to climb a ladder for that purpose, which was secretly a great relief to me. Falling off ladders is one of those things you need to get out of your system when you are young; several other things fall into that category, but let's not get distracted here by *that* tempting subject. So I spent a lot of time tediously putting the storm windows back up after they had finished and am, by now, rather sick of this whole tiresome window-painting project. It is high time to spend my energy resources in the spring garden, where breaking my arms and legs is most unlikely.

This weekend, I had to kill another two dozen or so dandelions, the little beasts, and was behind-hand enough in doing so that several of them had gone to seed already, so we shall have plenty more next year after all, and despite my earlier gloating, not to mention all the dandelions and who knows what other weed horrors I have brought down upon myself with the horse manure caper. Which I think illustrates the principle that when the gardener is just starting to feel competent and pleased with himself, he should look out, for nature is about to serve up a very humbling surprise. Hubris, I believe it is called, classically. I had gone out of town this week on business, and this short absence was my undoing with the dandelions. In future years, I should remember that late April is a time for almost daily vigilance, for that is when these creatures are most up to no good.

Our twelve dozen red and black tulips were very successful and dramatic, and Cosimo The Wonder-Dog has diligently kept the beastly rabbits away from them. As I write, I am looking at a bouquet of them, plus three stalks of the palest white iris, plus some purple honesty. In our former garden in Colorado, I badly wanted the happy color of tulips dotting the landscape, even though they were rather inappropriate in that wild, rugged terrain, so I planted dozens and dozens of them. And the rotten rabbits came in spring and gratefully and gracefully nibbled the tiny, delicious bloom buds out of each one, so I needn't have bothered after all. Annoying, that. This year, our transplanted lilac produced just two small cones of flowers, which went in a small vase to our daughter's room with some purple tulips. I am sure she does not think twice about the gorgeous fresh flowers that regularly appear in her room, perhaps supposing that that is just what flowers do, or what dads do, or that she is some sort of princess to whom these tributes come naturally. More likely, she does not think about them at all. But a day will perhaps come when she realizes what a love offering they always were, and that is a future realization that is like money in the bank to me now.

I was looking through an iris catalogue the other day and saw that the bi-color iris that, to myself, I call "tuxedo irises" (white flags and purple falls), and that I have fondly grown for many years and in many gardens, are actually called 'Wabash' and were the most popular iris in

1936, of all things, though you do not see them much anymore, as fanciers seem to cravenly prefer the much bigger, much gaudier pastels popular today. Honestly, sometimes I think humans have the brains of bumble bees because, like them, we seem to fall for the big and obvious and vulgar in our floral tastes, and the flowers themselves are certainly happy to oblige us evolutionarily and become as big and tasteless and trashy as we require them to be. Possibly you have noticed this? Anyway, see if you can find any 'Wabash' irises, or ask a steady, reliable sort of gardener, if you know of any, and you can grow something that was, at one time, considered the epitome of beauty and refinement. Some of us think it still is.

The now numerous pink azaleas around the yard are starting to light up; ours run the gamut from the simple clear pink on the corner (a shade I like, but which you don't see much anymore in the nurseries, having been replaced by the more garish and electric shades) to bright magenta and almost true red. The old azaleas, which you can tell by their size have been here a very long time indeed, were simple, dignified colors: red, white and pink usually, and nothing more. Perhaps that is all they had then, or was it evidence of a more sober, steady esthetic in older times? Then the hybridizers and experts got busy, and now you have almost any kind of color or monstrosity you like in the azalea department, including, God help us, yellow and even orange. So far, and happily, I see no evidence of this same corruption affecting, say, peonies, which still come in only red, white and pink, as far as I know (and purple, in tree peonies), but no doubt some insane scientist somewhere is trying to come up with an orange peony.

On the other hand, I must admit to loving the loud, tacky, and showy Kwanzan cherries. I know it is very wrong of me and would be deplored by more sophisticated gardeners, who have a settled animus against them, but I have to say I love these unsubtle creatures, and I suspect there may be something more than just a little bit vulgar in my own gardening esthetic. But I do think that, if your heart yearns for these things, then you should have one, and stick it in the middle of your front lawn, and to hell with anyone who doesn't like it. At least I haven't gone that far here, though when we lived in Virginia, I certainly did, and it was just fine.

Each of our tree peonies has two large, purple blooms, with many more to come, and they look very blousy and grand, absurdly beautiful, really. The pink clematis on the tuteur is flowering nicely, but will probably look better next year, when it is a bit fuller. The first flower of the dark blue clematis on the grapevine opened just this morning and looks very well near all the light blue of the bluebells jangling in the porch bed: sort of a Cambridge blue and an Oxford blue. And speaking of blues, the dark purple irises on the corner are nearly finished, and the very pale gray-blue-white (white, really, with a very slight undertone of bluish-gray) irises are just opening, but no other colors of iris have yet volunteered and these two, as always, are the earliest. I have great hopes for the iris bloom this year, having divided them all last summer and created many, many more than we have ever had here before, possibly even more than we had at our former garden; but perhaps they will wait until *next* spring to be in their best form. The pink dogwoods around town are long finished, but our whites are still looking great, with some of them more than forty feet tall.

In the world of food, we are followers of those who recommend the famous Mediterranean diet, which reduces heart disease and other serious disease by more than 30%. And all you have to do, if you want to follow this healthy and life-saving discipline, is eat great food! Well, yes, you can't eat anything you want, and you are going to have to eat less meat, but we are not talking great hardship here. The main idea is to eat a lot of fresh vegetables, little meat but lots of seafood, take moderate amounts of red wine, and use olive oil as your principal source of fat. There are, of course, many books on the subject, and excellent cookbooks, so I won't go on about it much here, except to say it really works and is really delicious. And in keeping with this tradition of great food that is very healthful, here is a recipe for Mediterranean tapenade that is out of this world.

Mediterranean Tapenade

8 oz. dried lentils
½ cup olive oil
¼ cup fresh lemon juice
1 tsp. salt
1 tsp. freshly ground black pepper
2 cloves of garlic, crushed in a squeezer
3 oz. toasted pine nuts
1 cup freshly grated *parmigiano reggiano*
½ cup chopped Kalamata olives
¼ cup finely minced fresh thyme
¼ cup anchovies
¼ cup finely minced fresh celery leaves (or Italian parsley)
1 loaf of French bread, baguette style
Celery ribs

Rinse the lentils and put them in a saucepan with 2-4 cups of water; bring to a simmer and cook for 30-45 minutes with the lid on but slightly open. While the lentils are cooking, add all the other ingredients (except the bread and celery) to the bowl of a food processer and process until very smooth, about 45 seconds. Yes, you do have to use the anchovies, even if you don't really care for them. Don't worry, we are just adding a few here for a mysterious hint of the sea; they won't overpower this dish. This excellent tapenade can be used as a dip for crudités, or you can load it onto short lengths of the celery ribs. Slice the baguette into rounds, toast them on both sides, and serve a basket of these toasts for dipping in the tapenade. This make a great hors d'oeuvre, but you can also make a meal out of it by adding a plate of whatever meat you have on hand, with some good cheese and olives.

Victory over Dandelions

Spring chores in the garden are endless, are they not? Last weekend, I finished weeding the fence bed and manured it, mowed the lawn for the first time, and put down lime, fertilizer, and crabgrass preventer on the lawn. Then planted seven new azaleas bought for $7 each and good-sized too, a great bargain in a weak economy, when we are all feeling too poor to spend money in the garden; they went into the hedgerow along the driveway. I also moved seven hydrangeas out into more sunny locations at the lawn's edge, where they will do better and be seen to greater advantage in midsummer.

Our small peach tree is a mass of pink blossoms against the dark black-green of the yew, just as I envisioned it four years ago. Rarely do garden schemes come off like this, just as you planned them. The tulips are starting to pop off their little colored flares all over the place, and most of the trees and bushes have tiny, spring-green leaves on them. The late forsythia in the corner of the yard by the benches is in its glory, though the weatherman says we are to have one last taste of the lash of freezing temperatures this week, rather surprisingly. The variegated hostas on the patio are growing so quickly you can almost see them emerge, as in fast-motion photography, and most of the plants in the crescent bed are already about a foot high.

This weekend, I put down two loads of manure and planted the canna lilies on the patio. I dug up two purple clematises and put one on the peach tree and one on the cherry. We grilled chicken outdoors for the first time Sunday, and scrubbed and filled all the birdbaths and the copper fountain. I note that the little birdhouse over the north side of the porch already has two occupants who are busily building a nest. The pink dogwood on the patio has buds that are swelling very promisingly, and the lovely redspire pear in the front yard is now in bloom and looks very smart.

I killed six tiny dandelions today, all that remained after the last few years of my ruthless suppression of them, and that was very gratifying. There is nothing like a bit of brisk killing in the garden to get things started off right and to put a spring in the gardener's step. This yard was infested with dandelions at one time, and that was hard for me to bear, because to me nothing says ill-cared-for-garden like dandelions about the place. Our first spring here, there were so many, I hardly knew where or how to begin; it was very demoralizing, but I decided to proceed methodically. Early each spring morning, weekdays not excepted, I would go out with an old steak knife and a weed bucket and kill all the blooming ones if I could, or if there were too many, I would get them the next day or the next.

The object was not to kill them all at once—that would have been quite impossible, as there were so many—but to let none of them (or not very many, anyway) go to seed, so that at least the problem would not get worse. It was very tedious work, weeks of it, but eventually I was pretty sure I got most of them. But of course, I missed more than a few (they are that sly), and the next spring, I had to repeat the process, but it was much more manageable. I was clearly gaining ground. Years passed in this way, providing hours and hours of harmless fun for the gardener. Now, however, they are almost all gone, and all I have to do is get the new colonizers that are brought here by the wind and our little bird friends, and compared to the labor of prior years, this is a lighthearted and satisfying task. Victory, for once, is mine. I must savor it, as it is so rare.

May

The Furtive Beekeeper

The garden is bursting with unopened blooms, with thousands of peonies, irises, and poppies, all swelling in their bloom buds on the eve of spring's main riot. A small but fruitful pod of irises, dark indigo and light blue, at the west end of the oval bed, is decked out with over 200 blooms in about 1.5 square meters or less, and already the first dozen or so are open. How well a dark rich color like that works in the garden, when you have masses of it. The first dark indigo clematis—

the same shade exactly as the irises—opened today on the fat white porch column, while not far away in the arch bed, the first, and only so far, orange poppy also bloomed today. This pairing, not far apart, of dense indigo and intense orange is very successful and captivating, and I make a mental note to see if I can establish some of those orange poppies in the porch bed, where they can be more closely juxtaposed to the indigo clematis.

I also planted the four rhododendrons we got inexpensively at a local garden center, and laboriously dug half the trench for the canna lilies by the neighbors' driveway. The red and white azaleas in the front yard, huge and very old, or old for azaleas anyway, are now somewhat past their bloom, and a giant infestation of bees, our annual visit, is trying to form on the north eaves at the top of the house outside the kids' playroom.

We do love bees, the helpful creatures, and try not to make their lives any harder, but they can be such a nuisance sometimes. It is a huge swarm, much larger than a basketball and very dense, with great gobs of honey dripping all over the patio. A great mess, but very interesting and rather delicious, and we look on with wonder. The American garden writer Elizabeth Lawrence said (in 1959), "The hum of bees is the voice of the garden, a sound that lends new meaning to the flowers and the silence; music that has not changed since Virgil heard it and wrote of Heaven's gift, honey from the skies." And that is what we have just now, honey dripping from the skies, just as Virgil said. But how awful a world without bees would be; unthinkable, really.

I once ventured to suggest to an important person who lives on the premises that I had a budding interest in bee-keeping. Well, *that* didn't go over very well. A broad and colorful stream of language poured forth, much of it in what students of language, as I am, would instantly recognize as the command form, together with a shadowing forth of numerous evil contingencies that would befall us, me really, if any further interest in bee-keeping of any kind was detected in the garden or in the gardener, and so on. In short, She Who Must Be Obeyed decisively put her tiny but perfectly formed foot down on my good-natured plans for beekeeping. I thought I even heard a loud crunching sound, but I must have imagined that. Well, we live in an oppressive time, it is sometimes felt, and when innocent helpful little creatures like bees have to become the object of such scornful and forbidding diktats, it is a sorry reflection of the mood of our times and the way of the world in general.

So my golden dreams of a honeybee hive at the back of the garden were summarily shattered and had to be laid aside, for now at any rate. It is exactly the same fate that befell my earlier plans for a toad house and a bat condominium, though it is hard to understand why these delightful, interesting, and useful beings should be persecuted in this cruel and prejudiced way. Brooding on these painful subjects, I sulked through the garden, cursing the evil era we live in and meditating on the shortcomings of mankind in general. It was prudent, I felt, to dwell on the shortcomings of mankind in general; I was not willing to come any closer to home than that.

But then, to my great joy, I discovered on the internet that there are things you can do to help bees that are short of building a hive and becoming a beekeeper, as enjoyable as that would be. Take for example, mason bees. These creatures like to lay their eggs in narrow tubes and to encourage them, you can buy inexpensive cylinders about a foot long, each of which is filled with about twenty small tubes. Each cylinder will produce hundreds and hundreds of bees. You mount the cylinder perpendicularly on a tree in the garden and there they go largely unnoticed. Except by mason bees, to whom this is a great help and of the greatest possible interest. If asked about these harmless-looking devices, I propose to say they are a humane method of repelling mice; that when the wind blows through the tubes, it emits a sound only mice can hear and keeps them off the premises fairly successfully. The person who detests bees detests mice even more. Problem solved! Peace returns to the household, and the gardener has a spring in his step once again, knowing that he has become a beekeeper after all, though perforce a furtive one due to unreasoning adversity and persecution.

But returning to the great swarm of bees, dripping great, golden gobs of pure honey onto our patio, what on earth to do with this delicious mess? It seems to me that even a furtive beekeeper should be able to savor the taste of raw honey from time to time, even though it does not usually pour down from heaven in quite this amazing way. So I go out and scoop up a fairly clean-looking half-cup of this bee bounty and bring it inside to the kitchen, where it is destined to be an anchor ingredient in a simple but outstanding chicken dish. The secret to its tenderness is the long cooking time in a moderate oven, so allow plenty of time for its preparation.

Honey-Lemon-Garlic Chicken

8 large chicken thighs
2 large cloves garlic, pressed (or very finely minced)
1½ Tbsp. freshly chopped rosemary leaves
½ tsp. allspice
½ tsp ground black pepper
1½ tsp. salt
½ cup limoncello
Nutmeg
Two bulbs of garlic
One lemon
½ cup honey (from heaven, if possible)
A loaf of really good artisanal bread

Pre-heat oven to 300. For the chicken thighs, by far the best is to use thighs with the skin on and the bone in, but you can suit yourself. Toss the first six ingredients in a large bowl until the chicken is coated. Pour the limoncello into a casserole dish and then arrange the chicken in the dish, skin side down, and grate a generous measure of fresh nutmeg over it. Cover tightly with foil and bake for 45 minutes.

While this is cooking, divide the garlic bulbs into cloves and peel all the cloves. Yes, it will look like far too much garlic, but never mind. Cut the lemon lengthwise into eight wedges. When the 45 minutes have elapsed, turn the chicken pieces skin-side up and tuck garlic cloves in and around the chicken pieces. Put the lemon wedges among the chicken pieces too, with the yellow skins up. Re-cover and bake a further 45 minutes.

Uncover the dish and collect half of the garlic cloves and 1/3 cup of the liquid in the chicken pan; set aside. Drizzle the honey over the chicken; this is the way they do it in Greece and it makes the skins extra crispy. Broil the chicken until the skins are crispy, about 5 minutes. While broiling, process the garlic and the 1/3 cup of chicken liquids with a hand blender or in a regular blender. When served, use the hearty bread to sop up juice from the chicken and to spread the roasted garlic paste. Pure bliss, and definitely something to buzz about.

The Emperor's Peonies and My Poppies

The Forbidden City of Beijing, the vast palace complex of the once omnipotent Chinese emperors, sits in the center of the sprawling capital city of China, an ancient labyrinth within a modern labyrinth. Still today, behind its high walls in several of its most treasured gardens, can be found a truly remarkable horticultural treasure: what must surely be some of the oldest, largest, and most stupendous tree peonies in the world, covered in spring with hundreds and hundreds of huge, absurdly beautiful flowers. I have seen them for myself just at this time of year, and it is easy to see why they were so prized by the Chinese emperors and their mandarin grandees in their massively walled gardens. They are superb, mind-boggling in their beauty and antiquity. When you think that they only put on one or two new blooms a year—and possibly if you have struggled with these temperamental creatures yourself, as I have—you just look on in awe at a floral specimen of that size, age, and robustness.

Probably my admiration for tree peonies is the only thing I have in common with the emperors of China. Here, in a more humble Mid-Atlantic garden, my own tree peonies are superb this year, covered with big lavender blooms though they are still very young; but they are the same imperious creature, to be sure. Sadly, this winter we lost a showy Kwanzan cherry that I have a craven soft spot for—some varmint appears to have burrowed in and eaten its roots. I suspect chipmunks, the rapacious nuisances. Now I know that, at this point, into some gardeners' minds creeps the thought of BB guns or mousetraps, but we must resist these murderous impulses. Live and let live, I say, even though we have to suffer for our benevolent philosophy. So I replaced the cherry with a redspire flowering pear, which should do better there. I built two eight-foot tripods for the extremely robust honeysuckle near the street to give it something to climb on, create a bit more interesting verticality in the garden, and try (probably hopelessly) to keep it out of the large azaleas it is meanly trying to get into and smother.

The deep purple clematis on the patio and the ones in the arch bed (pale pink) are blazing very strongly. This plant has many great virtues to recommend it. If you just plant them correctly (rich soil, cool and shaded roots, please, and not too dry a location) they can be left on their own. They grow like weeds, look sensational, come in a variety of beautiful colors, and are normally not bothered by pests. But the point about shaded roots is critical. Perhaps their greatest virtue, after their interesting, star-shaped flowers, is that they take up very little space in the garden, and for most of us, this is a considerable virtue indeed. They make an excellent companion plant, growing up next to and inside a tolerant host plant and adding to its interest without harming it or bothering it in any way. I have set them to clamber up fruit trees, grape vines, roses (what a lot of interesting combinations you can make with roses and clematis), and wisterias (imagine the broad pink stars of the clematis spangling the light purple panicles of the wisteria), and so on, and of course they are quite happy to festoon your mailbox or to dignify a common stop sign or street sign, the agreeable creatures.

After a long week on a business trip to London, I was unpacking last week and realized my coat pockets were full of all manner of botanizing debris – in this case, mullein seeds, early spring wildflowers and whatnot, all collected on a long spring walk in the English countryside. Of course, I often forget exactly what I have and where I got it. It's all part of the lucky dip of gardening, I imagine, and quite a good way, really, to ease into the eccentricity and dottiness that is no doubt my fate when I am older: the absent-minded gardener, with pockets full of seeds and weeds and other rubbish, walking along the roadside mumbling and laughing to himself, lost in an unfathomable interior world of great gorgeousness. My children are of course appalled, and think me far more eccentric than I really am, and one hates so much to disappoint them.

The poppies are in fine form just now, adding their discordant dash of shocking, electric orange to the landscape, and they are likely to finish just in time, before the more mellow colors of the irises appear and the very creamy pinks and whites of the peonies fully open. The acidity of the poppies is moderated and neutralized somewhat by the large clumps of chives adjacent to them, with their golf ball-size purple pompons, and similarly by the purple honesty, which looked well this year and is just now finishing. I finally achieved a life's gardening goal by purchasing a very large wisteria last weekend, from a local nursery whose stock is good but very expensive, and drove it home streaming merrily out the back of our convertible. It has been planted on the corner of the garage, and is intended to grow along the roofline, a rather traditional look for an Arts and Crafts bungalow such as this. I planted clear blue lobelia in the urn by the arch to simulate a water feature, and it seems to be thriving. Lastly, the Colorado lupines, grown from seed here, are all very large already and are sending up very handsome spires of blue and violet.

The chives are looking good now, as I say. Mostly, I grow them for their cheerful flowers, but every spring at this time their profusion reminds me that they are destined also to be the garnish of many delicious soups and salads, but none as good as our annual spring treat, Stilton soup. You can use any blue cheese in this soup if the real Stilton is hard to get in your area, although Stilton is much better. The cheese is so rich that, in the old days in England, it used to be brought to the table seething with maggots, and you were given a special maggot spoon to eat the poor things with. Nowadays, we don't have to do anything so dreadful, and you can just enjoy the famous cheese in this delicious soup, without the bonus protein. The recipe comes to us from an English friend who is a superb cook.

Stilton Soup

2 Tbsp. unsalted butter
1 onion, finely chopped
5 sticks of celery, finely chopped
4 Tbsp. flour
½ cup dry white wine
2 cups chicken or vegetable stock
½ cup whole milk

8 oz. Stilton cheese, crumbled
½ cup whipping cream
Salt and pepper
3 Tbsp. chopped chives

Melt butter in a saucepan. Add onion and celery and cook over a medium heat until tender but not browned, about five minutes. Add flour and cook for one minute, then remove from heat. Stir in wine and stock, then return mixture to heat. Bring to a boil, stirring continuously, until soup thickens. Then simmer over a low heat for 30 minutes. Allow mixture to cool slightly, then process it in a food processor. Return mixture to the rinsed saucepan. Add milk and heat the soup, but do not let it boil. Stir in the Stilton cheese and the whipping cream. Season to taste with salt and pepper. Garnish with fresh chives. Serves 4-6.

Must Your Get Your Hands Dirty?

It's true that many busy professionals choose to hire a landscape firm to install and maintain their gardens and general landscaping. While it may turn out to be pleasing to the eye, it cannot achieve what you yourself can do by actually getting in amongst your own garden and getting your hands dirty on a regular basis. Gardeners know this strong feeling of connection, satisfaction, and well-being that comes from contact with their own soil, and what a power of good it does for each of us. It is almost *mystical*, we have always known and felt. But now, science has proven that it is real and demonstrably *chemical* as well. It turns out that working in soil raises your spirits, at least partly because you pick up good germs while gardening.

Christopher Lowry, who is a researcher at the University of Colorado, injected some mice with bacteria that live in dirt (*Mycobacterium vaccae*) and, as a result, found significantly increased levels of serotonin (the biochemical feel-good agent in humans and other animals) in their prefrontal cortex. That's the official scientific reason gardening makes us feel good, or part of it anyway, and it's further proof that the garden uses microbiology and crafty evolutionary tactics to manipulate and control the gardener in ways that are subtle and symbiotic. It is fascinating; it turns out that the gardening high is real.

Not everyone is fit and energetic enough to leap about the garden as we used to do long ago, and perhaps a bit of help with tedious tasks or tasks requiring great stamina is fine as far as it goes, though for myself, even at my age, I can't conceive of paying anyone to have the fun of my garden. And other ways of obtaining assistance in the garden—pleading, bossing about, complaining to teenagers and so forth—I have not found to be very often crowned with success. Ahem, perhaps the less said about that the better. Also, few of us can spend as much time in the garden as we would really like. A daytime job in the "real" world, for example, interferes shockingly with the time that would be far better spent in the garden. And too, other people who share one's house can be surprisingly critical of the time one spends in the garden, as if it were time somehow taken, unfairly, from them.

But in general, if you are the gardener and the garden is yours, then you must get your hands dirty, yes. If you hire the work done, much of it anyway, you are really more of a garden designer than a gardener. A connection with the soil is critical, and with the labor that creates and sustains the garden as well. This connection keeps us grounded, and not just figuratively. In my own daytime job, I live the ordinary life of a much-pressed and harassed businessman (as what person in business is not, these days; times are pretty tough, as possibly you will have noticed), and the chance to dig in my own earth like a common farmer, or to tinker with a design for where some new lilies would look especially good, is a way of staying focused on what is real and proximate, staying humble and centered, caring for what is important to me, and linking myself with chains of beauty to the small world I presently live in.

Thinking of the beauty all around us, I was recalling a spring walk around town I took a few weeks ago with the companionship of my old canine friend. Winter jasmine was blooming brightly along near Main Street and several homes lucky enough to have snowdrops (or gardeners hard-working enough to have planted them, as I in my laziness did not again this year) were enjoying this first bloomer in our town, often in very large, naturalized patches from which you may deduce that they have been there for a very long time indeed. In our own garden, spring had sort of arrived (not really), as it always does, with the hyacinths, of which we had one small pink flower blooming with precisely three tiny pink bugles open. So it was a rather modest beginning of all the promised glories to come, and which now in May have been largely realized, and even then, you had to get right down on your knees by the ivy near the stone walk around the garage to appreciate their beauty and get a tiny whiff of the hyacinth perfume.

Further along on my walk that day, and here is the colorist point of this reverie, I noticed one otherwise rather nondescript home with half a dozen large bunches of primroses growing in the front yard, their bold colors making them look almost fake in their cheerfulness. One does not see these grown very much in this country, though they are such a staple of English gardens, and indeed of the English countryside, that you may wonder why not. Perhaps they are too common and unpretentious, too easy and simple, to attract serious attention from gardeners here. We have a national mania for pansies, it would seem, which is rather harmless as national manias go, but the primrose is far superior to the pansy, in my opinion. Perhaps their bright chromatic colors are thought unsophisticated, with serious gardeners always preferring the more subtle blending properties of pastels. On the whole, though I also like pastels, I think this a color prejudice and a very unfair one.

I find the acid yellow of forsythias, for example, to be rather unattractive as an abstraction, and yet as a splash of bright paint on the dull canvas of early spring, it is thrilling, and who does not rejoice to see it? Some of the colors of azaleas are loud to the point of bizarreness, and yet who would complain about having these colors to light up the woodland shade (except perhaps for the yellow and the orange)? Only think of daffodils and tulips in their bold primary colors and how delightful they are, and you soon see how unreasonable it is to think chromatic primroses common and pastel pansies always better.

So while we ponder whether pastels are innately superior to primary colors in the garden, we remember that we simply must get our hands in the soil. We must keep our feet on the ground, on our *own* ground; we must get in amongst the plants that we admire and care for and the weeds that we do not care for, and all the birds, the insects, the wildlife, and the plant life of which we are, for a short time, the benign curator and the wondering admirer. This is life and death and art and beauty, after all, and we cannot stand at the back of our studio sipping iced tea and telling the boy with the paint buckets where to apply dabs of color to our landscape, where this plant should go, whether this weed needs lifting right now, and whether it really is time after all to divide this clump of peonies.

This mystical connection is a very important part of the interior discipline of gardening: it *must* have an exterior expression and your own hands must be the operative agent of the interior-ness of it. Being separate from this aspect of gardening is not to garden at all, at least not in the sense I mean. You must live the life of the garden of your mind; you must also be alive and present in the garden out-of-doors, and your physical activities are the critical thing that connects the two holistically.

❀

Beautiful Despite Flaws

Most Hollywood movies are about beautiful people with some serious flaws they have to either overcome or be undone by. As in Hollywood, so it is in my garden; there is so much beauty, but all beauty is flawed, no creature is perfect, each has its own drawbacks and problems. Surely you have noticed this?

Even though there is no such thing as a perfect flower, every gardener has favorites. I would be very hard-pressed to name a single variety as my overall favorite, just as I would be hard-pressed to name one favorite book, piece of music or superlative food. Most people would have roses, tulips, dahlias and irises on their short lists, but gardeners are funny and some are nuts for grasses, native species, even zinnias and marigolds, for heaven's sake. Honestly, the zeal of some people for native species is sometimes rather alarming. They speak as if it is downright *immoral* to wish to grow something that may have come from somewhere else. I bow to the principle that we should honor what grows naturally where we live, but what a boring thing gardening would be if we were to limit ourselves to that. And our gardens would of course be full of weeds and other weed-like plants. Awful.

And the didactic edge in people's voices when they talk about natives can be rather alarming, have you noticed this? You have the feeling you are about to be drafted into their moral army to proselytize the Congo. Geologists tell us that most of our continents were fused together at one time in one great mass, with common plant species— this is certainly true of Africa, North and South America, Australia and Antarctica—so to suggest that now for some reason we all have to live and garden in our own botanical silos and resist the temptation of a broader palette of life and experience and world history…Well, to me that sounds absurd and smacks of bossiness, just the thing to put the stubborn gardener's back up.

But as I was saying, all flowers have their strong points and their flaws, as every gardener well knows, and learning to love them despite their flaws and to make allowances for their shortcomings is actually pretty good training for coping with the people one comes across in a long life. A rose, for example, despite its considerable virtues—gorgeous and copious blooms, wonderful scent, immense variety of color, and varied growing habits, and so on—is notoriously greedy for nutrients, hogs the best sunny spaces in the garden, is very prone to pests and disease, and is covered in cruel thorns.

An iris, to give another popular example, can tolerate xeric conditions; has long stalks with often a dozen huge, flamboyant, orchidaceous blooms; comes in a rainbow of amazing colors, each more envy-inducing than the next; is relatively pest-free (though some people have fatal trouble with borers which I, thank God, do not); and has leaves that are gorgeous all the time and add structural interest to the garden, even when the iris is not in flower. And yet some gardeners, proving once again that there is no pleasing some people, incomprehensibly affect to find the irises' sword leaves ugly. Such folk are unwholesome influences in life and should generally be avoided as much as possible by the steadier sort of gardener.

I guess the iris comes closest to perfection in my mind, partly because of its inherent virtues and partly because I have been planting and enjoying this wonderful creature, man and boy, for oh, say, fifty years or so. But even they have not-inconsiderable faults: their individual blooms are relatively short-lived and every stalk soon has ugly blobs of slimy or shriveled (depending on how wet it has been) faded blooms on it, definitely disfiguring the general effect.

Orchids are a sealed book to me, as I have never lived in the tropics or been lucky enough to have a greenhouse, so I am painfully ignorant about them. But they strike me as being close to perfection in many ways: their blooms last an absurdly long time, they are extremely interesting to look at, they obviously come in a huge variety of colors and growing habits, and they do not even require soil. And yet, many of them are very difficult to grow and to get to flower. Still, they grow all across the world in the most amazing places. I remember as a boy tramping through the Australian bush, looking for these delightful beasts. They were very tiny there, but not hard to find if you looked down and really concentrated on their modest beauty.

Lilacs are also a good illustration of my theme, because the virtues and flaws are both so pronounced in them. The blooms are so beautiful, simple, wholesome, traditional, and wonderfully perfumed, but the plant itself is far too large for the small amount of blossom it produces. Weedy natives and xeric flowers, while extremely hardy, are another example of the same flawed principle: a low proportion of bloom to plant material. Even peonies, with all their virtues, have this flaw, plus the drawback of being so top-heavy that they are ruined more years than not by the not-uncommon rains of May. But their flowers are so absurdly gorgeous that we devotees put up with these serious drawbacks for the sake of the occasional May when their magic is at its unspoiled peak and they weave their lifelong spell ever deeper into the tissue of the stuff the gardener is made of.

I do have a special soft spot for our red peonies, I must admit, despite their being rather gaudy. I am pretty sure they are the variety known as 'Lowell Thomas,' named for the travel adventurer and news broadcaster of that famous name, who was a boyhood hero of mine. I once, as a student, got to meet him. I was waiting in the outer office of the University of Denver's great chancellor, Maurice Mitchell, one day on some frippery of student government business, when the door to the chancellor's office opened and out came the charismatic chancellor and, to my very great amazement, the legendary Lowell Thomas. It was he who popularized the phenomenal exploits of Lawrence of Arabia, and his name is synonymous with news broadcasting. Mitchell introduced me to him and I was, of course, enthralled. So I grow his eponymous flower as a dutiful and happy tribute.

As I was saying, reflection on the strengths and weaknesses of plants makes us mindful and tolerant of the strengths and weaknesses of all our fellow creatures; even people, when we are being especially broad-minded, and possibly even of ourselves, if we are being scrupulously fair and generous. And thinking of the vicissitudes of life in the garden teaches us much about anticipating, accepting, and enduring the vicissitudes of life generally. These last especially, acceptance and endurance, are two of the great teachings of the garden for the gardener, and the gardener would do well to study the example so patiently, so modestly, and so beautifully spread before him by the plants who have chosen to befriend him.

Before I close, I can't resist giving one recipe with which to capture the bounty of the spring season. We are presently engulfed in green, our eyes are surfeited with it, and of course we rejoice in it. Now is the time to gather up all the fresh green produce you can and make this tasty and exuberantly healthy Spring Harvest Salad.

Spring Harvest Salad

For the vinaigrette:
8 Tbsp. olive oil
2 Tbsp. white wine vinegar
1 tsp. sugar
Salt and freshly ground pepper to taste
6 Tbsp. freshly grated *parmigiano reggiano*
2 Tbsp. fresh lemon juice

For the salad:
2/3 cup chicken stock, divided

1 clove garlic, finely minced

11-13 oz. fresh baby spinach leaves

1 bunch of asparagus

1 lb. Brussels sprouts

½ cup vinaigrette

1 cup thawed frozen fava or lima beans

1 cup thawed frozen peas

1 large shallot (or 2 smaller ones), sliced as thinly as possible

Searing flour (or regular flour)

1/3 cup olive oil

4 slices bacon

2 Tbsp. chopped chives

Combine the ingredients for the dressing in a jar and shake well to combine. Put aside. Combine half of the stock and all the garlic in a covered saucepan and cook over a medium heat until the garlic is tender. Add the spinach leaves to the pan and cook, tossing occasionally, until it is just tender; do not overcook, a minute is plenty. Remove spinach from the hot pan and put it in the bottom of a large salad dish or platter. Cut off the bottom ends of the asparagus spears if they are woody and then cook the asparagus in the saucepan with the other half of the stock until just tender. Remove the asparagus spears and arrange them on top of the bed of spinach.

Heat oven to 425. Cut the white ends off the Brussels sprouts and split each in half. Throw the halves, including any loose leaves, into a mixing bowl and toss with half the vinaigrette. Place the sprouts on a rimmed baking sheet and roast them until they turn brown and are slightly caramelized, about 25-30 minutes. Then add them to the dish with the spinach and the asparagus.

While the sprouts are cooking, prepare the beans and peas according to the packet instructions. You can of course use fresh peas and beans if you can get them, simmering them in 1-2 cups of water until they are tender. Add the beans and peas to the salad, arranging the vegetables so that some of each can be seen. Pick apart the sliced shallot, into delicate onion rings if possible. Dredge them in the flour to coat them, then fry them in the hot olive oil until they are crispy, and put them aside to drain. Cook the bacon until it is crispy, then drain the bacon as well. Chop the bacon into small bits. Spoon the remaining half of the vinaigrette over the salad, then garnish it with the fried onions, bacon, and chives. The onions and bacon make this a surprisingly hearty-tasting salad, bursting with green goodness.

Jennings Irises

Now comes the season of the iris, and pictures of these gorgeous creatures flash up often in the gardener's mind, with their long stalks of corsage blooms in all their vivid colors. The mind of the dreaming gardener also teems with visions of irises admired throughout the years. He remembers, he remembers.

I am crazy about irises; I might as well admit it. I love them for their vivid colors in all the hues of the rainbow, which is what their name means in Greek. I love how gorgeous they look in flower, like orchids, only more so. I admire them for their rugged hardiness and their drought tolerance, something unusual in a plant that is so beautiful and delicate. They are easy to grow, and they repay the effort with absurdly generous dividends; just the thing for a very young gardener.

My first irises were given to me as a boy for helping to weed out and then divide a large established iris bed planted by our neighbor. He was Bob Jennings, a tall man of few words who looked to me like a cross between Gary Cooper and Noel Coward, if you can imagine such an improbable hybrid. He was a highly intelligent engineer and a truly gifted gardener, having created an amazing gardening oasis in the harsh, high and dry climate where we lived. He was a high-ranking civil servant in the Bureau of Reclamation that made our western deserts bloom.

Everything about Mr. Jennings' yard and garden was a marvel, and he worked in it whenever he could, from the first to the last daylight. As he got older, however, the tedious chores like weeding and dividing choked and overgrown irises fell to me, and I was well compensated. I was paid $0.50 an hour for backbreaking work in the Colorado heat. But I also got many of his cast-off plants for my own little garden and irises were luckily among the first plants I received. I must have been about twelve years old at the time, perhaps thirteen, and I was in love with them. They were a beautiful pale white, with a shade of almost bluish gray to them that made them a fresh and cool foil to other irises, particularly all the classic blues and purples. I think, in retrospect, they may have been the iris known as *purissima*, but they sometimes look to me like they have a bit more of a pale gray tone in them than the dazzling white *purissimas*, so I am not sure.

I grew these in my garden for many years; then eventually, as kids do, I left home to go to college, studied law overseas, and then began working in Washington, D.C. Meanwhile, the back yard of my childhood home went through many changes and my little garden was wiped out in a landscaping reform my mother implemented, turning the back yard into a large, grassy park-like area dotted with trees, which she called "Waverly." It was beautiful in its way, though rather idiosyncratic, like most garden designs, and to my horror, my small garden disappeared in the general change-over. In the middle of this park, where my garden had been, was a long kennel area and dog run for a pair of schnauzers my parents then had.

Many years later, while living still in the Washington area, I was thinking one spring about those Jennings irises of long ago and longing for them. Bob Jennings had died in the interim and his widow had sold their beautiful house. Their miraculous garden was gradually neglected and dismantled by the new owners, who had no appreciation for it; they thought it was too much work, which it certainly was. So out went the magnificent rose garden with dozens of gorgeous mature plants, along with its ingenious irrigation system designed by the gardener himself. Out went the prolific strawberry beds, out went the sprawling tulip planters—one large area held nothing but hundreds of pink tulips under the deep russet of a fat berberis hedge—and out came the dark, prickly berberis themselves, eventually. The amazingly productive orchard died from studied neglect, tree by tree, and it was painful to see.

The hundred feet of redwood fence that had eight-foot-high red roses growing against its entire length with, above that and in the far distance, the red rimrock curtain of the Colorado National Monument, all came down to open up the vista. I will never forget the sight of those extremely vigorous red roses against the redwood fence, backed up by the red sandstone of the Monument. It is quite likely that the red roses were 'Don Juan', the classic red climbing rose. It was all red on red on red, and going on forever, seemingly. Each time I visited my parents, it grieved me to see each new increment of "progress" at our neighbors' place. The iris beds were, of course, among the first to go, and they were long gone by the time I reflected on the disappearance of this complete garden marvel and realized the important lesson it taught, which at first I thought of as a rather bitter lesson, but which I now think of as a rather mellow, stoical one.

And that is that gardens are necessarily ephemeral. They are different even from day to day in subtle ways, as every attentive gardener knows, and certainly month to month and season to season. They are wildly different from year to year, even under the care of the same gardener; the gardener is changing too, of course, and so are his tastes and skills and interests in the garden. The fact that the garden designer has to operate in four dimensions, and include change over time in his design, is the very thing that makes gardening so extremely complex and challenging an art.

Architecture is something like it, as an architect has to consider a structure over time, but mainly as a way to keep it looking the same, while a gardener has to think what all the components will look like season to season, year to year, even decades later, as they layer change upon change. It is enormously complex and difficult. And I think we have to admit that this constant mutability is a great part of the charm of the gardening art. In some gardens, especially important historic ones like, say, Monticello or Mt. Vernon or the great gardens of England, great care is taken to try to keep the gardens unchanged, to keep them just as they were when Mr. Jefferson or General Washington or Gertrude Jekyll walked there, but this is, of course, futile and hopeless really, as even these museum-like gardens are changing all the time in subtle and unsubtle ways.

Even the royal gardens of England, some of the most carefully and expensively looked-after gardens in the world, are vastly different today from what they were a generation ago and definitely different from what they were before World War I, when labor was abundant and inexpensive and there was no practical limit to what such a garden might become. Beauty is ephemeral, as every gardener and indeed most non-gardeners know, or should know, but a gardener has this lesson burned into his heart and not in a way that is bitter, but rather in the way that all the facts of natural life are. They simply are. Youth and vigor are ephemeral, and so is happiness, and for that matter, sadness too, in case you never noticed. And so too is the gardener himself, who, if he is wise, knows he is not trying to create in his garden a durable masterpiece, or even something that will look familiar ten years after the gardener has left it. The certainty of the transitory nature of all things is one way wisdom begins in the garden. Accepting it is a step further on the road to enlightenment. Being pleased by it and then rejoicing in it are only for the very advanced, and few people progress to that level of enlightenment, but let us not get too far ahead of ourselves here.

And so one day, musing on these things, I was walking around in the back yard of my boyhood home, when I noticed a single, slim blade of iris leaf that had woven itself into the wire fencing of the dogs' old kennel, which location had protected it from being cut down by the repeated mowing of the grassy park over the years. Eureka! I carefully dug it out, wrapped it up elaborately, and took it back to my small garden in Northern Virginia. This single small survivor flourished and eventually flowered, and I cannot express the joy I felt when I saw that this was indeed one of the old Jennings irises, the only one to survive from that old, far away time, a pale white one with the characteristic blue-gray undertones.

All of my other irises had long since failed, all of its peers in the Jennings garden had perished, and even the original gardener himself was long gone. Only this single bloom remained from that garden and that far-off time, true to its nature and striving to fulfill its destiny in difficult circumstances, as we all are. In my devoted care, from it grew many hundreds, perhaps thousands, of Jennings irises over the years. I have divided them and moved them with me to every garden I have since tended. I have given them to many friends and strangers. At our former garden in Colorado, we had a huge patch of them and they were magnificent in bloom, perhaps a thousand at a time. I have a picture of that iris bed on my desk, as I write this as a much older man, in stupendous bloom. The bed of irises is in stupendous bloom, that is, not the man so much. Plants come and go, the garden changes, gardeners themselves come and go, and the great and lovely cavalcade of life rolls and rumbles amazingly on. Ah, beauty.

June

Hope, Persistence, and Stoicism

June, of course, brings some of the finest days of the year for the garden and the gardener. Today, it is simply spectacular outside, a brilliant summer day. To celebrate, we successfully released the fledgling wren that Cosimo and I rescued last weekend and were nurturing in a birdcage on the patio. He flew away after a moment's hesitation, and it was a great feeling to see him successfully restored to his parents and to nature. Cosimo, of course, was thrilled and fascinated, his eyes glowing with joy and, I even thought, a kind of paternal pride. He had found the creature in its distress, and had led me to it and to its rescue, so his ownership of its restoration was well-deserved.

I am glad to see I lived long enough with this garden to see the immature wisteria on the garage bloom, though it was not much of a bloom. In fact, it was only a single panicle of blossom, but it reminded me strongly of the gorgeous wisteria that grows on the ancient stone embrasures of the cloisters at Magdalen College, Oxford, and how, every spring when it bloomed, the cloisters were filled with its distinctive perfume. We would throw the windows open to spring for the first time after the long, grueling English winter, and the perfume of wisteria always speaks of the fresh advent of spring to me, in a distinctive way. It reminds me of a fragrant oil cooking in a hot skillet more than a floral perfume, and I have always loved it, though not everyone does. Sometimes, we know, beauty in the garden comes in small, singular ways, like that single panicle of wisteria-bloom. Or the single stalk of *Allium cristophii* in the oval bed that was somehow overlooked by our normally very thorough chipmunks, blooming magnificently in all its singular glory. It can't escape its fate another year, surely, so we must admire it while we can.

The glories of the season have put me in a philosophical mood. It is a fact universally acknowledged that gardeners are the most likable and admirable people one could hope to know. But why is this so? How could so many virtues and laudable character traits be packed into a single sort of person in this excessive and attractive way? It really is most remarkable. As a group, we are steady, well-adjusted, extremely hard-working, persistent, thrifty, brave, cheerful, kind, and generous.

Okay, perhaps we gardeners are a bit shaky on the last one or two of those virtues, generosity being especially difficult for some of us where plant material is concerned. I certainly struggle with that, and it is like pulling teeth for me to part with any plants, even ones I don't like very much, absurdly. Probably in my case, that comes from being raised as a gardener plagued with extremely poor soil, scarce water and even worse weather conditions, things that induce lifelong character traits of horticultural miserliness and avarice that are perhaps a bit unattractive, but surely forgivable. Or at least understandable.

Why is it true, though, that as a rule, we gardeners are pretty much paragons of virtue? I believe it is because gardening teaches the gardener three really valuable virtues: hope, persistence, and stoicism.

To garden is to hope. The planting of a seed or the tending of a small plot of vegetables or flowers is founded on hope—a belief, and a certainty about a better future. It is a curious thing about gardening that the reality often disappoints—a color scheme does not look quite right after all, a hoped-for beauty does not materialize, a beloved tree is destroyed by pests or hungry animals in winter; or all our best laid plans are so often ruined by the ravages of weather, disease, and the gardener's poor judgment or deficient skill—and yet even a lifetime of disappointment strangely only feeds the gardener's hope rather than diminishes it. We are cheered to plan the garden of midsummer in the depths of winter; we lay the plans for next year's spring garden glories in the shambles of the exhausted and dying autumnal garden; we ignore our failures and revel only in our successes. In our mind's eye, we can see the world as it ought to be. We are bedazzled by the beauty of optimistic hope.

And yet, gardeners are firmly planted with their feet on the ground, and never let their optimism become unhinged, deranged, or foolish. Rather, it is a different way of seeing altogether, a kind of far-seeing idealism that takes in the world as it is, but lives within it as it really ought to be and can perhaps be. That slip of a ponderosa seedling that I found growing in a hopelessly wrong location and transplanted to an open spot in the garden was only pencil-sized at the time; three years later, it is four feet tall and is off and running now, with foot-long candles of fresh new growth put on just this spring. It is going to be a huge success, you can see it already, and it cheers my heart every time I walk past it. Long after I have left this garden and probably left this life, it will still stand, strong and true, and I see its future grandeur plainly already. *I know it.*

Hope is surely one of the keys to a happy life and persistence goes well with hope; combine the two and you have a very powerful mixture for goodness and happiness. Every year—indeed every week—brings heartbreak and disappointment in the garden: death, loss, frustration, and disappointment. But every season also brings with it delightful surprises, unplanned beauties, and undeserved successes that mix with the disappointments and offset them, obscure them. It does not actually matter if the successes exceed the disappointments, as long as the gardener will only have the temperament to focus on and retain the former and endure and ignore the latter. This sort of disciplined, impressionistic editing is essential to gardening happiness, or to life happiness, for that matter, and leads to persistence and to taking the long perspective.

One of the few real advantages of aging is that it gives one, finally, the long perspective, so that one can take the rough with the smooth, the good with the bad, and know that, over time, with hope and persistence, it will all even out. We will come home again, safe and sound and reasonably happy at the last. The persistent gardener stands out there in his garden, being shredded and beaten with foul weather, the decaying vegetation of the expiring garden all around him on a cold and bitter late autumn's early evening. His face is aglow with a knowing and slightly odd expression of joy, for he is holding a paper bag of cherished crocus bulbs in one hand and a bucket of daffodil bulbs in the other. His mind is alight with the warm and colorful dazzle of the spring garden to come. Not just persistence then, but persistence in the face of failure and adversity; *that* is what we gardeners prize and aspire to, that is our great characteristic. And not just about the little things of the garden, either, but by extension, about all the big things of life.

And finally comes stoicism, by which I mean a courageous acceptance of what must be, what is ordained, what just cannot be otherwise. The Roman emperor Marcus Aurelius, in his magisterial memoirs, left us one of western civilization's great gifts of thought and one of its most inspiring and personal accounts. The personal philosophy of this philosopher-emperor is impressive and surprisingly modern in its outlook. For the gardener, it can be summed up like this: we may be as full of hopeful plans as we like, but when the blight strikes and our plans are dashed, the gardener knows to accept the judgment of nature, to bow to it and move on. We gardeners have each been humbled countless times in our gardening lives.

Stoical gardeners are alive to the passage of time in the garden and to the fact that the garden exists in and changes over time. In Europe in ancient times, when clocks and timepieces were extremely rare and largely beyond the means of individuals, prosperous towns would install a public clock in the main square, and often these timepieces had improving or admonitory slogans carved on them, like "*Carpe Diem*," "*Tempus Fugit*," or "*Memento Mori*." A very common one was "*Vulnerant Omnes, Ultima Necat*" ("They All Wound, the Last Kills"), referring to the hours marked by the clock. That is rather too gloomy a concept of time for my liking, but at least it does remind us that each hour and each day is precious; they came to us as gifts freely given and we should not take them for granted.

Gardening has an improving way of sandpapering the pride and hubris right off of us. Other things do that too, of course: raising children, professional or personal disappointments, illness, and so on.

But gardening does it in a thousand small ways, rasping and refining us gently but ineluctably into the smoothly polished and weathered old stoics we all become in the end if we are lucky enough and cooperate even just a little bit. At the last, provided we are paying attention and are not too stubborn, we are humbled even by our successes and joys, and we accept them too as what is and must be, and not as an artifact of our will. It is required of us, in the difficult and complicated lives we lead, to accept stoically what must be while persistently toiling and planning and hoping for what yet *might* be and *should* be.

A gardener knows all this by instinct and experience. Hope, persistence and stoicism; these are the cardinal virtues of the gardener, the sustaining triangle of virtues, each one touching and reinforcing the other two and creating the moral tone, the fit tension, and the inner structure of a great gardener's mind and sensibility.

Good Things We Don't Deserve

It is a perfect summer morning, clear and cool and sunny, with low humidity. Cosimo and I got up before the rest of the household at 6:30, with me taking my Voltaire biography and a cup of coffee outside to watch the sun climb up through the large trees, while he patrolled the garden, looking for furry malefactors. And sure enough, a chipmunk ran right across the patio—just feet from both of us, the bold thing—and the chase was on to start the day. It is hard to think the chipmunks actually mean to tease him or enjoy risking their lives to bother him, but they are so cheeky and daring that sometimes it looks like it may just be a great game to them. Personally, I would not like to be a chipmunk with Cosimo chasing me.

And as the sun gradually climbed through the branches of the great trees at the eastern edge of our property, I was thinking about those trees and how, when you inherit an existing garden, you inevitably get things you like along with a lot that you may not care for, and a gardener knows how to take the rough with the smooth. We are past masters at that sport. I suppose if you pay for new construction in a new development, as we have done with a few homes and their gardens, you can start your garden design with a blank slate, and every plant can be selected by you. But the drawback of that, as certainly we learned in Colorado, is time, for that is what it takes a lot of for things to grow to any meaningful size. In Colorado, it takes three years just for plants to establish themselves and very little growing takes place in that time. Then, when plants do start putting on size, it is a very slow affair. Here, in the Mid-Atlantic States, things grow much more rapidly. In any event, inheriting a well-loved garden is better than starting from scratch, even if that is possible, which usually it is not. And so you have to edit out the plants you don't like, divide and increase the ones you do, and put up with the large things that define the property.

Gardeners, as a rule, are fairly well adjusted in putting up with things that have to be put up with—weather, pests, disappointments, geography, unwelcome indoor tasks assigned by non-gardening members of one's household, and things like that. There comes to mind the somewhat facetious prayer: "Lord, give me the strength to change what I can, the humility to accept what I cannot, and the wisdom to know the difference." Gardeners live this prayer every day, and in all they do.

One of the things about this property that is very much in the category of needing to be put up with, and which probably cannot be changed without a great deal of expense, is the dratted hemlock trees. I have never been partial to the hemlock. Actually, I am being too mild in an effort to seem more open-minded than I really am. The truth is: I don't like them. I think they are unattractive and even border on the ugly. While some admire their small needles and blurry, feathery growing habit, I see only effeteness and a lack of self-expression.

Too, they are a very untidy tree, shedding dense clouds of green pollen that cover the cars, the windowsills and the porch furniture, and which is followed by millions of small unpleasant seed cones, and they drop needles profusely all year round. Their lower branches die off rapidly and you have to either limb them aggressively, which becomes more and more difficult and expensive as they age and also causes them to look unnatural, or let them go—as I do, always preferring laziness and thrift, especially when it can be disguised as a natural look and as a design ethic—leaving the winter snows to bring down an occasional dead branch. We have the bad luck of having three of these unpleasant creatures, big ones too, all standing in a row on the southern edge of our property. It is better than having nothing there at all, but only just. And yet, as I say, we accept what we cannot change (or are too cheap or too lazy to change).

On the other hand, gardeners know that life also brings us good things we don't look for or expect, and almost certainly don't deserve. For example, holly trees. For years, I have loved these creatures, though I could never grow them myself, and not for lack of trying. I planted them at all our Colorado homes and they never did well, rarely even surviving and never really flourishing. But when we lived in Virginia, we had two enormous holly bushes (not the tree form, but the large, dense bush form) growing in front of our house, and they were so large and vigorous that they came to overwhelm the front porch of our little bungalow and looked very out of proportion. So I actually had to harden my heart and remove one of these venerable things. Much easier said than done, that turned out to be. They have an enormous and very deep taproot that is made of a heavy, wet wood that is remarkably like concrete to cut through. That was a very hard job, but eventually, it was accomplished and the front of the house was re-opened to the light and the view. The twin of that holly remained and was a favorite hiding place for birds and, of course, supplied the house with masses of holly for Christmas. And here in this long-established garden, to my very great delight, we have half a dozen or more enormous holly trees, some so old they must be forty or fifty feet tall, and they rejoice my heart every time my glance falls on them. What luck!

We also have, as a great compensation for putting up with the hemlocks, another half-dozen Serbian spruces growing on the land of our neighbor to the east, but seeming to be in our yard, so emphatically do they define the long vista from our patio down to the far end of our back yard. This borrowed view is sublime, and we often sit on the patio of an evening, looking east and admiring the light of the setting sun shining from behind us and being reflected in the tops of these great trees. We call it "The Golden Hour." We have only one of these great Serbian spruces on our own land, but it is far larger than any of those on our neighbor's land and was perhaps their progenitor. It is almost three feet in diameter, and towers above our house, a colossus.

Do you know this unusual being? It reminds me of that beautiful, sheltering tree that is the subject of the lyrical and classic children's Christmas book, *A Possible Tree*. It has, for an evergreen, a very distinctive growing habit. Its very long branches droop downward, but then curve back up near the end of the branch, giving its limbs a very characteristic and graceful appearance, as of a lady lifting her old-fashioned skirts to step over a rain puddle. They drop very large pine cones, which we gather to burn in our outdoor fire pit for their piney aroma. The trees are supposedly very rare, and certainly, I had never seen them before living here. At one time, long ago, they were only available at a single nursery in Princeton, and while rare elsewhere, one now sees them everywhere in central and southern New Jersey. Personally, I would put up with ten hemlocks just to have one of these noble spruces.

Speaking of good things that life brings us, yesterday evening while I had the house to myself, I made the cold summer salad we call "Japanese salad." This is a really great recipe for many reasons. You can make it in advance; indeed, its flavors are supposed to be allowed to percolate at least overnight. It is fresh and cold, and makes a great summer dinner *al fresco*. The nuts and chicken make it very proteinaceous and satisfying, and it is a real crowd-pleaser.

Japanese Salad

For the salad:
6 cups diced barbecued chicken breast
8 oz. toasted slivered almonds
6 Tbsp. toasted sesame seeds
3 3-ounce packages ramen noodles
6 finely chopped green onions
2 cups shredded red cabbage
1 cup shredded bok choy

For the dressing:
3 Tbsp. sugar
¾ cup olive oil
¼ cup sesame seed oil
1 Tbsp. salt
1½ tsp. freshly ground black pepper
¼ cup rice vinegar
3 Tbsp. Szechuan spice (if you can find it)

Combine all the salad ingredients in a large bowl after breaking up and cooking the ramen noodles as directed (discard the "flavor packet"). A comment about the chicken: be careful not to over-cook the chicken breasts on the grill. Use a meat thermometer and remove them from the heat when the temperature of the thickest part of the breast is 160 degrees; there is no need to cook beyond that, and some authorities even say anything above 140 degrees is safe. The idea is to keep them moist and tender. Put all the dressing ingredients in a container and shake well, then pour it over the salad and allow to percolate at least overnight.

We often make this when we are going to have company in the summer and want something that is easy, tasty, and fresh. It keeps for days and people will have it for breakfast, or lunch, or any time. For dessert, you can serve very cold cantaloupe and pair that with a dessert sauterne, if your taste runs in that direction. Or you can serve it with a nice cold Provençal rosé wine, as indeed, they really do in Provence. I remember sitting out on the graveled garden terrace under towering columnar cedars on a soft, velvety Provençal night at our friends' rambling old house there, eating cold melon and drinking the cold local rosé: fabulous, and you are very close to heaven there.

Or you can have it with my own personal concoction, which I call the Yellow Bird. You take equal parts of limoncello (homemade if you have it, store-bought if you must) and pineapple juice, served over crushed ice. You can drink it just like this or you can dilute it with club soda to make it less sweet and more refreshing. It is very simple and the taste is out of this world. If you want to serve something that is really astonishing and will have your guests devoted to you and your genius for the rest of your life, you can put balls of lemon sorbet in a parfait glass (a large wineglass will do also), then pour a generous measure of ice-cold Yellow Bird over it and serve quickly. It is so good, the police will likely have to be called, but there you are.

❦

The Tao of Ironing

Personal fulfillment gurus advise us to have a period of quiet time each morning to reflect on our life, our short-term and long-term goals, and the agenda for the coming day. Well, I too like to have a quiet moment to re-energize and think about the new day, and usually it is spent walking through the quiet garden in the early morning hours. But we have had so much rain for the last month, and so very little sun, that there has been precious little morning reflection time in the garden. What's a gardener to do? I find I have to rummage restlessly about inside the house for more mundane opportunities of coming across the occasional epiphany, hoping always not to run into others in the household, trotting around the place purposefully with an unwelcome and distracting "to do" list in hand.

It is pouring with rain again early today, and the gardener's eye falls upon a large pile of ironing in the laundry room, awaiting attention. The great American philosopher Erma Bombeck once said that her second favorite household chore was ironing, her very favorite being hitting her head on the top bunk until she faints. I cannot agree. Give me a big pile of ironing and soon I am dreamily lost in this steamy, soothing, and satisfying task. My dog differs with me profoundly on this. Though he is normally lucid and perfectly logical, he has a lifelong hatred of the ironing board, which he thinks is an implement of Satan and is somehow connected with Satan's right hand and equally evil sidekick, our mailman.

But what is it about ironing? Can the door to true bliss and spiritual enlightenment really be…*ironing*? It seems most unlikely, and yet, there is something about ironing clothes that is very close to holiness somehow. Did you know this could be a spiritual discipline and have you ever tried this? You get a great pile of laundry that needs to be ironed, you go into a room with nothing but yourself, the hot iron and the simple task at hand, and you proceed to smooth out all the wrinkles of life, with the hot steam and the starch and the sizzling cotton, and the quiet and the concentration. Your mind is wholly within your work. Your simple task is all-absorbing. You are decidedly in the present and you get lost in the Zen-like calmness and intensity of the uncomplicated, repetitive task.

Laborare est orare, as the Benedictines say, and surely they have that right: to work is to pray. In Hebrew, significantly, the verb *avad* means both to labor and to worship. With ironing, the wrinkles disappear, the fabric of life is smoothed out, you move on, beyond. It is hypnotic, so soothing. Other members of the household cruelly lampoon the gardener's love of ironing and the trancelike state it induces in him, and yet he can't help noticing how happy they are to drop off their shirts, pillow cases, and pajamas to be added to the ironing pile and to be returned fresh, starched, and folded.

It does not have to be ironing, of course. Any simple and wholesome task will do. It could be reading a good book, weeding the garden, taking a long walk with someone you love through a familiar landscape, or making food for sorrowing or celebrating friends. God is not found in the big obvious things, we know, but in the little subtle things, the simple things. Ironing is as good as anything, better than many; give it a try. Go into a cool room on a hot summer day, a cool basement is perfect. Close the door, fire up your iron, get a good-sized can of starch, and find grace in the little things, for that is surely where it is, waiting as always.

Outdoors, the garden loves all the moisture, with just enough brightness for everything to grow quite well. It's an English climate, really, and for now, the garden grows like an English garden. We have our full Shasta daisies opening, almost shoulder high, which is a bit excessive. I can't remember ever having to walk through the daisies before, parting them like towering corn stalks or jungle foliage. Perhaps I am shrinking, I think. And the helianthus have just cleared the tops of their four-foot frames, too. The cautious, tropical cannas were slow to start, given the cold spring, and a few other stalwarts like the helianthus and the black-eyed Susans have been holding back. The cannas are so conservative in their outlook and temperament that, if they could vote, they would all vote Republican, to be sure. The same with cats. Dogs would be more dividedly bipartisan.

The summer solstice is, of course, the classic time for roses, which overwhelm the garden at this time of year with their ostentatious beauty. The popular 'Knock Out' varieties are among the first to bloom, and what they lack in form and fragrance, they certainly make up in robustness and color. I like the pinks better and they seem to bloom more profusely and longer than the red, but suit yourself. The fact that they don't need to be fussed over with sprays is certainly in their favor, in my view.

Many rose growers worry fanatically about the lower parts of their more elegant, less bushy roses, and how bare their knees typically are. They think they are ugly and want to under-plant them with something that will cover up their imagined unsightliness, but then, of course, it is hard to get at the rose to feed and cultivate it appropriately. Happily, I have never suffered from this odd malady and am content to just leave their lower stems bare. Actually, I rather like their stems, and frankly admire the tough, thick stems—trunks, really—of a really venerable old rose. I have sometimes seen them three inches thick, and I think they look just fine.

I tend to take plants as I find them and even like the shape and color and glossiness of rose leaves, which even most rose enthusiasts think are rather poor and unimpressive, so there you are. But if you have a Victorian fetish about bare rose knees, and therapy has been to no avail and you feel you simply have to do something about it, then by all means consider under-planting them with a companion like salvia, whose abundant purple blooms are a great foil for the pastels of most roses, or stachys, with its cool gray foliage and mild lavender colored flowers. Or speaking of lavender, you could do much worse than just using lavender itself with your roses, or Russian sage, which though not as elegant, I find rather easier to grow.

I notice with great satisfaction that the single clump of rare, pale lavender phlox we have is blooming pleasingly next to the hostas, whose blooms are exactly the same shade of pale lavender. I actually planned it that way, and how well they look together in reality. And how satisfying it is to see a simple scheme like this come off in the garden, for once. When the two are blooming together in arrestingly identical shades of pale lavender, life does not get much better than that, really, when you think about it.

This weekend, I cut our first hydrangeas, light blue, and have them in a vase with pink flags of astilbe. Our three mulleins are already chest high, and I intend to dig up three first-year mulleins, to have them on hand to bloom next year. I spent a lot of time drinking morning lattes and reading Margot Asquith's superb autobiography and Buchan's *Greenmantle* on the porch, with my loyal sheltie looking very regal on the steamer chair next to mine, watching all the birds and the leverets dash about on the lawn in the occasional rain showers.

And now the rain has stopped, the ironing is all finished and put away, and it is time to make the most of a summer day and whip up a quick batch of crab cakes for tonight's dinner. Really good crab is now available year-round in most cities, and what a treat this is any time of the year.

Classic Crab Cakes

16 oz. lump crab meat
3 eggs, whisked
1 cup Panko bread crumbs
3 oz. chopped fresh chives
2 cloves garlic

4 Tbsp. good mayonnaise
¼ tsp. salt
¼ tsp. cayenne pepper
½ cup olive oil
½ cup canola oil

Combine the crab meat, egg, bread crumbs, and chives in a mixing bowl. I know, purists will not like using a third egg and so much bread crumbs but, while I bow to their zeal for crab cake purity, I find the cakes just don't hold together well unless you use this minimum amount of bonding ingredients. Using your hands, shape the crab mixture into six patties and place them on a plate lined with wax paper, in the fridge. Process the garlic cloves in a press, and combine it with the mayonnaise, salt, and cayenne, stirring until the mixture is smooth. Put this in the fridge and allow several hours for the flavors to combine. When you are ready to fry the patties, combine the oils in a covered saucepan and put it over a medium high flame. When the oil is hot, cook the crab cakes in one batch, turning once, until they are golden brown. Drain on paper towel, then serve warm with a dollop of the garlic mayonnaise on each cake. Serves 4-6.

Alpine Solstice, Maritime Solstice

Circumstances so arrange themselves that, on the longest day of the year, we find ourselves deep in the heart of the Rocky Mountains, at the foot of the great gray wall of the Continental Divide, in fact. We are visiting our daughter, who has landed a great summer job as a horse wrangler and kid counselor at a high-end dude ranch for well-to-do city slickers. The ranch is very beautiful, and she seems very happy there, introducing us to one horse after another, and describing the personality of each. We take her out to dinner miles from the ranch in the resort town of Winter Park and sit outside on the restaurant patio, eating dinner and altogether enjoying the dying sunlight of the solstice, long after eight o'clock, vowing together to remember this golden moment half a year later in the darkness and cold of Christmas week.

I delivered myself of a long-winded, closely reasoned parental discourse artfully arranged to prove something our daughter did not particularly wish to hear, I forget what it was exactly. Her not wishing to hear it, though, I remember plainly, because after listening to me politely while I rabbited on for some time and then finally came to the end of my tiresome oration, she cheerfully replied with her famously devastating one word dismissal: "False!" And that was the end of my credibility and influence on *that* point, whatever it was. She is a marvel of willfulness, this daughter of She Who Must Be Obeyed, I thought to myself, and I wonder where she gets it.

I remember once we were having breakfast at a restaurant when she can't have been much older than twelve years old, and I admonished her to break her bagel in half before applying cream cheese to it. "Why?" she asked, not really interested, but only mildly curious.

"Because," I explained patiently, "it's traditional good manners to do that. You always break your bread in half before putting something on it; it's just the right thing to do."

"Well, I think it's dumb, and you are going to have to give me a better reason that that," she said.

"It is simply what civilized people do. If we do not keep up the standards of civilized people, then civilized life as we know is doomed to come to a bad end and collapse into a lot of heathen people eating their bread any old way and without any regard for tradition and propriety," I waxed on, warming to my theme a little too much. I probably carried my point a bit too far in predicting the end of civilization; I admit it now. She stared at me hard a moment and then, never taking her eyes off mine, coolly applied the cream cheese defiantly to the unbroken bread and ate it with extra satisfaction. Ah yes, as I say, a marvel of willfulness.

We part with her on this day reluctantly, knowing we will not see her again this summer and feeling the poignant pangs that every parent knows in saying goodbye to our not-quite-emancipated children. Then we drive away over Berthoud Pass. Often this difficult mountain pass is treacherous, especially in winter, but this particular evening, it is magical. First, we see a regal moose, of all things, at the edge of the forest not far from the road, and what a spectacular sight this is. But it is nothing compared to what awaits us as we crest the long winding pass and get a full, horizon-to-horizon view of the mountainous spine that is the Continental Divide: a sheer wall of pale green tundra and jagged gray stone heights far above timberline, overtopped by fleecy white clouds that are peeking over from the other side of the divide, boiling high up into the heavens above the ragged dentition of the angular peaks. All this fantastic geography is lit in roiling pinks and yellows by the pale fire of the fading light of the longest day, and the scene is utterly fantastic.

Strangely, like a dream sequence, there is no traffic on the pass, and this amazing light show on the top of the world seems to be put on for us alone. We actually decide to pull over and watch the show, amazed and grateful. After a time, we get back on the road. We don't speak, but descend slowly from this empyrean height, feeling like Zeus coming down from Mount Olympus, solemn and pre-occupied, and every turn of the steep and winding road brings to the hungry eye a new vista of this magnificent tableau. It is like a vast canvas by the western painter Thomas Moran, the pink and gold light painting and repainting the scene in infinite variety. Eventually, we reach the lower regions of the valley at the bottom of the pass; the light of the dying solstice is now lost and the landscape returns to normal, from celestial to merely terrestrial. We return to our daily lives, but we are slightly transformed interiorly.

The next day, we fly back to our home in the east, and late that night, I am sitting alone in the garden on the border of the dense, dark forest that is on the other side of our garden fence. We have been gone for more than a week, and in that time, the fireflies have come out in great number. And I see the dark forest is lit with literally hundreds, perhaps even thousands, of them. It glitters and sparkles with their twinkling lights, as if the entire forest had been bedecked in our absence with a myriad tiny fairy lights. I walk over to the garden fence and peer deeply into the forest, sparkling with the brilliant firefly lights. And I think about these two lights of the summer solstice, one alpine and one maritime; I pack them carefully into my memory, hoping to carry their light with me for a long time.

I shrug off my melancholia, take one last look at the glittering, sparkling dark forest, and go back inside, where I find that my wife's mind is operating in this same wistful, parental groove. I know this without her saying anything, because she is making one of her ultimate comfort foods, cheddar cheese popovers. And so we sit down for a quiet dinner together, just the two of us, with the Popover of Consolation.

The Popover of Consolation

4 Tbsp. butter, melted
1 cup flour
½ tsp. salt
¼ tsp. freshly ground pepper
1 cup whole milk
3 eggs
½ cup shredded cheddar cheese
½ cup grated Velveeta cheese
2 cups frozen broccoli, thawed and drained

16 saltine crackers, coarsely crumbled
4 pieces bacon, cooked and chopped

Pre-heat oven to 375. Spray 6 cups of a popover or muffin pan with vegetable spray. Drizzle half of the butter in the bottom of the 6 cups. In a bowl, whisk together the flour, salt and pepper. In another bowl, whisk together the milk and eggs. Add the wet ingredients to the dry and whisk for two minutes, then whisk in the cheese. Fill each cup 1/3 full with the batter. Divide the broccoli evenly between the 6 cups, then cover with the remaining batter. Top the popovers with the crumbled saltines and the bacon, then drizzle the remainder of the butter over the tops. Bake for 20 minutes, then reduce heat to 325 and bake for 12 more minutes. Remove from oven and allow popovers to set for 10 minutes. Serve warm.

July

Toads of Yesteryear

If you happen to have friends who live in the very cosmopolitan city of Hong Kong, it is very likely they are going to get plenty of visitors from around the world. Well, this month it happens to be our own sixteen-year-old son. What a lucky boy. With only a little trepidation, he flew the sixteen-hour non-stop route from Newark to Hong Kong. Our friends have generously taken him on a trip to Xi'an to see the terracotta warriors and the tomb of the first Chin emperor. He, of course, is having the time of his life, and we are getting daily updates via email and text. They were dehydrated by the heat today and naturally could not drink the unsafe tap water, so he had to drink beer and got a little tipsy, he was happy to report.

Suffering ourselves from the oppressive heat closer to home, we decided to get a break from it and drive down to Stone Harbor to stay at our friends' cottage at the seaside. We passed through mile after mile of southern New Jersey's vast blueberry belt. I noticed a stunning blue heron flying over the blueberry fields in a perfectly blue sky and I thought to myself, well, you don't see *that* very often: blue in blue over blue. In other wildlife news, last night we were sitting out on the patio here at the beach, sipping wine after dinner and talking, waiting for it to get late enough to go down to the beach for the fireworks display, when I felt something large and rather solid drop past my shoulder. Startled, I looked down at the ground and there, to my surprise, was a toad, literally the first I have seen after living in New Jersey all these years and the first I have seen anywhere in a long time. This little guy apparently lives in the moist gutters of the cottage roof (I would guess, as that is where he fell from) and likes to come out in the evening and take up his position near the outdoor light that attracts bugs, the fat lazy thing.

Honestly, where have all the toads gone? Said another way: *Où sont les crapauds d'antan?* Probably there is something wrong in their ecosystem and I don't want to be an alarmist, but no doubt our own species is somehow implicated. Toads do not have many friends, though it is hard to see why, but for an unreasoning prejudice against their appearance and thousands of years of superstition against them. One of their great champions was the celebrated botanist and naturalist of the eighteenth century, Joseph Banks, who loved to nuzzle with toads. He wrote in a letter to a friend, "I have from my childhood, in conformity with the precepts of a mother void of all imaginary fear, been in the constant habit of taking toads in my hand, and applying them to my nose and face as it may happen. My motive for doing this very frequently is to inculcate the opinion I have held, since I was told by my mother, that the toad is actually a harmless animal; and to whose manner of life man is certainly under some obligation as its food is chiefly those insects which devour his crops and annoy him in various ways." And quite right too.

Really, one sees toads and frogs and even turtles very seldom these days. Their habitats are so under attack and are everywhere shrinking, and I think the ubiquitous use of chemicals, particularly insecticides, is very hard on them and their habitats. Perhaps our children or grandchildren will rarely, if ever, see them except in zoos. It is a sad thought. But just the other day, Cosimo found a magnificent tortoise the size of a large grapefruit bathing in a pothole at the foot of our driveway, no doubt lured out of hiding by this tiny accumulation of moisture in what has been a pretty dry season. I haven't seen one of those since I was my son's age. Cosimo was thrilled and worried by this strange creature, dancing around it and barking excitedly, getting close to examine it in extreme curiosity, then darting back in alarm or amazement. He was enthralled; we all were. In the end, we decided to move it carefully to our backyard, which borders on acres of untouched woodland, where it should be perfectly safe and which is no doubt where it came from.

After all the excitement about the tortoise, I was finally able to go back to the patio and pick my current book back up. Recently, I saw recommended *A Time of Gifts*, the first of Fermor's great, three-volume memoir of walking from Holland to Constantinople at age nineteen in 1933, across what is now a completely vanished world, of course. Imagine walking across Europe at that young age and in that time, walking across Germany just as the Nazi terror was coming to power, strolling observantly through a wonderful world that was about to perish forever in flame and death. These books were first published in England late in Fermor's life, the first one in 1977, but somehow I completely missed them until now.

I am enchanted by the reveries he invokes. The way the books were composed is most interesting. They grew out of his travel diaries, written at an age when he was open to the wonders of the world as a young man, boy almost, with considerable observational gifts. Then the diaries were put away—and much of the original material was lost through bad luck in World War II—and the books themselves were written much later, when the boy had become an old man, a great writer at the height of his powers. And in the books, you can hear both voices, see both points of view, read the one writer enthusing about a wonderful experience while understanding it is being told by another writer who knows all of that world disappeared forever in an evil conflagration. So you get both perspectives, one feelingly perceived by an adventurous boy and the other well-crafted by a gifted older man, both writing about a beautiful and bucolic world the boy perceived and from the perspective of the older man who knew it was a doomed world. Enthralling.

A few days ago, I was likewise sitting on the patio, engrossed in Fermor's memoir. I had been cleaning up the yard and watering everything thoroughly, so I could be away from the garden at the beach for a week in high summer. I had just sat down on the patio for a moment to rest when my attention was attracted by a lot of bird commotion, and suddenly, a harassed blue jay flew right down into the patio. He landed in the dogwood and prepared to drink thirstily from the fountain, but was followed by an angry escort of no fewer than four irate wrens, a couple of robins, and a scolding scarlet male cardinal. Whatever the jay had been doing, it had not met with acceptance by our resident bird population; probably bothering nestlings, I would guess, or perhaps they were just escorting him off the property based on prejudice and his kind's (deserved) bad reputation among the avian gentlefolk.

Anyway, besides toads and tortoises and so on being so rare in our present age, it also occurs to me that not many young men are walking across Europe these days. They are no doubt too busy with more important concerns like Xbox and Facebook and suchlike diversions, but I can't help thinking the world would be a better place than it is now if we had in it a lot more toads and tortoises and even just a few more dreamers and wanderers like Fermor.

Granola, the Real Thing

I came by my interest in granola honestly. As a child of the sixties (a very young child of the sixties, I hasten to say), I was there when America discovered this rich and earthy cereal. It was a tiny part of the hippy culture of the time, because it was cheap, wholesome and a calculated rebuke to corporate America, which had (and let's be honest, still has) corrupted the market of breakfast foods by making them loaded with sugar and salt, lacking in food value, low in fiber, and generally processed almost past the point where they are any good for us anymore. It is time for us to take back the morning, and nothing is easier than doing that by making your own granola.

Growing up, we had an uncle who was (and is still) a painter of considerable talent, and in the 1950s, he went off to Paris to study painting. As a kind of beatnik artist, he really was more of the Jack Kerouac generation than the hippy generation, but he definitely lived a different life of art and no rules. Of course, we kids all thought he was fabulously glamorous—no rules and art, what could be better than that! —and we got to go visit him and his wife in turns. They lived in a small shack, improbably right on the water's edge on the spectacular, halfmoon beach of Morro Bay, California, with its postcard-famous rock monolith protruding from the center of the picturesque bay. I cannot conceive how they came to live in such a gorgeous spot, but property laws were somewhat more lax in that free-wheeling era. Think Gidget and Moondoggie: totally fun, no parents in sight, and surfing whenever you wanted to. At any rate, from the point of view of a visiting nephew, living in a shack on the beach and making a living, sort of, as an artist who made his own rules and worked his own hours…it all seemed fairly perfect. All I had to do was fall off the dock into the bay to go for a swim, and I learned how to bait a string with chicken bones to pull up crabs from below the dock, who, in their greed, would rather be pulled out of the water and captured alive than let go of their prized drumstick. (I have known more than a few humans who were likewise simple-minded in their unlimited avarice, as who has not?)

Every day began, before a swim, with homemade granola and whole milk, and I became a lifelong devotee of this great way to begin the day. I have given several recipes for other things here, and the thing most of them have in common is that they are simple ways to re-introduce wholesomeness and good taste into our family food preparation, to replace corporately manufactured foods that have been dumbed down: over-processed, over-cooked, stripped of food value, loaded with sugar and salt and fat, and basically adulterated in every way our large food companies can think up to make us crave a product that is really not very good or good for us.

Wouldn't it be nice to try a different path, something that is more nourishing and interesting? So, without wishing to be doctrinaire about it, we should just eat lower on the food chain, eat more organic food, more locally grown food, and food that is less processed…and less cooked, if you can bear it. And while we are at it, we should make our food taste better and more authentic, simple, and fun. Easier to prepare would be nice, too, as we are all very busy, and we can't spend the whole day finding and preparing food, as our ancient ancestors had to do and as, indeed, some people still do in poorer parts of the world.

And so here is a great and practical way to strike a blow for food that is rich-tasting, good for you, and loaded with fiber and heart-healthy ingredients. And it is easy, inexpensive, unusual, authentic, and nostalgic all at once. What could be better?

California Granola

Vegetable cooking spray
18 oz. old-fashioned, uncooked rolled oats
1 cup sliced almonds, toasted
½ cup apple juice
6 Tbsp. maple syrup
2 Tbsp. brown sugar
2 Tbsp. vegetable oil
1 tsp. vanilla extract
½ tsp. salt
1 tsp. allspice
1 tsp. cinnamon
1 tsp. freshly ground nutmeg
1 cup dried blueberries or cherries (or raisins, if you must)

Pre-heat oven to 325 degrees. Lightly coat a rimmed cooking sheet with the vegetable spray. Add the oats and bake them until they are crisp and fragrant, about 30 minutes. Some, but not all, of the oats should be a bit toasted and the perfect time to take them out is when they just begin to smoke a tiny bit from the toasting process. Scrape the toasted oats into a large bowl and add the almonds. In a small saucepan, combine the remaining ingredients (except the dried fruit) and stir over a low heat for a minute or two until dissolved. Pour the mixture over the oats and nuts and stir.

Do, by all means, at this point stick your nose deep into the bowl and inhale this extremely fragrant mash of roasted oats and sweet spices. Heaven. If you are lucky enough (and crazy enough) to have a horse in your life, as we do, this is the point at which you scoop out a cupful or two of this fragrant oat mash and put it in a re-sealable bag; whenever you go to the barn, you can give your horse a discreet handful of this and he will be your friend for life, if he is not already. Oh the heck with it; you can make a double batch, so the horse can have a more generous portion. They do not stint in their love for us, after all, so why should we?

Anyway, leaving the barn and returning to the kitchen, you spread the combined granola back onto the cooking sheet and return it to the oven for 30 more minutes. Then turn the oven off and leave the mixture in it until the oven is cold, so it dries out thoroughly. Finally, add the dried fruit and then store the granola in a re-sealable container. It keeps for 2-3 weeks. Remember that the pan is red-hot while you are handling it; I know this because I have burned myself on it many, many times, in my haste and carelessness. I can show you many granola scars, emblems of my haste and folly. You, however, are not as foolish as I am and will take more care.

You can combine real, homemade yogurt and the granola to form a power food combination that will make you a force to be reckoned with for the rest of the day. Try it; you'll be amazed, and you will like how elevated your energy levels are. Sometimes, when I am on a tear around the house and am accomplishing things right and left and driving everyone nuts like a whirling dervish, She Who Must Be Obeyed will pointedly ask me if I have been eating this power-food granola with yogurt again. After I admit it, the granola bin sometimes turns up empty the next day. Hmmmm, a message of some sort in that probably. Anyway, here's a wicked suggestion, try this granola with cold whole milk, or even cream; hell, it's not illegal yet, you know, so why not live a little while we still can. And, once you have this fabulous staple on hand, try using it to make oatmeal cookies. Just use your favorite oatmeal cookie recipe, and substitute this granola when oatmeal is called for.

Cheese Grits and Rock & Roll

After a particularly grueling slog at my day job in the metropolis, I emerge from our silvery, over-air-conditioned skyscraper into a stifling, shimmering haze of stunning heat and humidity. It is like stepping out of a chilly Las Vegas casino into the overheated radiator of an oncoming, cross-country semi-tractor. It is 105 degrees at 6:00 p.m., with humidity of about, oh, say 189%. I feel like I am being abducted by kidnappers who wrap a hot, wet towel of chloroform around my face, except that instead of chloroform, it is just the humidity and odors of a big city, grilling and sizzling like a big piece of meat on the hot July gridiron, just the way poor St. Lawrence was martyred. With a whiff of sewer gas, car exhaust, and cigarette smoke thrown in to round off the offensive urban smells.

We are a very traditional company and I stand there, stupefied by the heat, in my nice suit and tie, wilting quickly and feeling like a forlorn and confused Dick Van Dyke in the black and white sitcom of my life. In this crazy episode, I yank my tie off and open my collar, and try to resume breathing somewhat normally. This is just what Dubai is like in summer, I think ruefully, and I've been there. Brother. By the time I reach my very hot car, I am withered like the bouquet of flowers I picked in the (relatively) cooler garden this morning, which I put on the patio table and forgot for ten minutes, instead of plunging it immediately into cold water. Ruined and wilted, of course, as I am now.

I dream of a cool evening indoors; it is too hot even to think about the patio tonight, even in the dark. Sometimes I hose down the patio and that cools things off, but it adds to the humidity, to be sure. So in weather like this, it is better just to stay inside with the AC cranked as high as we dare. It is shocking how expensive our utility bills are, with all of our deliciously chilled air pouring out of the millions of cracks and leaks in this handsome old house. We have the reverse in winter, of course, when it is the *heat* pouring out and the delicious chill pouring *in*. There should be a way to balance that out somehow, but I can't think of it.

We have music and cold white wine after dinner, and my mind wanders down the avenues of memory, the music calling to mind long summer nights when, as children, we would be allowed to stay up later than during the school year and listen to music. We all loved music, naturally, as much as this generation or as any modern generation of young people, but music for us in Western Colorado was a lot harder to come by. I speak of the time, of course, before personal music players, the internet, file sharing, and so on. For us, music came from records, and vinyl ones at that, and they were frustratingly expensive. It was all a long time ago.

You could listen to the radio. Because we lived in a small western town, there were only three radio stations: there was the old fogey station that basically played music for our parents, a country and western station that I disdained, though now I rather like it, and a single other station that had to cover everything else, from rock and roll to R&B, soul and Motown, to the wild musical innovation that was happening in the late sixties and early seventies, before music fell into the black hole of disco for a while. You could listen on your parents' hi-fi, which was lame, or you could listen on your own stereo in your room, if you were old enough and lucky enough to have one. But most of us had to make do with small transistor radios. I would tuck mine under my pillow as a kid and fall asleep at night listening to music, half the time forgetting to turn it off and rapidly burning through a kid's fortune in transistor radio batteries.

The great thing about those summer nights, or one of them, was not just that your parents let you stay up later and didn't care how late you turned the radio off; it was that late at night was when the radio choices broadened, mysteriously. For reasons I don't understand, the FCC let some Midwestern radio stations boost the power of their antennas up to 50,000 watts at midnight. Probably because other stations signed off, so there was less interference? Anyway, it was enough to boost the signal of KOMA in Oklahoma City over the Rocky Mountains and into my little radio under the pillow in my boyhood bedroom. And this was *so* much better than our local rock and roll station. I listened to it like a guilty pleasure, like a zealous devotee of some obscure sect, hearing ethereal intimations from another world. Or like teenagers half a world away were doing in Eastern Europe in those Cold War days, hungering for real information and real western music, listening to Radio Free Europe and the Voice of America. Improbably, I grew up thinking of Oklahoma City as the cutting edge of style and modernity.

Well, as fate would have it, my wife is from there, and so Oklahoma City has never let me down or lost its charm for me. Nor has she, come to think of it. Not everyone is lucky enough to marry a southerner, of course, (all right, southwesterner, if you are a stickler), no matter how hard they may try or want to, but I can't help that. People have to look out for themselves in some things, after all; I can't do everything. So you might miss out on some of the great things about southern living.

Like cheesy grits, for example. Try this recipe for cheese grits, a major food group for all right-thinking people. To make it even more interesting, we add shrimp and an amazing new way to deep-fry eggs. Yes, deep-fry them, the way God intended them to be. Just forget that it is hot-as-hell July. Instead, imagine that it is a blazing hot, fresh morning in February on Duval Street in Key West, you are home after a long run and a quick dip in the sea, drinking a Bloody Mary, with somebody else doing all the work, and with classic late sixties rock and roll playing in the background. Heaven, and you are there. We make no claim that this is a healthy breakfast, only that it is fantastically delicious, and you will love this new way to make eggs.

Duval Street Cheese Grits with Deep-Fried Eggs and Shrimp

To soft boil the eggs:
8 whole eggs
1 Tbsp. vinegar
1 tsp. salt

For the meat:
8 pieces of good quality bacon, thick cut, if possible
1½ pounds of large fresh shrimp, peeled and cleaned

For the grits:
2 cups of stone ground grits
2 cups chicken stock
2 cups whole milk
1½ cups sharp white cheddar cheese, grated
2/3 cup freshly grated *parmigiano reggiano*
Salt and freshly ground pepper to taste
2 Tbsp. bacon grease
A bottle of your favorite hot sauce

To deep-fry the eggs:

½ cup flour

¼ tsp. salt

¼ teaspoon cayenne pepper

2 eggs, lightly beaten

½ cup Panko (Japanese-style) bread crumbs

Vegetable oil for deep-fat-frying

Put eight whole eggs in a saucepan, cover with at least one inch of cold water; add the vinegar and the salt (they prevent cracking, make the eggs easier to peel, and prevent the white from leaking if the eggs do crack). Bring to a boil, watched closely. The *second* the water begins to boil, turn the heat down so the water boils gently for a steady count of exactly 180. To get the slightly runny egg you want for the finished product, it is important to start with a precisely three-minute boiled egg. With a slotted spoon, transfer the eggs to a bowl of cool water; run cool tap water over them, the idea being to stop the cooking process. Then very gently peel them, taking care to keep the eggs as whole as possible. Make a few extra the first time, until you get the hang of handling them, as they are wobbly and break easily. Return them to the refrigerator.

Fry the bacon in a skillet until it is slightly crispy but still juicy. Transfer to drain on paper towel, reserving the bacon grease. When cool, chop bacon into a quarter inch dice and set aside. Fry the shrimp in the bacon grease until just cooked. Reserve 2 Tbsp. of the shrimpy bacon grease.

Put the grits in a bowl with 4 cups water and stir; allow to rest for five minutes, then drain. In a saucepan, bring the milk and the stock to a boil, and then slowly whisk in the grits, for at least one full minute. Yes, home-made stock is *much* better for this purpose but yes, you may use store-bought stock if you must. We try to let everyone rise to their own level around here, you know. Reduce heat to medium low (barely bubbling) and cover. Then cook the grits, stirring every so often, until they thicken; it takes about 15-20 minutes. If you use "instant" grits, just follow the instructions on the packet, using equal parts milk and stock instead of water, for a richer taste. Add the cheeses until melted and whisk the mixture until it is smooth, then stir in the bacon grease; if the grits are too thick, add more stock until you get the consistency you want. Season with salt and pepper. Use a heavy hand here; the grits are a bit bland even with the cheese, so knock yourself out.

Move on to finish the eggs. Place flour in a shallow dish. Stir in ¼ teaspoon each of salt and pepper. Place lightly beaten eggs in a small bowl. Place the bread crumbs in a shallow plate. Remove boiled eggs from refrigerator. Gently wet each egg with tap water, then carefully roll each egg in the flour mixture to coat, and then roll each in the egg batter. Roll each coated egg in the bread crumbs to coat; set aside. In heavy saucepan, heat two inches of vegetable oil to about 350°F. Fry the eggs, two or three at a time, about one minute or until golden brown. The yolks should be runny when eggs are broken open. Sprinkle the grits liberally with chopped bacon and assemble the shrimp on top of the grits; place two of the deep-fried eggs on each plate. Add lots and *lots* of hot sauce; don't be a cry-baby. Serves 4.

Roadside Farm Stands
God made July for going to the beach, as everyone knows, and if you are lucky enough to live within an hour or so of the coast, that makes it easier to get away often. A lake will do nearly as well in a pinch, but it

is not quite as good as the beach. There is just something special about how good saltwater feels on your skin. Not to mention the healthful therapy of the hot sun and the cold seawater, endlessly alternated all day, with the fresh air, some really good books, friends and family, and the complete impossibility of doing household and garden chores, no matter how much you may want to.

The heat inland has been quite amazing lately, rather overpowering, in fact. The garden is looking pretty ragged, of course, as are we all. Even the hydrangeas, one of the indefatigable stalwarts of the midsummer garden, are looking a bit droopy, sunburned and the worse for wear unless they are pampered by being watered every day. Once you let them dry out too much, you have lost them, and they look frowsy and unattractive for the rest of the summer.

It occurred to me while driving down to the beach that some of the best-looking flowers this time of year are not in our gardens at all, but are growing wild on the roadside, like the weeds they are. Consider the charming Queen Anne's lace and the blue cornflowers that are blooming everywhere now, the common tiger lilies along the highways of the eastern U.S., and the noble mulleins that grow practically everywhere. I love how, in the Carolinas, they plant whole acres of wildflowers in the medians of the interstate highways there, which make a delightful and lasting impression, even when you speed by at seventy miles per hour. Okay, eighty.

If you want to see flowers looking really fabulous this time of year, you need to go to higher elevations. Check out some of the ski resort towns in Colorado during this season, for example. The growing season at high altitudes is very short and very intense, and so in late July, flowers there are a riot of color and healthful vigor in the cool and refreshing alpine air, with regular afternoon showers but intense sunshine most of the day. Beaver Creek or Aspen in late July are fantastic places to visit, and the flowers blooming everywhere make them look like immaculate Swiss villages at the height of an alpine summer.

If you are more into extreme sports and adventure, you can go up to timberline in our Rocky Mountains at this time of year, when lower elevations and lower gardens are staggering under the burden of century heat, and find vast, fresh meadows filled with miles and miles of vivid and varied wildflowers. There's a town called Ouray (pronounced "yerAY") in Western Colorado, for example, where in late July, you can go jeeping up to Yankee Boy Basin at timberline and see vistas that you thought only existed in calendars or Thomas Moran paintings. You need a four-wheel-drive vehicle to do this, so you either bring your own or sign up for an escorted tour at one of the local mountain towns.

At 12,000 feet above sea level, the sheer, vertical gray walls of the Rockies rise straight up out of vast, green, flower-bedecked meadows. The air is refreshingly cool, the sunshine is intense, and the peak blooming season is very brief. The year's first snows are only a few weeks away, and the last of the winter's snow can still be seen lining the deep couloirs and crevasses of the jagged walls of stone. Everything must happen on a compressed schedule here, so everything blooms at once, basically, and it is a visual extravaganza. In our garden at sea level, there are a leisurely seven months minimum, sometimes eight, between the last frost of winter and the first frost of autumn. But here in the high alpine meadows, all of spring and summer and part of the fall are packed into six riotous weeks.

July is definitely the time for a pick-me-up, whether it's alpine vistas or the beach. And the roadside farm stands on the way home always attract us like magnets. These have so many good things to offer, and they are varied, fresh, and delicious. Plus, you earn the good citizenship points of helping local farmers instead of our giant food processing companies. Without too much trouble, you can now find local produce that is organically grown as well, so you can add organic to local and feel good about the part of the food chain from which you are consuming your food, for once.

There is a roadside stand on our way home from the beach that sells roasted chickens as well as local produce, and what a treat it is to stop there on the way home and pick up a couple of roasted chickens and a bag of whatever is ripe that week on local farms. And by this time in the summer, a lot is. The corn! The cantaloupes and onions and eggplants! And don't even get me started on the ripe, local tomatoes.

Nobody really wants to cook after a long day at the beach, do they? And sometimes you just don't have the energy to go out to eat. Here's a really good recipe for a farmer's market pie to quickly throw together, which maximizes the fresh produce in an interesting and delicious way without taking much time or fuss. So have a go at:

Farmer's Market Pie

For the pie crust:
2 cups flour
1 tsp. salt
½ cup olive oil, chilled in the freezer for one hour
4 Tbsp. ice water
(Or skip the above and just use a frozen pie crust)

For the filling:
4 large tomatoes, cut into ¼-inch slices
Olive oil spray
1¾ lbs. eggplant, cut into ½-inch rounds, then cut in half
(Zucchini can be an alternative to eggplant, if you prefer)
Kosher salt and ground black pepper
2 Tbsp. olive oil
3 large red onions, sliced thin

1 Tbsp. fresh thyme, chopped fine
1 Tbsp. balsamic vinegar
½ cup freshly grated *parmigiano reggiano*
1 cup pesto
Fresh basil leaves

Let the tomato slices drain on paper towel while beginning the prep work. Pre-heat oven to 375 and coat a large baking sheet with olive oil spray. Whisk the flour and the salt together in a large bowl. Add the olive oil and mix until the dough has the consistency of peas. Add ice water until the dough just holds together in a ball when kneaded. Shape into a six-inch disk, wrap in plastic, and chill for an hour. Or just use a frozen crust and allow it to thaw while prepping the filling. I love to do things the hard way, so making my own crust certainly has some appeal. But even I am tired after a long day at the beach, and let's face it, nobody really wants to get out the pastry knife at this point, do they? So it's okay to cheat a bit here with frozen crusts, because the whole point is that this is supposed to be quick and easy. I give the olive oil crust recipe above for the hard core.

Spray the eggplant slices with olive oil and season them with salt and pepper. Put them on the baking sheet and cook them for about 20-30 minutes, until they are just golden, then remove from heat. In a large saucepan over medium heat, brown the onions in the olive oil until translucent, about 5 minutes. Add one tsp. salt and the fresh thyme, then cook over low heat *uncovered* for another 30 minutes, until they are soft and brown. Add the vinegar and remove from heat to caramelize.

If you made your own crust, roll it out on a floured surface into a 13-inch circle and then transfer it to an 11-inch springform tart pan that has been sprayed with olive oil, and build up the edges of the crust. Put the onion mixture on the tart first, then the eggplant pieces, then the tomato slices. It is fine to overlap the tomatoes. Sprinkle the parmesan over the top. Bake tart 30-45 minutes or until the tomatoes and cheese are golden-brown. Remove from oven and cool on a baking rack. While the tart is still warm, remove the outer ring of the tart pan and transfer the tart to a serving dish. Serve with liberal helpings of pesto and garnish with fresh basil leaves.

Home-made pesto is much the best thing to use here. If you still have not tried it, perhaps you could take the time while the pie is cooking to reflect on what a lazy, wicked person you are and resolve to do better in the future. You probably have some fresh basil growing in the garden, or you can get some at the supermarket. Just stick it in a blender with garlic, olive oil, parmesan cheese and salt and pepper; you hardly need a recipe, and it is hard to go wrong. Or you can use store-bought if you must. And if you are really desperate, you might use a bottle of olive tapenade, which no pantry should be without for very long.

Anyway, you do all this while everyone else is having showers, you see, and while the pie is cooking, you quietly make yourself an extremely cold martini, the kind that makes you shiver when you take the first gulp. Then you serve this with a baked chicken and a fresh, cold rosé. We recommend a really great California rosé from The Withers winery near Healdsburg (http://thewitherswinery.com/a-true-story/), which was recently praised by the Wall Street Journal. It is made in the traditional way of Provence, by a direct press of the grapes, and is superbly balanced, with both a mineral edge to it and a smooth cherry note that lingers wonderfully on the palate. High summer in a bottle! You can go on drinking it after the meal, with a chilled cantaloupe for dessert, peeled and seeded and cut into big succulent pieces. Life is good, is it not?

Birds and Bees, and Lucy

When I was a boy, at Thanksgiving our tiny Irish grandmother would journey by train from Racine, Wisconsin, where she had lived all her life, to our small town in the west. She was my mother's mother and we all adored her. We loved all four of our grandparents, but Granny was the most special. Her eye was more twinkly, her smile more kindly and crinkly somehow, and she was a kid magnet in a mysterious and powerfully irresistible way. Anyone who has Irish in their family pedigree will know what I mean. Too, she traveled with what, even as kids in those long ago days, we recognized as funny, old-fashioned suitcases, the small hard cases with battered leather trim, like the ones Carol Lombard might have put aboard her last, fatal flight. She was glamorous, funny, and kind, and smelled good; we were enchanted. And one of her small suitcases was always packed nearly full with candy, contraband absolutely forbidden to us for most of the year, but our mother looked the other way when her mother visited, and let her spoil us rotten. We were quite happy to be spoiled, if candy was involved, and we were each allowed to pick one piece of candy out of her suitcase each day.

On one of these visits, family history was made. My suave older brother, an impossibly lofty two grades ahead of me in school, had recently participated in what in the sixties passed for sex education. The way this worked was, schools sent notes home to parents, warning them that their child's health class was going to have a presentation on "reproductive information"—boys in one class, girls in another—and seeking written permission for the awful truth of the birds and the bees to be communicated to them. This thunderbolt was hurtled down upon students in fifth grade, when the average kid was ten years old. I am not sure what happened to the kids whose parents did not give consent; I think they were sent to the library, to struggle on in ignorance for a while longer, but usually not very long, because about ten minutes after the awful information was handed down, eighteen people would tell them the exciting and rather surprising news. Of course, the essential kernel of new information was that babies came from eggs and sperm. This was a fascinating but highly improbable new theory that now had to compete with all the more impressive former theories about storks, cabbage patches, Christmas trees, and so on.

And of course, this is what happened in families, as a rumor of sex was coolly passed along in authoritative whispers from the older kids to the amazed and rather abashed younger kids. I remember my own reaction when the basic outline was set out didactically by my worldly older brother: "Something about that does not seem quite right, that just seems impossible, are you *sure* that's the whole story?" He assured me it was true; they had a special teacher come all the way from Denver to tell them about it, so it must be so. Besides, he argued, it must be true because, only that summer, our father had taken us fishing and the two of them were cleaning the trout we caught. One proved to be a female heavily laden with eggs, so our dad took that moment to explain that females lay their eggs and a male comes along and fertilizes them with his sperm and that is where baby fish come from. So this powerful corroboration from the world of fishing supported his whole sperm-and-egg theory for humans, and he made me admit that it did. And then he thumped me, to seal the credibility of his revelation.

Shortly after this, Granny visited us as usual for Thanksgiving, and one night, we were all watching TV after dinner. She had this nervous habit of crossing her legs and bouncing the uppermost foot up and down with her shoe half on her foot, and she was bouncing away as usual while we were all watching the "I Love Lucy Show." That night was one of the episodes from the year that Lucy was pregnant with "Little Ricky," fascinating a rather backward America, which had not been allowed until then to see a pregnant woman on television. Out of the blue, my brother said: "Well, it looks like Lucy sure got the sperm, all right!" My shocked grandmother violently twitched her bouncing leg, sending her shoe flying across the room to land firmly in family lore, and exclaimed: "Where did that boy learn about sperm?!" Well, that cinched it – it had to be true. My brother shot me a meaningful and triumphant glance.

Many years later, a great friend of mine had married and was raising a family, and their eldest boy, who was also my godson, went through a more modern but still incomplete version of this health class episode. They had a tradition of "family bed" on the weekends, when all the kids piled into their parents' bed and talked or snuggled or read papers and had coffee together, until gradually everyone got up to start the day. One Saturday morning, the oldest was in family bed and had a puzzled expression on his face, so his mother asked him what was troubling him.

"Well, you know that health class this week that I told you about?" he asked. "There's something about it that doesn't make sense."

"What's that, darling?"

"Well, I understand about the egg and the sperm of course, but what I don't understand is, how does the sperm *get* to the egg?"

"That's a very good question, dear, and I think your father should explain that to you while I go make us a nice breakfast," she said, giving the poor father a meaningful glance of encouragement.

And so the crucial missing information of the basic mechanics was communicated, to the boy's amazement. His eyes goggled and he exclaimed: "You're kidding!"

"No, that's really how it happens."

"Wow, they'd have to be pretty good friends!"

Which is true and pretty much sums up the whole sex thing among humans. I don't think we have to go as far as Evelyn Waugh, who famously observed in a letter of 1954 to his friend and fellow English writer Nancy Mitford: "Of children as of procreation—the pleasure momentary, the posture ridiculous, the expense damnable." Among plants, it is much simpler. Sex is why we have flowers in the garden, as everyone knows. And sex and flowers are why we have gardeners too, come to think of it.

So what is happening in the garden, back in the current day and as a beautiful summer is getting under way? Well, what I am most excited about lately is that the cardoons are coming up very vigorously for the first time. They arrived in the mail from White Flower Farms last year, mere slips of things, and now they are four to five feet high, with sharply incised, prickly gray leaves and stunningly architectural, artichoke-style fruits on them, which is not surprising, as they are of course in the artichoke family. They are topped by eye-catching flowers with an inch-long fuzz of filaments that are a stupendous violet and have a heady perfume that is not sweet, exactly, but rather sickly and smelling of an exotic oil of some kind.

This plant, with its bizarre, violet flowers, looks like something growing on another planet. Venus, perhaps. They are amazing. I have so enjoyed growing them; they have such an unusual growing habit and personality, like fantastic thistles. The English like to grow cardoons—and actual thistles too, for that matter—in their herbaceous borders, where they are allowed to get quite tall and commanding. They also grow things like dill, papyrus, and fennel in similar positions, for height, distinctive growing habit, and surprising variety. I like the boldness and freedom of that. Of course, if you want to risk growing thistles, you must be very careful never to let any of their flowers go to seed, or next year, you will have rather more thistles than you care for and will probably never get rid of them. Do not ask me how I know this, but here's a hint: it involves more sex in the garden.

August

Funny Thing Called Parenting

Today I noticed those brilliant, canary yellow American goldfinches working over the seedpods of the rudbeckia and I realized that means summer is drawing to a close. The birds have raised their clutches of nestlings and are loading up on fatty seeds and protein for their long journey south. In a similar way, in the human world, kids are preparing to fly away too; they are packing to go off to college, and the sentimental, back-to-school mood is definitely in the air.

In my new end-of-summer and back-to-school state of mind, I notice the garden is making its late summer checklist of chores to be completed by the gardener before the growing season draws to an end:

The helianthus are putting on a spurt of growth and are enjoying one crazy last hurrah of flowering. Check.

Nearby, the sedums are putting up their fuzzy green flower umbels prior to their eventual rosy display. Check.

The hummingbirds are busily sipping nectar from the large flowers of the red canna lilies before these tropicals close up shop in the cooler days of autumn. Check.

The new wave of long-throated "obedient plant" (*Physostegia virginiana*) has begun blooming, freshening the late summer garden with another fog of pinkish-purple haze. Check.

And yesterday, we saw the first blooms on the new flour o'clocks burst into view as August begins. Check.

But wait! They were supposed to be purple, and instead, I am disappointed to see they are yellow…Not, as I have lamented, my favorite color in the garden, but there you are. It's just a personal preference, no hard feelings. I find yellow loud and a bit vulgar, to be honest; I don't know why. It clashes with other colors in the garden and does not cooperate well with them; overall, I think it lacks subtlety. A bit of pale yellow here and there is okay and works well, especially with blues, but the yellow I don't like much is that brassy orange-yellow, as in common daylilies and black-eyed Susans (*Rudbeckia*), a vigorous member of the coneflower tribe, though I grow them both and copiously too.

At the same time, yellow has taught me a valuable life lesson. I used to ruthlessly edit yellow out of my garden, but noticed that the more I uprooted it, the more successful I became in growing plants that were yellow. Naturally, this was very frustrating for the gardener, so the gardener (as if he were a very simple-minded cartoon character; Elmer Fudd, say, as I sometimes think of myself) foolishly redoubled his efforts to get yellow out of his garden, and yellow flourished there more and more, in the perfectly predictable way. Finally, the rather obtuse gardener got the message and changed his view (progress!), accepting that the garden is not all about the gardener and what the gardener wants, but is actually more about what the garden wants, in the long run. Possibly it is entirely about that and not about the gardener at all, I have even thought, in a rare modest moment.

That is part of the Tao of gardening; to the uninitiated or a casual observer, it looks simply like the gardener is making a garden, but the greater reality is that the garden is all the while *making the gardener*. And this is more and more true over time; the longer we have been gardening, the more we are products of our gardens, rather than the other way around. People, even some gardeners, think that the garden is that patch of flowers in the front yard, but really, the garden is behind the gardener's eyes, not in front of them; the garden is *interior*. As I have mellowed, in the fullness of time, yellow has come more and more abundantly into my garden, and I am truly at peace with it. At last. Wise, no?

And so, to return to my original subject, of course the four o'clocks *would* turn out to be yellow. I might have known they would. What else could they be, as I ironically observed to myself on seeing them in bloom for the first time yesterday evening. Soon everything in my garden *will* be yellow, and no doubt after a while, I will come to be at peace with that too. I suppose that is how I will know my life is at its natural end, fulfilled.

This morning as I went off to work, I had to laugh as I noticed the bright yellow American goldfinches furiously working the seeds out of the yellow black-eyed Susans below the yellow showers of blooms on the helianthus and above the fresh new yellow blooms of the four o'clocks and daylilies. So it can't be long now for me, really, before that whole natural end thing. Probably I will find heaven is like a big yellow orb of golden sunshine over an all-yellow garden, and eternal peace will descend upon me at last.

And just as the garden teaches us that it will be what it must be, so our children teach us the same lesson over time; they must be what they must be too. We gardeners, and we parents, have our plans and hopes and expectations, but we soon learn that we are not the only creatures with these attributes of willfulness and foresight. Here is how this funny thing called parenting works: we get to be helpful and benevolent influences, we parents/gardeners, and we get to be proximate observers as the miracle of life unfolds before us upon the canvas of our allotted time. Our gardens and our children find their own ways in life, and how much more interesting life is for that, I say.

One night many years ago, they place in your wife's arms a tiny sleeping bundle with fine red fuzz for hair and you are instantly enchanted, and remain so for life. You are cast under a spell and enter into a deep, trance-like state. The next thing you know, she is eighteen and about to go off to college, and you wonder, *how did this happen so fast,* and how can we slow down the sometimes too-dizzying speed with which God's grace bears us along through life?

Saturday, my daughter and I drove to Spring Lake in the convertible with the top down and the music blasting, on a cool summer morning that was simply ideal. It was indeed a rare thing to spend the whole day at the beach, just the two of us, and it was perfect. After a stressful week at work, I could go into the refreshing ocean, then lie in the warm sun and just feel the stress pour off me like the seawater rolling off my skin. It was heaven, and sorely needed. And my daughter was such a delight to be with—a poised, accomplished and funny adult, just a marvel, really—and I felt the melancholy of her leaving in two weeks creep stealthily over me like a drug, infusing me with sadness, though I particularly didn't want to be sad that day. I wanted to be happy and upbeat, or at least to seem that way, which is nearly as good.

When I went to college, I felt nothing but excitement. I had no idea what my parents were feeling at the time, selfish creature that I was and that probably most teens are. For myself, I couldn't wait to start the great adventure, and I know she feels that keenly too, unaware of how poignant it is for us. That night at home, after she and our son had gone off with their groups of friends, my wife got home from work and we just sat on the porch and had sandwiches and cold cantaloupe with wine, enjoying the cool summer evening and having this time for ourselves. Soon, we shall be two little old things in a porch swing on a summer night, holding hands and waiting hopefully for the phone to ring.

On the way to work today, I summarized the weekend to myself as I often do: I got to spend an entire day alone with my daughter just days before she leaves home to go to college; I went to the beach, which I love to do; the weekend was beautiful; I got to have quiet time alone with my wife; I got to take my son driving for the first time and to relish this small rite of his long passage into manhood; I took long walks with my dog; and I worked in my delightful garden, but not overmuch. All in all, pretty nearly perfect. I am a lucky man, really, and the world bowls along in a happy groove.

And thinking about our children and how completely besotted we are by them, especially in those tender times when they are about to leave us, I wonder if they are perhaps adored too much. Is there a word for the excessive love of one's children, as uxoriousness is the excessive love of one's wife? There should be. If not, perhaps I will invent one, I think, and I add it to the list of things to be worked on, things needing thoughtful attention. Because, as the garden slows down on the approach of cooler autumn weather and as the children fly from the nest of their childhood home, I can tell I am soon going to have a lot of time on my hands.

Red-Right-Return

The many successes we have in life, both big and small, help us establish self-esteem and give our lives pleasure and, sometimes, meaning. Gardeners get to experience many successes (failures too, of course), but mostly our gardening successes are on the order of small triumphs. But one day, I had such a big gardening success that the police actually showed up to put a stop to it.

I had weeded the sidewalk on the corner where the Russian sage was standing up nice and tall, which I thought looked very fresh and fine. Then the *police* showed up and, much to my surprise, complained that our handsome and thriving Russian sages were *too* tall in that spot and were, in fact, a traffic hazard on the corner because people couldn't see oncoming traffic over them. The upshot of this visitation is that they have to be moved, by order of the local constabulary. Honestly, everyone is a garden critic in this town, but I have never had a visit by the forces of horticultural law and order before. So it looks like they will have to go to the oval bed this weekend, and some more irises will go to the corner in their stead. It would be absurd and annoying to get arrested for growing plants too well.

As a boy, one of my small successes was learning how to spot satellites as they passed over the northern hemisphere. This past week, we were at the beach at Stone Harbor again, and my wife and I and Cosimo took two beach towels to the beach Saturday night to stargaze and had the entire beach to ourselves on a remarkably lovely night. It was the first time Cosimo ever saw the ocean, but he took it in stride, of course, as he does everything. While stargazing, we saw *two* satellites pass overhead—I had not been able to see any since we left Colorado, because you need a very dark sky and a wide swath of night sky to scan for the fast-moving satellites—and I was so tickled to see them. My father taught me as a kid how to spot them in the dark, open western skies, and I always used to hunt for satellites with him. It is funny how the little things like that define and recall the relationships we have with the people we love in this life.

Another garden success occurred last week. Actually, it was more of a carpentry success, but it happened in the garden. I decided to do something creative about the aggressive patches of Virginia creeper that we have growing in the ivy, and rather than trying to rip them out every year, as I have been doing, I thought I would instead give them something to clamber up. Observe how the gardener obstinately pursues the wrong path year after year, while nature stands there, patiently and politely pointing out a better way, which the gardener is too dim to see. So my son and I went to the hardware store and got eight treated 1x1's in eight-foot lengths. Four of these were to be the uprights of two tall frames. Then we got some treated 1x2's, sawed them into two-foot lengths, and screwed them into the uprights at four feet high and at the top, at eight feet high. The uprights made the corners of a tall, square frame, and the 1x2's connect the uprights and make the frame sturdy. Then we bought eight milled, ornate finials and screwed them into the four top corners and painted the two frames all black.

They look fabulous, like antique tuteurs you would see at Dumbarton Oaks or Sissinghurst Castle. A fun job and surprisingly easy to do. Inexpensive too. I was at a dinner party just the other night, and a woman complimented me on our garden and asked me where on earth did we get those fabulous iron frames and were they terribly expensive. I laughed and said they are just painted wood that my son and I put together; they cost a few dollars each, and we would be glad to make some for her if she would like.

And they do look grand, like cast iron towers, framing an entrance to our driveway. It was my son's idea, in fact, to pair them off as gateway pillars to define the driveway entrance better and provide a bit of drama there. Unseen by him, I tied the ivy and the creeper to their respective columns, and the next day, he came racing in, breathless, saying, "Dad, Dad, vines are already growing up the towers!" It charmed me entirely and reminded me of the heavy spring snow we had one year in our Colorado garden that melted so fast on a sunny spring afternoon that the usually dry stream bed in front of our house actually did its duty for once as a storm drainage, with melted runoff from the golf course pouring down it. And seeing it, my then very young son came running into the house hollering, "Dad, Dad, come quick, there's water in our river!" Just as we can experience our own childhoods in our gardens and in the plants we tend, so we can experience our children though our garden, and our garden through our children, can we not, and it is lovely that it is so.

Oh, and one more word about the tower frames by the driveway, just to show how goofy gardeners can be, in the unlikely event that the goofiness of gardeners has escaped your notice until now. I trained English ivy up the tower on the left as you come into the driveway and Virginia creeper up the one on the right. That way, in the fall when the Virginia creeper is brilliant red, the tower on the right will signal the way safely home: "red-right-return," as the sailors say about harbor channel lights. No one will ever notice this nautical whimsy but me, I feel fairly certain, but I know every year it will get a chuckle out of me as I see the brilliantly lit red tower at the right of our driveway. And the secret, profound delight of the gardener in a simple but satisfying success like that is a very fine thing indeed.

❁

Roasted Corn

It is late August and there is a changing of the guard in the garden. The jolly yellow helianthus has bloomed and the rose mallows continue to sound off gloriously with their dazzling white and red trumpets; they are almost too big, really. We also noticed, sitting on the patio late the other night, a single firefly signaling in a desultory fashion in the back yard. Surely he is one of the last to find a mate, blinking balefully around the patio and no doubt wondering where everyone had gone. Dude, where's the party! Perhaps he left romance too late in life. We all know people like that.

One of the great things about summer around here—and something you definitely don't want to leave too late because, like young romance, it does not last—is the abundant availability of fresh, locally grown corn. This is an amazingly versatile plant, which in our ingenuity, we have made into thousands of edible products. It is one of the earth's great staples and feeds millions of people, but it was not always thus. Five thousand years ago, this life-giving plant was an obscure grass in the highlands of South America. For what it is to human civilization today, we owe our thanks to the genius and attention of the Incas, who began cultivating and improving it from a simple grass that could feed their livestock to the ubiquitously versatile staple that it is in our own era. In our household, several people give it "best vegetable" status.

We roast corn at our house most weekends in mid- to late-summer, and whatever we cannot eat gets stripped from the cob and goes straight into the freezer. Then all winter we have fresh-roasted summer corn to put into soups, salads, and pastas. It is only a little more work for the person staffing the grill, and it is incentive enough to think of all the good meals of autumn and winter that are being made possible. And corn should be part of a simple household ecosystem. We usually roast and strip ears of corn by the dozen, putting the stripped cobs into the freezer too, until we are ready to make one of civilization's great hallmarks, roasted corn soup with crab.

Roasted Corn Soup with Crab

12 ears sweet corn
Olive oil
Garlic salt
Ground black pepper

For the corn stock:
12 corn cobs
2 medium onions, coarsely chopped
1 medium carrot, coarsely chopped
1 stalk celery, coarsely chopped
1 medium bulb fennel, chopped
4 cloves garlic, peeled and smashed
1 medium sized jalapeño pepper, split and seeded
1 bay leaf
8 sprigs of thyme

For the soup:
4 Tbsp. butter
16 oz. fine crab meat
One batch of corn stock (see instructions, below) or 4 quarts
    vegetable stock
2 Tbsp. olive oil
1 large carrot, chopped
1 large onion, chopped
2 cloves garlic, pressed or minced fine
½ tsp. salt

¼ tsp. ground black pepper
6 Tbsp. butter
6 Tbsp. flour
½ cup heavy cream
Sage leaves

This recipe is best with fresh, locally grown sweet corn, which is not usually hard to find, but may not be available in all areas. You husk the corn and remove the silks, then arrange the corn, three cobs at a time, on a large piece of aluminum foil. Drizzle the corn with about a tablespoon of olive oil and add garlic salt and black pepper to taste. Wrap up the corn tightly in the foil; you finish with four packs of three cobs each, the cobs lying flat, side by side. Put these packs on your grill, set on high. The cobs need about 15 to 20 minutes per side, but you may need to do this a few times before you get the hang of it. The idea is to cook it thoroughly and to get just a little bit of grill scorch on each ear. I listen for the first kernels to start popping, and then I know they are ready to be turned. When the corn is done, put it aside to cool. Strip the corn kernels from the cobs with a sharp, broad-bladed knife, and reserve both cobs and kernels.

Put all the ingredients for the stock in a large stock pot and cover with four quarts of water. Bring to a boil, then reduce heat. Simmer, covered, for 1½ hours. Strain the stock through a fine mesh sieve and discard the solids.

Melt the butter and toss it with the crab meat in a mixing bowl. Put the buttered crab meat in the fridge to cool and congeal. In a large stock pot, cook the carrot and onion in hot oil for 10 minutes, or until it starts to brown. Add the garlic and cook one minute more. Increase heat to medium-high. Stir in reserved corn kernels and cook for five minutes. Season with salt and pepper. Add corn stock and bring to a boil. Reduce heat and simmer, uncovered, for about 10 minutes, then remove from heat. Cool slightly. In food processor, puree soup in small batches until smooth. Strain through fine mesh sieve, discarding solids. Season to taste with salt and pepper.

In the now-empty stock pot, melt the butter and, on low heat, gradually add the flour while whisking. The idea is to make a nice roux to thicken the soup, and cook the flour for about two minutes to cook off the floury taste. If the roux gets too thick and pasty, add *small* amounts of the hot soup to thin it. After the flour has been cooked two minutes, gradually add the hot soup back to the stock pot, one cup at a time, whisking constantly so the soup does not get too thin. After all the soup has been added back in this way, slowly stir in the cream. To serve, place a dollop of the crab meat in each soup bowl, then pour the hot soup around it. Garnish with a whole sage leaf. Makes 12 servings.

This takes a bit of work, but wow is it good! To go with the creamy yellow soup, maybe I'll cut some yellow flowers from the garden for the centerpiece tonight.

Scent Garden

It is a common shortcoming of gardeners—and I know this because it is certainly a shortcoming of my own—that too often we focus excessively (perhaps obsessively) on the flowers in the garden to the exclusion of other attributes of the plants we care for. This is odd when you think about it, because most plants only flower for a few weeks each year, but they are otherwise with us year-round in their non-flowering state. I often think it would be better to garden the other way around: for the leaves and the structure of the plant and the contribution it makes to the overall garden structure, with the flowers a remote secondary consideration. But this is easier to say than do for those of us who are flower-besotted. Still, some of the most beautiful gardens I ever saw were foliage gardens, where the flowers were rare and were certainly not the point.

So I think foliage is overlooked by most gardeners in our zeal for blossom nirvana and bliss; certainly it is our loss and it serves us right, I suppose. But perhaps one of the most delightful and easily overlooked attributes is the scent of our plants. Some plants have powerful fragrances, some have subtle perfumes, and some have none or almost none. But the rich and fruitful diversity of scent in the garden is something that we can all profitably be more attentive to.

Many flowers are far gone in gorgeousness without having developed scent as part of their strategic repertoire. Many things that we think of as beautiful flowers are not properly flowers at all, but only plants with specialized leaves called bracts that only look like flowers: dogwood, impatiens, bougainvillea, and hydrangea, to cite some common and very lovely examples. The main purpose of both scent and flowers is to lure pollinators—bats, bees, birds, and moths—but a plant does not have to have both a flower and a strong fragrance. There are many beautiful flowers that flourish perfectly well without scent. Consider tropical examples, such as orchids, begonia, brugmansia, anthurium, hibiscus, mandevilla, canna lilies, nicotiana, birds of paradise, dahlias, and amaryllises. Probably there is a theory that explains why such plants evolved obvious and enormous flowers instead of scent to attract pollinators. My guess would be that they rely more on birds, bats and moths than on bees for pollination, and it is a sweet scent that attracts the bees, but a large flower that attracts the other pollinators; but I am not a naturalist, except in the broadest sense.

Outside of the tropic zone, there are many other plants that have little or no scent, at least as far as fragrances humans can detect are concerned, but instead have large and attractive flowers. Just think of things like yucca, rhododendron, lupines, hollyhocks, foxglove, delphiniums, squash, and pumpkin blossom. Also such diverse flowers as tulips, poppies, clematis, and the whole group of rudbeckia, gaillardia, echinacea, daisies, and sunflowers. The pollinators easily find them and love them. And so do gardeners, by the way; we find these big flowers irresistible as well. We are not much less susceptible to these flowers than the pollinators and it has occurred to me (and others) that possibly flowers are evolving to please us and to enlist us in their evolutionary plans more than we realize. They are manipulating us at least as much as we are manipulating them, and sometimes it is hard to be certain who is the dominant personality in this relationship.

I often think it would be a good experiment, and good garden design discipline as well, providing I had a larger garden, to design an area that was meant to be plants and leaves only, no flowers allowed. Similarly, it would be fun (again, if space allowed such experimental gardens, which for most of us unfortunately it does not) to have an entire garden area devoted only to fragrance. This garden would certainly have to have some of the great icons of floral scent. In early spring, masses and masses of hyacinths would perfume the bower, followed quickly by lily of the valley. These have a wonderfully intense fragrance, but outside in the garden, you have to kneel down with your nose just inches from the ground to savor their perfume, and this posture naturally cultivates a reputation for eccentricity. Much better to cut a generous handful or two, leaves and flower stems and all, and put them in small vases or glasses in the house. Heaven. And certainly, you would want to have two trees each of peach, plum, cherry, orange, and mock orange, if only for their wonderful blossoms after a long winter and their lovely light perfume on the evening air of spring.

Later, in May, you would want several varieties of lilacs to overwhelm the senses in an old-fashioned sort of way, and for this, we would overlook their absurd proportion of flowers (small) to plant (large), like an elephant carrying a nosegay with its trunk, because this exercise is not about the rational use of garden space; rather, it is about intoxication, plain and simple. In June, you would have the stupefying perfume of honeysuckle, which I would train to grow up columns or other supports, the better to disperse its heady fragrance throughout the garden. You could probably afford to have one magnolia tree, if only for its enormous, pre-historic flowers; you cut these when they are just open and bring them indoors, where they sit in a shallow dish of water and release their heavy, besotting perfume.

Roses, of course, you would grow all summer, and only the ones that have powerful fragrances; you would not really care what their blossoms looked like. Mostly, these would be old varieties, before they were hybridized away into gaudy, unscented blooms. In Hollywood, they talk about "Coppola's Law," coined as legend has it on the movie set of "Apocalypse Now," when the famous director hung a sign on his trailer saying: "Fast, cheap or good: pick two. You can never have all three." The same is true of roses, I find; you can have any two of hardy plants, perfumed blossoms, or beautiful flowers, but never all three. For myself, I will take hardy and perfumed, and I am pretty sure I have made the wisest choice. Lilies, of course, would be grown all summer, adding their own swoon-worthy fragrances, as when you walk into the lobby of a great hotel and there is an enormous display of lilies and you almost faint from their perfume, not to mention their gorgeous blooms. And remember this is only a fantasy, so why not bring out a dozen pots from your greenhouse of the exotic tiare flower, that great emblem of French Polynesia and a member of the gardenia family. Or just use a dozen pots of regular old gardenias; they are nearly as good.

In addition to the strongly scented flowers, there are of course many whose fragrance is more subtle and understated. Daffodils, for example, though their fragrance is often unnoticed. I can tell you exactly what they smell like. Go right now to your pantry, open a new jar of honey, and put your nose right into the jar: daffodils. I love the very subtle scent of irises, ranging from sweet to spicy to indefinable and other-worldly. Speaking of spicy, the whole family of pinks is in this category, from cinnamon to allspice. Wisteria has a faint scent of perfumed oil, the white autumn-blooming clematis is a great favorite, and hostas and peonies have faint but well-defined sweet floral fragrances. And even the humble petunia, greatly prized for its masses of flowers and long flowering season, has a lovely perfume, though it is often overlooked as well. Bluebells are a special favorite of early spring, and buddleia in mid-summer, and on and on. And don't forget the extended family of herbs, whose leaves are prized for their scent and taste. Of these, by far the most fragrant are dill, mint, basil, rosemary, lavender, sage, and thyme. Planted in full sun, they sweat their precious scented oils into the air of a hot summer afternoon.

It is curious how a fragrance transports us in time and place to where we first strongly registered it. This is much more potent with scent than with, say, music, but the principle and the effect are the same and many people have observed this common phenomenon. Brush the leaves of a chrysanthemum or a geranium, and I am instantly a ten-year-old boy again, in my first tiny garden, noticing for the first time that leaves have fragrance as well as flowers. Bruise the needles of a piñon pine, and I am a little kid, bursting with excitement at Christmastime. Wave a branch of orange blossom or philadelphus in front of me, and I am in Seville, Spain, at Easter with thousands and thousands of orange trees all blooming at the same time and perfuming the entire city. Every time I smell almond blossom, it can only be Paris in spring on a cold, sunny day. With lilacs, I am walking to school and I snap off a few stems of blossom to give to my favorite teacher, or else I am walking home and doing the same thing, to give them to my mother.

The perfume of honeysuckle reminds me of when all the neighborhood kids would come over to our house in June to feast on the honeysuckle blossoms, pulling the stamens down through the fragile neck of the flowers to capture a tiny drop of the sweetest nectar imaginable. The mysterious perfume of wisteria, faint and exotic, for me signals the end of a long and bitter English winter. Sage reminds me of my boyhood home, for it grew all over the hills behind our house, and whenever I go on a long trip, I pack a sprig of this in my suitcase in case I get homesick and as a remembrance that eventually I am returning home again. With tiare or any member of the gardenia family, I am once again newly married and on my honeymoon in exotic and gorgeous Tahiti.

Through the scent of flowers, the years melt away, time dissolves, we travel the astral planes through space and distance, long-gone friends and family members spring back to life and crowd joyfully around us, memory mysteriously unspools, and we are magically transported to beauty, peace, and grace—all through the simple but compelling chemistry of plant fragrance. Life is rather wonderful, is it not?

Summer Fruit

I really made an effort this summer to eat more fruit, and have gorged on cherries (we got some fantastic ones from the Pacific Northwest that were dark and sweet and almost as big as walnuts), blueberries, cantaloupes, and now pears. And even our poor raspberry canes, ruthlessly exploited by the birds, have managed to yield us a bowlful of berries every now and then. It doesn't get any more local than that. Our tomato strategy has paid off only moderately; they were delicious, but not very numerous because of the dry summer and because the gardener has another, less important but still full-time job and cannot be on hand to give the tomato plants a deep and refreshing drink twice a day, though both the tomato plants and the gardener would much prefer that agreeable arrangement.

What I find myself really missing are the fresh, ripe peaches and apricots of my youth. I grew up in a fruit-growing region where fresh summer fruits were taken for granted as part of the natural rhythm of life. Late every summer, my mother would pile the kids into her station wagon, and we would go to the roadside fruit stands in Palisade and on Orchard Mesa to load the car up with the peaches and tomatoes she would preserve and the cucumbers she would pickle. For days, our house smelled interestingly like a cannery—with the sickly sweet smell of sliced ripe peaches, the rich aroma of parboiled tomatoes, and the sharp tang of dill and boiling vinegar for the pickles—and the kitchen was full of steam from the boiling Mason jars. We had a room in the basement under the stairs where our freezer was kept, and that room was called "the fruit room," because that was where all the jars of preserves were stored, glowing red and yellow and green like traffic lights for tomatoes, peaches, and pickles.

In early summer, my mother would come home with paper bags full of local apricots for us kids, and they were the big, juicy apricots that have a flavor that only local, ripe-picked apricots can have—not like the sad and tasteless, merely apricot-colored things we have to buy in grocery stores these days. Possibly the modern ways are much better, though in some not-very-obvious respect. One summer, when I must have been around ten years old, I was sitting on our front porch with my brothers and sister; we were eating our way through a bag of these amazing apricots and spitting the pits into a planter near the front door that held a tangle of honeysuckle and vinca mixed together. A few weeks later, I noticed a tiny, sprouted seedling there when I was pulling some weeds, and I must have seen the cracked apricot pit, because I decided it had sprouted from that day of the apricot feast a few weeks before. I carefully dug it up and moved it to our back yard, and planted it in a tiny little garden I was then tending, which didn't have much in it except a few irises I had scavenged from the neighbors' yard.

That garden was also where I buried my tropical fish when they died, after a brief, but heartfelt and tearful, religious ceremony that usually consisted of me solemnly reading the 23rd Psalm over them and trying to get my sister and our Boston terrier to be suitably reverent, or at least to sit decently still, something that was just not in either of their natures, my sister squirming even more than the Boston terrier.

Well, the apricot seedling liked that garden spot and rapidly grew into a whip-like stripling. Perhaps it was the fish fertilizer that provided the magic ingredient, because that stripling eventually became a very large tree, whose spreading canopy was more than twenty feet tall and twenty feet wide. And to my childish delight, it always fruited heavily, though I never did anything more for it than find it in the first place and water it fairly regularly when it was small. One year, much later, we had a perfect season for apricots and this great tree fruited much more heavily than it ever had before, with every large branch burdened with its golden freight of fruit, some branches bowing down almost to touch the ground. At that time, our back yard was a dog run for a brother and sister pair of standard schnauzers. The female had a weakness for these sweet apricots; she stripped the branches bare as far as she could reach. She was in perfect apricot heaven, a place I knew well, carefully spitting out the pits, and amazingly, she suffered no ill effects from her golden binge.

That tree became the tallest and shadiest tree in our back yard, and I spent many happy hours in its cool shade as a boy, reading. For all I know, it is there still, and I hope it is, bearing mute and lasting witness to the way that small things in our lives become big things and some of the best things that happen in a garden are not planned, or even foreseen or dreamed of. And so the gardener goes on being instructed and humbled over the years, man and boy, and the marvels of horticulture continue to fall promiscuously from heaven, or from a brown paper bag of cool summer fruit held for a brief moment of time between the bare feet of children on a hot summer day.

September

Ceremony in the Garden

As we get older, we occasionally fantasize about how great it would be if more of our friends and relatives had private planes, large yachts, and vacation homes in great destinations where they could invite us for weekend getaways. Well, one out of three ain't bad, and we just spent the weekend on the Chesapeake Bay with some friends who have a big boat there. How great it is to be on the Bay on a fine weekend in early September.

Ah, the good life! There was much wine and good conversation, and spectacular marine scenery. We saw many ospreys and one huge owl, who swept down to the docks not more than twenty feet from the back of the boat where we were sitting, a few blue herons, and even a pair of majestic swans in the backwaters of the harbor. I got up early on Sunday morning and slipped off the boat to go to the harbor inn for coffee and a quiet read of a good book. And how special a morning like that is: the vast watery world of the Chesapeake, a mellow old inn in rural Maryland, a superbly imagined tale to read, the still morning as yet all to myself, and the day not even really begun. The morning had an almost *ceremonial* feeling to it.

I am a bit of a traditionalist and I believe in ceremony. I think life is meant to be lived with some seriousness, dignity, and *gravitas*. And for us humans, some at least of our purpose and meaning comes from tradition and ceremony. Anybody who has had a boat or spent much time on one knows that a lot of boating involves particular ways of doing things and ceremonial duties and traditions. There are maritime rituals that are essential to the way a boat skims over the surface of the earth with almost magical powers. The garden, too, teaches us over time that, in general, the traditional ways are the good ways. Except, of course, when they aren't. And learning to recognize those exceptions is one of the great skills of a serious gardener.

Here is how I think it works for us mortals, thrashing about here on earth. Our preferences become our habits, in gardening as in other things, and at length, our habits become our customs. In time, our customs have a patina of sentiment glossed over them and they become our traditions. Then, when traditions become invested with meaning (either personal or universal, or ideally both), they become ceremonies. Eventually ceremonies become rituals, freighted with transcendent meaning and implication, and the stuff of devotion, metaphysics, and spirituality. WHOA, big fella, now I think you're going too far!

Perhaps this is a good place to say I am not here going to plunge off the speculative cliff into the vast abyss of metaphysics, but I do want to talk about the *ceremonial* aspects of gardening, which I think is rather safer ground.

You would, I think, have to be a pretty vague and not at all an introspective sort of gardening chap to have overlooked this extremely interesting aspect of gardening, especially its connection to the interior aspects of gardening. Many of the garden tasks we perform have been performed by us over a lifetime. And by other gardeners in other places and times, too. We have ways of doing the things we do over and over, during the gardening calendar, and then year after year. We like our gardening tools cleaned and sharpened and put away just so. We like that Japanese split-leaf maple to be barbered so sunlight can fill it inwardly and shine out through its leaves, giving it the characteristic interior luminosity that is so striking. We like it when the lawn is newly edged and the ivy is sharply trimmed back and the roses are thoroughly deadheaded so that, for a day or two, they give a fresh and robust show and do not have an unwelcome suggestion of decay hanging over them. You get the idea. There is a meaning and a measure to each of these processes and habits that are larger than the literal activity itself; there is a stateliness to them, and eventually a dignity and a ceremony to them as well.

We gardeners all have our own ceremonies. Weeding can be one; deadheading another. For me, pruning can only be ceremonial. I love that weekend in February when it is mild enough to spend the whole weekend outside, pruning roses and grapes, and cutting down the buddleias. For me, that is one of the best weekends of the year. It ends with a brilliant fire of buddleia branches in the reading room fireplace, and the incense quality of its perfumed smoke is almost a religious offertory. I am obsessed with pruning azaleas, and we have dozens of them, so this obsession is given very ample scope for expression. I have some lovely Japanese pruning scissors I am very fond of, and at least once a year, every single azalea in our garden is given a thorough pruning. When I've finished, each branch has a light and airy texture, and when it blooms, the effect is a clouds-of-blossom appearance that to me is the characteristic azalea look.

I concentrate intensely while doing this; I live decidedly in the moment. I cannot think of anything else or look away, even for a second, or I will cut myself badly with the fast-moving scissors whizzing around my fingers. I speak here from bitter experience, having often cut my left hand when my attention wandered, even momentarily. Imagine a spiritual discipline where you will be seriously hurt if, for even one split second, you fail to live conscientiously in the present moment. It concentrates the mind wonderfully, and is not to be attempted lightly or by a novice. If I had my way, I would prune our trees this way too, but other persons in our household (She Who Must Be Obeyed foremost among them) are on to my obsessive ways and are alert to any unhealthy or excessive expressions of them, so barbering azaleas like Edward Scissorhands is about all I can get away with. For now.

Mowing the lawn is ceremonial for me too. I don't mow in boring old vertical or horizontal stripes. Instead, I first mow around the entire contour of the grass and then in the next pass I mow inside that contour; this is repeated over and over until finally I end in the middle of the grass, inside concentric iterations of the shape of our yard and the gardens that define it, the garden form dizzyingly reiterated like an Escher etching.

Cutting flowers for the house and collecting garden produce for the table have always been fraught with more meaning than just picking a tomato or a rose; it is *gathering beauty*, providing for your family from nature's bounty, connecting your physical body and your esthetic sense to the land and the plants that provision and sustain them both.

The garden interior—that sense of the garden that we have inside ourselves—is alive to the larger significance of these customs, traditions, and ceremonies. They ground us; they give our actions purpose, dignity, and meaning. They bind us to the garden and the garden to ourselves. They invite us to consider whether the garden might not, in fact, be a metaphor for life, or the world, or life-in-the-world—or all of these things at different times or on different levels. They are in large measure the reason why serious gardeners find meaning and joy in what they do, working with loving devotion at the very interface between the individual person and the wide, universal creation.

Getting Your Fill of Plants

Ah, the Labor Day weekend, the end of summer, good times with family and friends, an extra day or two in the garden! I love early September for its fine weather: fresh without being cold. The quality of sunlight as the fall equinox approaches is vivid and clear; the garden revives, but the gardener is not yet overwhelmed with garden chores or the end-of-season blahs. Soon, fallen leaves will claim a lot of our attention, shorter days mean nothing can really get done on weekday evenings, and a thousand other cares—and perhaps one or two other people who live on the premises—unfortunately summon the gardener away from the garden for indoor chores.

This is a good time to crack down on weeds in the garden. If weeds are let go now, they will slip into winter, and you will spend your precious spring days in the garden subduing a weed population that looks like Upper Amazonia. This is extremely good advice, as I am sure you appreciate. I have never actually followed it myself, and likely won't have time to do so this year either.

This is also a really good time to divide all the plants you were thinking of dividing, though spring is when we commonly think to do that important chore. Autumn is just as good a time as spring for this task, and most of us have more time on our hands now than in the busy weeks of early spring. Most of us, too, are severely limited in what we can spend at garden centers. Some, like me, are even watched like hawks by certain people where garden expenditures are concerned, so dividing plants is necessarily a critical part of our clandestine expansion plans.

It is also a great time to tramp through garden centers, nurseries, and even the big-box hardware stores, because they all put their remaining nursery stock on deep discount. Sometimes you want a very specific creature for a particular site or planting solution, and only that very specimen will do. Then, you have to order it, usually from a specialty company, and you know it is going to cost you. But if you are willing to be a bit flexible in what you plant, fall is the time to shop for value locally, and it is shocking sometimes, in a good way, how inexpensive plants are at this time of year. For a big garden like ours, there is always something I want and can find, usually at a good price and in relatively good shape. My wants and needs as a gardener are so vast, I find, and money is so annoyingly finite.

It is another hallmark of September that the gardening catalogs one receives now are, of course, full of spring bulbs, among other things, and how I love to paw through these, with the light of pure greed burning in my febrile eyes. Garden porn, is what I believe it is vulgarly called by publishing professionals. It's indecent, really, with summer not even over, to be already greedily thinking about all the glories of next spring, and I upbraid myself (gently) for my unseemly avarice. Really, at my age, I should know better and get a grip. And so on.

And all this makes me think about my fevers for plants. I think, with this large garden, that I have finally burned out a few of those fevers: for azaleas, rhododendrons, hollies, peonies, daylilies for sure, and possibly for hydrangeas too. We have so many of each that I am finally content, and while my fingers still twitch spasmodically when I pass them on the sale table at local nurseries, I can usually steel myself and walk AWAY from the table!

Not that I am tired of them, you understand—far from it, in fact—but at least I don't lust for more and more of them like I used to. It turns out that the cure for flower fever is growing plants until you've had your fill of them. Don't, of course, go to fatal lengths, like the wicked and stupid King John, who was said to have died in 1216 "from a surfeit of peaches." What a way to go (though it was probably really dysentery). It was nice of him to get Magna Carta signed and pave the way for 800 years of English, and later Anglo-American, democracy before he went on his ill-advised binge in the royal peach orchard.

Getting your fill of plants is very satisfying, and is not against the law, even here in New Jersey, where everything is famously either forbidden or required and nothing is left to chance or discretion. And at the end of the process, you are cured. Sort of.

Take peonies, for example. I divided them and divided them in this garden until, in the end, I have more than six dozen of them, almost all whites and pinks, which I admit is a bit excessive, but I love each and every one of them, and they are an important foundation plant of this garden. It is the same with several other plants, and I thank God I had the space and the strength of body (if not mind) to grow these plants to this level of self-indulgence and satisfaction. And it is nice to think that after a long life, lived with so many of these good friends and admirable creatures, contentment and maturity could descend upon the gardener. Well, okay, I may be overstating *that* a little bit.

But it is curious, too, how the fever still burns for some things. Roses and irises, for example; I doubt I will ever get enough of them to be content. And spring bulbs, oh my goodness. If my wife's vigilance wavers even for a second, I will be buying a dilapidated farm in the middle of nowhere, just so I can plant daffodils, crocuses, hyacinths, squills, muscari, and glorious tulips by the acre. Maybe that would cure me. But I doubt it.

Labor Day was as it should be this year. We went to some friends' house for the classic afternoon in the back yard by their pool, followed by a barbecue and far too many cold drinks on the porch as the heat of the day fell away. We scored a success with our Santorini salad, so I will just give the recipe here, to be enjoyed on one of the many fine September evenings that are left to us.

Santorini Salad with Grilled Shrimp

1 package of couscous, enough to make 2 cups when cooked
½ cup chopped cilantro
3 oz. pine nuts, toasted

1 lb. large shrimp, shelled and cleaned
2 Tbsp. fresh lemon juice
1 Tbsp. olive oil
1 tsp. fresh chopped oregano
1 Tbsp. minced shallots
Salt and freshly ground black pepper to taste

2 tsp. finely grated lemon zest
1 Tbsp. fresh chopped oregano
1 cucumber, peeled, seeded, and cut into ½ inch pieces
1 yellow bell pepper, seeded and cut into ½ inch pieces
1 green bell pepper, seeded and cut into ½ inch pieces
1 pint cherry tomatoes, cut in half
3 doz. Kalamata olives (checked for pits)
1 lb. feta cheese, crumbled
Salt and freshly ground black pepper to taste

1/3 cup olive oil, for finishing

Cook the couscous according to the packet instructions. You can use vegetable or chicken broth instead of water for more flavor. When it is finished, stir in the cilantro and pine nuts and put aside to cool. Put all the ingredients in the second group into a bowl and toss; allow to stand for at least ten minutes.

Put all the ingredients in the third group into a bowl and toss; put in fridge to chill. For the feta, use the real thing from Greece if you can get it, especially if it is barrel aged. Because the dressing is basically just the lemon zest and the olive oil that you drizzle on last, use the best olive oil you have on hand. Thread the shrimp onto bamboo skewers and grill, preferably outdoors and over charcoal. Refrigerate.

Serve Santorini salad very cold, on chilled plates if you can. The classic version of this recipe does not include couscous, but we like it and so compromise by serving it to the side. Heap the plate with the salad, drizzle with the olive oil (more if you want), and serve the couscous and shrimp on the side. Serves 6.

Are Gardeners Really Necessary?

The first chilly night of the late summer is always a welcome respite from the hot and muggy nights of August. And the freshness of the equinoctial mornings is welcome also, chilly and delightful, as the garden gathers its green force for its last brave hurrah of the season and the descent into the deep and dark winter to come.

The sedums were superb this year (that would be the excellent horse manure again, no doubt), swarmed most of the time with more than a hundred butterflies of various kinds. Pure magic. I have been training the wrens, who live in the pyracantha on the patio near the steamer chairs where we often sit, to come down and get bits of crackers or pretzels. They are becoming very tame and soon, at my command, they will no doubt be whipping up a ball gown for my wife, like the birds did for Cinderella. That may take a few more pretzels. The little colony of them now seems to number a dozen or more, and they are constantly very busy and twittering, flying in groups of three or four from pyracantha to wisteria, from wisteria to rhododendrons, from rhododendrons to the gutters, from the gutters to the large trees, and back again to the pyracantha to talk it all over excitedly. They are endlessly entertaining. And today I saw some more of the tiny but brilliant goldfinches, which come every year to eat the seeds of the helianthus when they are ripe, matching the helianthus yellow to yellow; they look almost like wild canaries, they are that yellow. For a moment, I am in a hammock in the tropical Canary Islands, off the coast of West Africa.

I have been rejoicing in a spectacular day, on the whole. I had no appointments at the office today, so what's a person to do except take the day off to do a final cleanup of the summer garden. I thoroughly weeded the herbaceous border, and the asters are looking fine, though they are in their final days. How fresh and welcome their sprightly colors are in the tired fall garden, and our tall purple ones look especially well with the bright chromatic yellow of the helianthus, who are their neighbors. Remember those favorite black and yellow or purple and yellow marbles we used to call "bumblebees" as children? This pairing always reminds me of them. They did rather better for us in our former garden than here; there must be something about the low altitude, or the humid marine climate of the Mid-Atlantic, that does not suit them quite as well.

I have staked the dahlias, which are fully coming into their own now, planted 150 more red and dark purple tulips by the arch and a hundred or so crocuses by the front walk, moved a lilac from the gloom of the hedgerow, where of course it was most unhappy (what was I thinking when I planted it there?), to the full sun of the front yard, and moved an azalea to replace a dead forsythia. Without unlimited funds flowing directly to the garden from the Treasury Department (meaning She Who Must Be Obeyed), the frugal gardener must be sure every creature he is responsible for is in the best possible place.

I tied the big, apricot-colored rose in the crescent bed to its new eight-foot tripod, and it still over-topped it by about two feet. Saturday, I bought two tons of beige pea gravel—the kind you see in the public parks in Paris—for the new patio area and then slowly shoveled it all into that area, completing that big project, and what a success it has turned out to be, definitely passing the old looks-like-it's-always-been-that-way test. And now our porch connects to the patio by way of a secluded and stylish Parisian garden "room." I put down a lot of new gravel back by the trash bins too, and yesterday, I cleaned out the fireplace and laid a fire for our first chilly night, no doubt coming soon.

A change of season always makes me a bit contemplative. And so I ask myself the big question that has been worrying me lately: Are gardeners really necessary? I sometimes doubt it. We tend to think of ourselves, egotistically, as the overseer, designer, architect, benevolent dictator, and generally brilliant organizing intelligence of our garden space, but the truth is, nature seems to do pretty well all by herself. And always has. No one is tending the wild dogwoods and rhododendrons in the hills of Appalachia, and they look as lovely as any fussed-over arboretum. Lovelier, really. Not to mention the natural, untended glories of, say, the Grand Canyon, the Rocky Mountains, the endless forests of Canada, Bora Bora in French Polynesia, and so on.

Still, we do sort of think of ourselves as in benignly despotic control of and imposing our will, brilliant or otherwise, on the gardens we tend. And yet, as the gardener ages, he begins to realize (at least the smarter and more introspective sort of chaps do) that perhaps this is not the way things really work after all. Little doubts emerge and are communicated to the perceptive gardener. What if the garden is in control of the gardener in the same very subtle and irresistible way that the hollyhock is in control of the honeybee and the canna lily is in control of the hummingbird? Perhaps the gardener does what the garden wants and needs him to do—provide useful things like nutrients and water, keep the weed and pest populations down, and so forth—so the plant population can flourish and go about its business of elegantly and manipulatively taking over the world.

Sometimes I think we are more designed upon than designing, more controlled than controlling. And every gardener has had the disturbing experience of finding an unplanned effect or an unplanted guest that arrived at just the right place and in just the right color to perfect a scheme that the gardener himself has failed at.

Early this morning, for example, as I was rushing off to work, I saw to my amazement a bright and dignified blaze of blue on the patio among the red and white impatiens. On inspection, I found it to be a perfectly gorgeous morning glory, the kind you wish you could find in garden centers but never can, which had volunteered to grow up the trunk of the dogwood and add its blue to the red and white design, achieving just the patriotic effect I had planned last spring when I planted the red and white impatiens and some blue petunias. My blue petunias, however, failed, ruining the point of the scheme, but here it was perfected at last anyway, and in a far more beautiful shade of intense blue than the one the gardener had himself selected. Humbling, that.

Last night, we sat out on the (now perfected) patio, on what is surely one of the last few nice evenings of this year, and to my surprise, I saw two fireflies signaling in the backyard, after not seeing any for weeks. In the second half of September! How is that possible? Anyway, they cheered me tremendously, and it was lovely to watch their tiny signaling lanterns slowly move around the darkened garden. It is nature doing what it has always done, without any help from the (likely unnecessary) gardener.

⚘

We Are Not Alone

Last week, precisely on the equinox, someone flipped the switch on the celestial thermostat from "heat" to "cool" for our part of the northern hemisphere, and that was the end of that for summer. Twenty degrees dropped out of the day overnight. We opened our windows and the hard-working air conditioners finally got a rest; we sleep now with our windows open and the comforter pulled up. I have decidedly mixed feelings about this. The air, of course, is deliciously fresh and crisp, and it has a sparkle and clarity to it that are truly wonderful. The garden has snapped back to life and lost much of its late-summer droopiness. But ah, I do love an eighty-degree day; that must be the temperature every day in heaven, I think.

Looking on the bright side, the garden is still producing some amazing color. The helianthus are particularly fine this year, with big sprays of yellow fountains erupting out of all six of the four-foot-tall tuteurs I made for them, and I don't think they have ever looked better. Nearby in the oval bed, there is a large patch of purple phlox blooming late and looking very well with the yellow of the helianthus. I put together two great bouquets for the house this weekend, though there is not a lot in the late garden to work with. In the kitchen, we have a big mass of purple asters as a base with two-foot-long sprays of yellow helianthus and purple phlox coming out of them. In our bedroom, we have a mix of mauve and purple phlox with an orange and a peach dahlia, coral carnations and a peach-colored rose; the peach and mauve and pink are a great combination and they make a lovely patch of intense color.

The lawn suffers terribly in late summer because I won't use sprinklers or chemicals, so when the weather changes, I really make an effort to help it along. I spent quite a lot of time this weekend weeding it by hand, which is rather back-breaking work, and I also mowed it with a much closer crop for the cool weather, so it looks very tidy and barbered once again. I also put down grass seed, with the hope that the rain scheduled for this week will materialize and help it to sprout before our bird population discovers it and all my work is wasted.

I am pretty much caught up with garden chores; thank goodness for that, because I feel I am coming down with a rotten, early autumn cold, and I am feeling rather sorry for myself. I'm told by the women in my household that men tend to be babies when they are ill, so I'll just keep my head down and quietly take my special cold remedy. It is a secret that comes to me from my mother, who is something of a famous medicine woman, or *bruja,* as they are called in the southwest where she lives. You put the contents of a packet of Emergen-C and two Alka-Seltzer tablets in a glass of water and drink it while it is foaming. Do this every couple of hours at the onset of the cold, and its severity will be greatly lessened. If you are lucky enough to have a steam shower, spend as much time as you can in the steam, too, and you will soon be right again. Or you can just suffer the old-fashioned way, as most of mankind does.

Anyway, as this cold formula was doing its job, I consoled myself by taking Cosimo for a long, rambling walk around our town, to patrol the front yards of our neighbors and see what they are thinking and doing. Gardeners are nosy by nature, and love to poke about everyone else's gardens and yards and see what is going on there, and certainly I am no exception to that rule.

Abelia is everywhere in its best and fullest bloom of the summer, I see, starting with the lovely old specimens of this fine creature that we have by our front porch. I think of them as the-birds-and-the-bees bushes: their dense and twiggy habit of growth makes a perfect habitat for small birds, and their heavy, sweet perfume attracts and intoxicates hundreds of bees at a time, who drunkenly navigate their heady blossoms in late summer when other food is relatively hard for them to find. I have never been stung by a bee, except once as a small boy when I carelessly stepped on one while walking barefoot in clover, so I deserved it really.

I have been stung often by the aggressive wasps that live in our stone walls, however, and I don't care for that very much.

Crape myrtles are everywhere in bloom at this time of year too, and as I do every year, I try ineffectually to decide which feature I like best about them: their lovely sprays of watermelon-colored flowers or their handsome, lean, and fastigiate stems. I have never grown them, but have always wanted to. Luckily, there are a lot of them about our town, so I can enjoy them fully without having to find space for them in my own garden.

I have a neighbor whose taste in gardening is decidedly eccentric. Well, whose isn't, really? But this guy is a bit round the bend in his enthusiasms and is, I think, a cautionary tale to all of us that the line in the garden between charming individualism and deplorable eccentricity is alarmingly thin. He likes caladiums and canna lilies. So do I, but he has gone too far. You can tell he likes them just by strolling past his yard, because his acre of garden is full of them and other tropicals too: hundreds and hundreds of caladiums and canna lilies, with here and there large elephant ears stuck in and even more enormous gunnera dominating the landscape, stuck in every container imaginable, even a rusted out old Jeep.

It is a surprising garden indeed, even remarkable, but in the end, not really beautiful. Good heavens, it is amazing to look at, and God only knows what he does with all these tender tropicals in the winter months, as he has no greenhouse. My guess is there is a long-suffering spouse somewhere in the domestic picture, as there usually is with round-the-bend gardening enthusiasts. Somebody like him is a real tonic for us all, making the rest of us feel quite sane and sensible by comparison.

A bit further on, I come across a scene that quite floors me. There is a place where the street crosses a small stream, and long ago, the town fathers erected an ornate iron grill in lieu of a railing where the sidewalk crosses the bridge. It is charming and someone has planted a most astonishing morning glory here so it can scramble up and cover this lovely grill. I have mixed feelings about morning glories. As a boy, I hated them, having spent a lot of time in the broiling sun struggling to dig the weed versions of them, the ones with the ratty little white flowers, out of our tough and rocky western soil. But their delicate, brightly colored cousins, the annual kind you can grow from seed or purchase at garden centers, I find quite lovely. Their colors are intense and luminous, and they have such a graceful climbing and draping habit, giving off a tropical air that is quite charming.

This particular morning glory was most arresting; it was a brilliantly electric indigo. Do you know this color? It lies between purple and blue, but is closer to purple. And this flower is so luminous, it literally seems to be somehow lit from within. Flowers like this need to be looked at intensely and up close, and we ignore for now how odd we look getting right in amongst a plant and putting its blooms right up to our eye. On closer inspection, you find that the throat of this flower is lighter indigo, and deep down in the throat, the color tapers off almost to white with tiny yellow traceries in the throat. That is where the luminosity comes from. The effect is very magical.

The grill was covered with literally hundreds and hundreds of these brilliant indigo trumpets. Seen under the dark bruise of the threatening, Mid-Atlantic sky, it was very arresting. And, as if this loveliness was not enough, some very discerning person had placed a large pot with an enormous, chromatic yellow chrysanthemum right at the base of the morning glory, so that the combination of the crackling yellow mum with the electric luminosity of the morning glory's indigo was like a bolt of floral lightning. I stood there, transfixed in admiration. Somewhere in this town, I thought, there is a true gardening genius on the loose, with extremely good taste and a very bold eye. We are not alone.

※

Cicadas and Fireflies

I cut another huge armful of mint, taking it inside to dry in the basement for next year's mint iced tea with lemonade. I cut down numerous chive plants, freezing them for use in making pesto and soup stock this winter. I always sing "Bringing in the Chives" to the tune of "Bringing in the Sheaves" to annoy other members of the household—and it never fails. I suppose they must take the rough with the smooth, just like the rest of us. I planted the last of the hundreds of irises I divided, and dug up two huge batches of daffodils from under the pink azaleas on the corner. I plan to divide them and colonize new areas with them.

Monday morning, I saw another sign of autumn's advance when I stepped off our back stoop on my way to go to work and noticed a large, iridescent blue cicada clinging onto a large, variegated, acid-green hosta leaf. It reminded me that the lovely summer chorus of cicadas is growing quieter and quieter, as more of this brood's members complete their lifecycle. Many people, I think, do not like the look or sound of cicadas. They are large-featured, blunt-headed creatures, and most people, probably thinking of the ugly exoskeletons found all over the yard in summer (the bugs', not the people's), find them more than a little repulsive. Personally, I think they are rather far gone in gorgeousness. Here they have vivid peacock colors: bright green and iridescent blue, with black and dark brown accent colors. And I find their whirring song charming, probably because I grew up in Western Colorado in a very hot and arid climate, where their humming and whirring were the song of my summer youth, so naturally those are pleasant associations, to me.

Once, when I was seventeen and living in Australia, I went on a trip to see, among other marvels, an enormous, 50,000-acre sheep station in north-central New South Wales, called "Raby," if memory serves, though that was a long time ago now. The people who lived there at that time managed the property for a giant English land-holding concern. Their house was very large and very gracious, built gloriously in the Australian colonial style, with thick stone walls and deep shady verandahs on all sides, tin roofs overall, and even a large swimming pool. It was situated near a river of sorts and surrounded by large shade trees. Not long before I visited, the Queen and Prince Philip had been in Australia, and the prince had been a guest at Raby and actually stayed in the beautiful room I was also given. Along the river by the house grew enormous old gum trees, and the cicadas in the trees were legion there. Once they all started humming their loud song, it was rather deafening, so the house was required to be strictly silent in the morning to postpone the inevitable start of the chorus for as long as possible, because the careless bang of a screen door would set them off, and they would sing almost maddeningly until you fell asleep, late that night.

Cicadas live an extraordinary, seventeen-year life cycle. After they hatch above ground and fall to the earth as larvae, they live in the soil as grubs, only emerging into the light as familiar insects in their final year of life, really just a season, and that scarcely three months long. Every year has a new generation, of course, but one brood is mysteriously called "Brood X" and is extremely large in parts of the eastern U.S., though no one knows why. I noticed them emerge in the summer of 1987, when we were living in the leafy northern Virginia suburbs of our nation's capital, and they were most astonishing. It was actually difficult to walk down the sidewalk without stepping on them, no matter how careful one was, and the noise they made was quite deafening for the three to four weeks that they were at their peak. Hundreds of them were on every tree trunk, and every screen door was covered with them; they were everywhere. They do no harm and are merely enjoying their brief time in the sun, as we all are, but people get a little overwrought about insects and try to kill them or otherwise harass them, which I am afraid makes the larger and more intelligent species look much smaller and rather foolish.

I remember that particular summer well, not only because the cicadas were so amazing, but because I had decided to ask my future wife to marry me, and I had selected a marquise diamond and two flanker diamonds that I was having made into a ring. My plan was to propose to her in August, after I had finished paying for the ring, which cost what I thought at the time an astronomical sum. I was thrilled to be the single person on the planet privy to this tremendous secret in my breast, and I well remember driving out into the humid, forested Virginia suburb of Maclean to the jeweler's store with a secret love song in my heart and all of creation shrieking its awesome, mechanically whirring love song back to me in reply as I flew into the forest on my secret-jewel-of-love's errand. She went on to say yes to my proposal, in case you were wondering, and wedding bells and wedded bliss followed in the usual way. But returning to the cicadas, seventeen years later, when this brood emerged again, we were again living in the East, this time in southern New Jersey, and while loud, their reappearance was not nearly as impressive there as it had been in northern Virginia.

Fireflies or lightning bugs lead a similar sort of existence, but they are much smaller and advertise themselves more charmingly, with light of course, rather than with sound. They are not really a fly, but rather a beetle, and it is not generally known that their larvae, and even their eggs, give off a soft, luminescent glow, hence "glow worm," as they are sometimes called. Where I grew up, it was far too dry for them, but every other year or so, we would go to Wisconsin, where my parents were both raised and where my grandparents and cousins still lived. And for two weeks or so, we would spend most evenings catching fireflies and marveling over them as many children have commonly done. We would keep them in fruit jars (this was in a time when every home had fruit jars on hand, as well as home-made preserves to put in them) and stay up late holding them, on my aunt and uncle's screened porch, listening to the adults talk and smoke and laugh over their highballs and bridge games while we grew sleepier, clutching our glowing, glazed worlds with their tiny pulsing lights. They would glow in our bedrooms at night, living nightlights, and then in the morning, we would let them go again.

One of the things I really like about living in the east again is having fireflies about the place once more. They seem to come out in the second week of June and to vanish again by August, though sometimes we have seen a few lonely, as-yet-unmated stragglers in late August, or even one or two now in September, I believe. It is wonderful to sit on our dark patio on a midsummer's night and watch their tiny golden lights flash on and off in the dark green bowl of our backyard, the sublimely hypnotic semaphore of summer.

October

Dogs Are Proof God Loves Us

I don't know why I like working for media billionaires so much. I suppose they are pretty interesting and stimulating to be around, on the whole, and I think it is a fairly harmless hobby. It is more interesting to me than stamp collecting, and certainly more socially constructive than, say, a career stealing toasters or hubcaps. When I worked for John Malone at Liberty Media, my wife used to introduce me as "the smartest guy at Liberty who is not a millionaire yet." This was always received with a laugh and I always thought there was an insult buried in there somewhere, but could never quite put my finger on it.

I'm thinking about my corporate bosses this morning because I see my canine boss is desperately trying to get my attention, with the topic of a walk clearly on his mind. What wonderful creatures dogs are, proof to be sure that God loves us and wants us to be happy. Well yes, I know that Ben Franklin originally said that about beer and not dogs. And of course, it has been said of many things since, and is true of many things too, beer—and horses, by the way—certainly included. But I am saying it now about dogs and who would disagree?

This particular dog is a marvel. I have loved all of the many dogs I have known in a long life full of wonderful dogs, and I would not be willing to give up the friendship of a single one of them, not for anything. And this one above all of them, for this dog is rare indeed. He is kind and keen, has the most lovely spirit, and is completely devoted to every member of our family, though over time I have become his favorite, an enormously humbling compliment and responsibility. I love the famous prayer, "Oh Lord, help me be the man my dog thinks I am!" If only I were.

Being a sheltie, he loves to obey, learns quickly, anticipates my every move, and knows what I am going to do, often even before I know it myself. And he is smart as hell, scary smart. We don't even leave our checkbook out any more, after we came home early one night and caught him on the phone, talking to the local pizzeria in a growly voice and ordering a "meat-lover's pizza." He watches me get dressed in the morning and knows that if I put on a suit I am going in to the office, but if I put my jeans on, I am staying home with him. Joy. Each morning, he goes over and puts his nose on my jeans to show me where they are, in case I forgot, and to show me what he wants me to wear. He is a sort of canine valet. It breaks my heart to choose the suit. On weekends, he will spend the entire day with me in the garden, indefatigable and endlessly interested, and the only words he likes better than "Do you want to go for a walk?" are "Do you want to garden with me?"

This morning is particularly fetching. It is barely light, and the sleepy world is suffused with dense fog, thrown up no doubt by the wave of warm, very humid weather we are having after the chills of last week. The days are growing speedily shorter and cooler. But today is warm, and the world is hushed and muffled by the fog. There are a few dozen stunning red maple leaves spangled on the blacktop drive, as if they were arranged by hand by a finicky florist for a community fall festival. But of course they fell at random, each one improbably landing face up. It is a day of exceptional beauty, much more beautiful than the average day, and I briefly reflect on the unfairness and unevenness of days, in respect of their inherent beauty.

I got up early this morning, fed Cosimo—the first thing as he requires of me—then grabbed the first cup of coffee from the coffee pot and went outside with him to watch the day come on. Our days often begin like this now, sitting on the back stoop with my arm around his neck as we watch the slow autumnal light infiltrate the new day. We watch the birds and squirrels moving about in the garden, and Cosimo seems to know intuitively that this is a time for quiet watching and not for chasing and barking. That will come later, as we both know.

It is a perfect dog-walking day, and we both reach this conclusion independently. Cosimo looks at me with an excited twinkle in his eye, to see if I have come to the same idea, and he knows by my answering smile that I have. A good, long walk is indicated, we both think. Of course, that means I will likely be late for work, so I briefly weigh the pros and cons of disappointing my famous boss or my dog. My mind flies though the realms of responsibility and affection and I choose my canine boss over my media tycoon boss. Once again.

On our walk around town, I notice the last of the cicadas are already whirring busily, but otherwise the world is silenced. It's like watching a lovely, dreamy Fellini film with the sound turned off, and the cicada whirring is the sound of the film spooling from real to reel. The birds are flocking together more thickly each day, great clouds of them wheeling shapelessly in the sky, settling on telephone wires and in trees in their many hundreds, soon to be thousands, before they depart, chattering excitedly about their upcoming big adventure. Every year in late September or early October, like clockwork, a few blue jays fly through our garden, and so far, I have never missed them; though we only have a few and then they are gone for the year, so you have to be quick-sighted. One of the great things about New Jersey is that it is located right in the middle of one of the most important American flyways for birds coming down from Canada in the fall, and of course, going north in the spring. So we are very spoiled and get to see a lot of wonderful birdlife here.

A bit of color is just starting to flush into the maples. And how beautiful the dogwoods are this time of year, when their leaves turn to an even, mellow russet and their graceful branches fan out their delicate, spreading russet canopies. It is exactly the color of russet that is echoed in the spent and faded floral umbels of the hydrangeas at this time of year. The humidity and warmth have caused an efflorescence of mushrooms around town, huge ones in a wide range of shapes. Kids cannot resist smashing mushrooms, which I mildly deplore because, to me, they are so interesting and rare; but I say I mildly deplore it because I smashed quite a few of them myself as a kid, and so I certainly understand the attraction of that.

Because our town is so old, some homes here still have the marble or granite posts near the street where guests, or the milkman, or the man driving the ice wagon would tie up the reins for their horses. A few even have the old stone mounting blocks for getting back on your horse. Whenever I pass one of these on my rambling walks around town, I step up onto it for old times' sake, as I think someone should from time to time, so they don't become entirely disused. The main street in our town was part of the old King's Highway that ran from Trenton to Camden, and then on into Philadelphia. At one point on this street, there is a worn, brownstone obelisk-shaped marker with the legend carved long ago in colonial cursive:

10

M

TO

C

which horsemen and coachmen of the old days would know meant "Ten miles to Camden." We get home after our long walk just as it is starting to rain, so I grab an extra cup of coffee for the drive in to work, when I would much rather this lovely autumn walk could go on and on, but reality intrudes, as it so frequently does. Duty and a city job call, and thank goodness I love that job or I might be tempted to do what my jealous canine boss seems to suggest I do…call in sick for an emergency gardening day.

Conversation of Owls, Fall Chores

Do you know the conversation of owls? I went to bed early Saturday with our bedroom window open and the cool air pouring in and, as I lay there waiting for sleep to overtake me, I heard *two* owls hooting to each other in the large trees outside our windows, and I fell deeply asleep listening to their mysterious conversation. Classically, they are associated with Athena, the Greek goddess of wisdom, whose favorites they were, and as a symbol, they represent both wisdom and protection from harm. Owls were thought to protect the armies of Greece, and if one appeared before a battle, it was universally taken as an omen of certain victory. I love living in a place where there are owls around; they have great dignity and gravitas, and their presence tells you that you are part of a healthy and robust ecosystem. There is certainly something reassuring and old-fashioned, almost primeval, about them.

It is three weeks after the equinox and most of the flowers are now finished. We mostly have just green in the garden, though the huge mums, the canna lilies, and the dahlias are still going strong, and the dahlias especially are impressive. How dull the autumn garden would be without mums, asters, dahlias, and helianthus. It was sunny and very fine all weekend, but the morning sky is not light until 7:00 a.m. I had seen a long red feather in the yard and had feared our cardinal had been taken by a hawk, but then I saw him again last week, so I guess he is all right. I got stung by a wasp again—about the sixth or seventh time this year, the aggressive little things—when dumping a pile of leaves too near the entrance to their home under a sidewalk paver. They are very protective of their homes, those wasps.

It was a busy weekend in the garden. I replaced an azalea in front that had perished in our summer heat, swept the walk to the side yard, and cut back the ivy around the giant Serbian spruce. I cleaned up and re-stacked the woodpile, and brought some logs inside for our first fires of the autumn. Cut back the ivy in the front yard, and I got our big ladder out and got into all our trees to tear the ivy out of them, some for the first time since we have lived here. Ivy is great: it is extremely hardy and covers a multitude of sins and flaws in the garden, I find, but if you are going to have it around, you have to be very vigilant in policing it and keeping it within bounds. It is a very dangerous plant to have around the place because of its invasive nature, as are bamboo, mint, and honeysuckle, to name a few of its aggressive and indefatigable pals. I don't like the look of ivy growing up tree trunks, though I know some people do. To me it is unkempt and unruly-looking, plus it can't be good for the trees, trapping moisture against the bark and providing a haven for all manner of pests.

But pulling it all down showed me a better, esthetic reason to oppose ivy on tree trunks: how lovely the bark itself it is. You really notice this when you strip the ivy off and see the different barks of the various trees, from the poured concrete of the smooth hollies to the red ridges of the cedars and the corrugated surfaces of the hemlocks, dogwoods, and maples. And sycamores are scaly and interesting, with their camouflage patterns, while crape myrtles are clean and limber. And so on.

I cleaned out some of the birdhouses while I was up in the trees. I finally stopped at 4:00 p.m. and then did something I have never done before after a hard day of yard work—had some aspirin and an early martini on the front porch in the lowering sunlight. Well, okay, maybe I have done that a few times before, but not in a while. Today, I was just marveling at the beautiful day and the strong, clear sunlight on the broad leaves of the canna lilies and flickering brilliantly green in the grape leaves on the porch columns. I had to concede that October is one of the better months. I didn't think I would be able to find any flowers to cut in the garden, but I managed a decent vase of roses and two other good bouquets, one of fall colors (cannas, sedum, and peach dahlias with two kinds of red chrysanthemums, "kiku" as the Japanese call them,) and one of magenta (two kinds of purple and pink chrysanthemums, the last of the phlox, and some magenta dahlias). Leaves are due to the curb for the first collection this coming week, so I will do that tomorrow.

Meanwhile, the northern world turns with daily greater haste toward the gathering darkness of winter. Two weeks ago, before the autumnal dark descended, we had one final glorious Sunday: it was sunny, with soft dry air and the temperature in the mild eighties. It was so clearly summer's last hurrah that a friend and I decided on the spur of the moment to go kayaking down the Batso River in the heart of southern New Jersey's Pine Barrens. No, it is true that it is not Colorado or Hawaii, but it is very lovely all the same. The river was still running very full from our wet summer and from being fully topped up by the late summer hurricane that dumped a ton of rain on South Jersey. The current was strong and the same hurricane had knocked down a lot of trees into the river, making it much more exciting to navigate than the previous time we descended it. There were very few people on the river. The leaves were just turning, the swamp maples were already in their full glory, and all for just a few eyes to see in the jewel-like wilderness a mere hundred miles from many millions of people. It was lovely, and by the end of the day, we were tired and sun-burned and happy. I felt like Henry David Thoreau in the empty and pristine wilderness.

The cooler weather of October naturally turns our minds to thoughts of autumn foods and wholesome, comforting meals and soups. The orange and yellow squashes of this season, and also of course sweet potatoes and yams, are excellent sources of beta-Carotene and vitamin A, and really should not just be thought of in autumn. Sweet potatoes are a great favorite in our house, but I think are not very popular in general. Their very sweetness tells against them, and I think people too often try to think of ways of preparing them that key off their sweetness. With marshmallows and brown sugar, for example. Yuck, I say. Far better, in my view, is to push them the other way, toward savory. This is a recipe that makes a great vegetable accompaniment to any meal at any time of the year, but especially resonates on a chilly fall day.

Savory Sweet Potatoes

3 medium sweet potatoes

1 Tbsp. salt

8 oz. sour cream

2 tsp. garlic salt

½ tsp. freshly ground black pepper

¼ tsp. freshly ground nutmeg

1Tbsp. Szechuan seasoning (alternative: 1 Tbsp. roasted ground cumin)

1 cup finely chopped cilantro

¾ cup freshly grated *parmigiano reggiano*

For the topping:

1/3 cup freshly grated *parmigiano reggiano*

1 tsp. sea salt

½ cup Japanese-style bread crumbs (such as Panko)

Peel the sweet potatoes and cut them into half-inch disks. Bring to boil a pot of water with the tablespoon of salt in it. When the water is boiling, add the potatoes and boil them until tender, 15-18 minutes. Drain them and allow them to cool until they can be handled. Mill them with a potato ricer or (much harder) mash them with a fork in a large mixing bowl. (A note on mashing root vegetables, in case you didn't already know this: they need to be mashed or milled and not processed in a machine, which breaks the cell walls and releases their starches, resulting in runny vegetables instead of the nice fluffy potatoes we are looking for. A potato ricer is a handy gadget and not at all expensive; it's a great investment or gift.) Add the sour cream, spices, cilantro, and parmesan, and combine well. In a small mixing bowl, combine the ingredients for the topping (which, by the way, is a great staple you can use on many dishes, for example baked pasta dishes like tetrazzinis). Spoon the potatoes into a deep baking dish, sprinkle the topping over them, then bake at 300 degrees for one hour before serving.

※

Treasure and History in the Garden

Just like the simple folk in that old TV show "The Beverly Hillbillies," I have found real treasure on my land. Unlike them, I was not able to buy a mansion in Beverly Hills, but I did find buried treasure all the same. On Saturday, when dividing some bluebells in front of our old stone porch, which is original to this 1888 house, I dug up an 1822 penny, the kind that is the size roughly of our modern quarter and is worth more than $100 to coin collectors today. Of course, I hoped there were many more and dug deeper, but no, there was only that one. Still, I treasure it. And the part of our back yard by the rose arch was obviously the home's rubbish tip many years ago, because digging there, I find so much broken glass and crockery that I finally have made a firm rule of always wearing gloves when digging and weeding there, I have been cut so often. But even the rubbish buried in this garden is beautiful, as I turn up lovely old broken bits of Delft porcelain, inexpensive blue and white Chinese export pottery, and interesting old-fashioned bottles, sanded smooth from a hundred years in the gritty soil.

There is also history in the garden, both literal and figurative, and we should be alive to it. The literal history is not hard to think about. We can look about the garden and ask ourselves, who gardened here before me and what were they thinking when this or that area was planted and this or that plant material was selected? We have lived several times in brand new construction, where no gardener intelligence preceded mine except the design intelligence of the Big Guy Himself, and we had the fun and the challenge of working with a nearly blank slate in planning a new garden. And we have also lived here, in a very old garden and a much older town, both of which were shaped by a lot of history and by many hands and minds.

Thinking of the great Victorian and Edwardian gardens of England, one realizes how ephemeral any garden scheme really is, even the great ones persisting into our own day by dint of slavish repetition and replacement. The great landscape architects Capability Brown and Humphrey Repton are perhaps examples of gardeners whose original work at the great houses of the English aristocracy has largely stood the test of time, but we mere mortals do not have the chance to express ourselves in the gardening vernacular of 300-year-old oaks and glades of giant London plane trees very often. Most of our gardens will not even outlive ourselves, in practice, and indeed, their mutable, ephemeral natures are a large part of their charm for many of us.

So it is well to look around and see what in the current garden is really old and is a treasure. We have a colossal Serbian spruce that towers over our back yard—it must surely be over a hundred years old—and we have many other large trees that have to date from the early part of the last century. We have quite a few very old and very large rhododendrons that must have been planted long ago. The basic structure of the garden, its backbone, I received as a given and I have been very pleased with it. I would not have chosen those three huge hemlocks myself; but still, I am not complaining and am reasonably glad to have them, having contributed nothing to their planting and care for fifty years or so.

But every garden, and all land, has a history before the current gardener arrived on the scene. Once, as a college student in Denver, I went to the Denver Public Library, which is justly famous for its collection of western Americana. In one reading room, there was a wall-sized map of North America, but instead of being divided into the states and provinces we are familiar with, it showed all the tribal areas of the Native Americans, as they were before the first European explorers and settlers arrived. I was fascinated by this very different way of seeing North America, now completely changed and largely vanished.

Do you know what Native Americans first walked the land you now inhabit? Every inch of America was part of the tribal lands of one native group or another. For my garden, it was the Lenni Lenape, whose name means "Human Beings" in their own language and who were called the

"Delaware Indians" by the European settlers because their land included the Delaware River Valley, as well as the Lower Hudson and western Long Island. Other tribes, for example the Algonquin tribes, considered the Lenni Lenape the "grandfathers" of younger tribes, and they were always treated with special respect and seniority in council. Only vestiges of this once-great people remain, mostly in Oklahoma, but there are some settlements also in Kansas, Wisconsin, and Ontario. They fished the Delaware, hunted deer in the forests of southern New Jersey, and in the fierce heat of summer, they went down to the Jersey Shore for fresh fish and oysters, just like the nomadic Real Housewives of New Jersey do on television today.

After the Lenape inhabited this area, its European settlement took hold. Our town is located a few miles from the left bank of the mighty Delaware River on a ridge in southern New Jersey with two abundant, sweet water springs that still exist and, in ancient times, would have been essential for wildlife and human settlement alike. One of these springs now feeds a long, serpentine lake in our town and the other, just a few blocks from my garden, has been trained into a series of lovely ornamental ponds. I suppose the people who live next to them now are largely oblivious of their natural origin and the fact that the reason our town exists where it does is thanks to these two fresh, life-giving springs.

In a nutshell, the English Puritans settled New England, the Dutch settled New York and Long Island, and the Quakers settled New Jersey and Pennsylvania. Part of the settlement was fueled by a quest for land, but a lot of it was caused by a quest for religious freedom, which had its roots deep in the Reformation history of the sixteenth century and the English Civil War of the seventeenth century. Struggles between Parliament and the king, on the one hand, and Christian fundamentalists who despised both the English and Roman Churches, on the other, resulted in civil war, regicide and the springing up of more than a dozen alternative Christian sects, the Quakers being one of the few that have survived to the present day.

Two syndicates of Quaker businessmen bought the two parts of New Jersey—East New Jersey and West New Jersey—in the 1680s, and European settlement began here in earnest, essentially all of it, in those early days, fueled by Quakers longing to escape from the official persecution of the established English Church and the English Crown. And one of the first foundations after these purchases was the town where we now live. That was in 1682, just a few generations after the landing at Jamestown and still a full century before the Revolutionary War would convulse the entire Delaware Valley. Then, General Washington would storm back and forth through our small town on the King's Highway from Trenton to Camden and on to Philadelphia, then the seat of government for the colonies in revolt.

One of the Quakers' greatest revolutionary ideas was education for all, instead of just for the upper classes. The Quaker educational ideals and philosophy of brotherhood and equality were to shape the political culture of New Jersey and Pennsylvania, which in turn shaped the founding documents of the new American Republic. The Mid-Atlantic is still full of great Quaker schools that carry on these philosophical and educational traditions in the modern day, and our kids attended one of them for many years, just blocks from our house. The Quakers would later become bitter and implacable opponents of slavery, and in our town, as in many New Jersey towns, Quaker farms eagerly enlisted in the Underground Railroad that smuggled escaped slaves from the South up through New England to freedom in Canada.

Solid Quaker farming folk built our town. What is now our acre of land, along with a new house that was built upon it, was originally a wedding gift in 1888 to the son of the family who owned the big farm next door. Imagine having the wealth to give an acre of land and a gorgeous house as a wedding present.

Possibly America's greatest botanist, John Bartram, came from this region and from the Quaker tradition. His travels ranged widely, from the shores of Lake Ontario southward to Eastern Florida and west to the Ohio River. He did more than anyone else in that time of open scientific inquiry to explore and taxonomize the American flora and to promote the exchange of information between botanists in England and in the American colonies. He lived just across the Delaware in Philadelphia, and there is a street in our small town named in his honor, just a couple streets from my current garden. And there is another distinguished explorer and naturalist who is linked to our town: Edward Harris was a local farmer who struck up a friendship with the ornithologist John James Audubon and helped fund the publication of his timeless classic, *Birds of America*. He accompanied Audubon on his famous birding expeditions to the Gulf of Mexico (1837) and along the Missouri River (1843).

This is the history of my garden—Lenape Indians; Quaker non-conformists; revolution; Penn and Washington; Bartram and Harris; a philosophy of egalitarianism, human dignity, and a love of the land; the pre-eminence of education—these are the ideals that percolate here in the very soil, that resonate in the rich marine air, and that still bubble forth in the long forgotten town springs, as sweet and as fresh as ever.

Nature, Red in Tooth and Claw

A dull, wet, gray fall week, the persistent gloom and rain lowering temperatures as well as spirits all around. Finally yesterday morning it first felt like fall, with the temperature in the low fifties and enough golden leaves spangling the dark wet blacktop to look like autumn is finally here in earnest. The last hearties of the garden are: the pinched-back mums finally coming into their own, late bloomers like the gardener himself, a few straggler roses, trying to go on until Christmas as they did when we lived in Virginia, the dahlias in their terracotta pots, probably wondering what happened to all that glorious sunshine they had all to themselves.

The cannas of course are still blooming, seemingly oblivious to the climate's growing less and less like the tropics and going headlong for broke like tropicals are meant to do, go big or go home as they say in the jungle. Or as they say in Vegas: Full blast, first class while the money lasts! Likewise the impatiens by the dogwood and a few cheerful petunias; nothing is going to stop them but a good, hard killing frost, but that is about it. I am going to pot up another half dozen amaryllises for Christmas; perhaps I am finally getting the timing of that chore right, though my vast experience of failure warns me to doubt it. It was so dull and gloomy last night, and just chilly enough, that my wife and I lit the candles and had our first blazing fire in the reading room, no doubt the first of many to come during what they say is supposed to be a much harsher winter despite the lulling mildness of this October, which draws darkly to a close.

I think gardeners have a lot of sentiment in them in general. We are famously kind and generous and hopeful—all winning personality characteristics. We have feelings for the things in the garden and its various traditions, attachments, and memories. But in other ways, we are completely unsentimental. We have no illusions or sentiment, for example, about nature and the forces of nature that we deal with every day and every season in the garden and that order all the living things in our gardens, our yards, and our neighborhoods. And of course the wider world too. We know nature is tough, unyielding, sometimes harsh, and never itself sentimental. In observing the interaction between animals, Lord Tennyson's memorable formulation of "Nature, red in tooth and claw" is the way it really works, by and large.

Not long ago, my wife and I were sitting on the patio one evening when we were very surprised to see one of the big, sleek hawks that patrol our town come sweeping into our patio just feet from us and, bold as brass, start attacking the pyracantha, where our nearly tame wrens were hiding and harmlessly chattering together. He could scarcely find a perch on the dense, prickly bush, but sort of held onto the vertical side of it, beating his great wings furiously to hold his position, and thrusting his killing beak into the bush repeatedly to catch one of the terrified wrens, who were creating a panicked commotion within. Red in tooth and claw indeed. But the beast was unsuccessful this time, and he flew off in a great sulk, to our amazement and relief.

Usually these hawks prey on the large squirrel population of our town, as do the silent and deadly owls. These squirrels, and their cousins the chipmunks which are not as numerous by us, are not my favorite animals in the world. They are quite a pest in our garden, and usually strip our peaches, apricots, and tomatoes, so that we can hardly hope for any for ourselves. But our grapes fruit too heavily even for the little beasts to eat them all, and they as yet have not discovered our fig tree, heh-heh. But I do feel sorry for them all the same, a bit, to be pursued by these deadly and efficient killers. Looked at another way, I love seeing the hawks and the owls and think they are perfectly marvelous in their way, and it is lucky they live with us, but I would prefer to look away when the ripping and tearing has to begin. We have some superb falcons who perch outside my office on the fifty-fourth floor of an office tower in Philadelphia, but when they fly up with a dead pigeon in their claws and commence tearing it to pieces, I just can't watch that. Surely there's enough of that happening already in the world of business, on the human side of the glass?

The main reason I put up with the squirrels and chipmunks, apart from the simple fact that I don't have a choice in the matter, is that they provide hours of wholesome entertainment and exercise for Cosimo, who goes nuts if he sees a squirrel in our yard, or even in our trees. Rabbits too, of course. They can do a lot of damage in a garden, but not in ours, as the word has gotten out in the rabbit community that our garden is patrolled by a very active sheltie with a particular animus for their kind. He has never actually caught one, nor would I wish him to, but I do like to see him active, and the squirrels, rabbits, and chipmunks all seem to take him very much in stride. We also have voles, and of course mice, but hardly enough to worry about and they have never been much of a problem. We also have seen bats, raccoons, groundhogs, and possums from time to time, and of course, toads and tortoises too, though these are far more rare. I so wish we had more of all of them.

Deer can be a terrible heartache in the garden, and are for many gardeners, but not for me in this garden, as I thank my lucky stars. They will certainly avoid specific plants they do not prefer, but no plant is really safe from them, and deer will eat anything on offer if they are hungry enough. Where we lived in Colorado, it was perfect deer and elk country, very wild and open and over 6,000 feet high. One morning, we were standing on the driveway with our kids, waiting for the school carpool, and I was shocked to see the distant ridge behind our house alive with movement. I focused more closely and it soon became clear that it was a vast herd of elk, at least several thousand strong, migrating past our house to higher spring grazing. Thousands of beasts of that size, all surging past you in a never-ending river of beefy quadrupeds, is quite an awe-inspiring sight.

In that same garden, I once arrived home to see a small group of four does in the new rosebed I had planted with special cold-hardy, Canadian-bred, high-elevation varieties of roses I had great hopes for. They were happily munching the tender leaves of all these new babies, acquired at great expense and considerable bother. I hollered at them and they just stared dumbly at me with that vacuous, unintelligent stare that everyone who has seen deer up close will recognize. I was furious and grabbed the first thing that came to hand, which turned out to be the driver from my golf bag, and began advancing down the driveway, whirling it menacingly over my head and hollering, and generally looking pretty crazy. The largest doe gave me a withering look that said: "Really? A crazy dude with a golf club? Whatever next. And I suppose we're meant to just run away, when we haven't even finished our supper of these delicious baby roses? Think again, loser!" But as I was practically in amongst them, they did finally move off, after each of them tore off a quick goodbye mouthful. The roses, of course, were ruined and never amounted to much because the deer came back and finished them off later in peace, as I knew they would.

But in our present garden, as I said, deer do not trouble us. We are just far enough inside town that we never see them here. Our dog keeps most other animal pests away and the birds dispatch most of the insect pests that bother many gardens and gardeners. The squirrels and chipmunks get most of the fruit, the wicked things, but we get all the fun of having the squirrels and chipmunks around and they amuse our dog endlessly. The flowers we have all to ourselves. So I have to say, I think we have it pretty good, all in all, in this most perfect of all worlds, and we have no wish to add to the hardship of the garden fauna in any way or to make nature any redder in tooth or claw than it already is.

Growing Connected to the Land

Driving into the city this morning, as I crested the Ben Franklin Bridge, I noticed a large, stage-prop harvest moon. It was just off full and barely gone to gibbous; the giant orb was hanging picturesquely over the chilly cityscape. Naturally, my mind turned to thoughts of the harvest, especially as the pumpkin patch is ripe with glowing orange orbs and we are going to have a lovely, late Indian summer of a week, sunny and high seventies all week.

The modern adult seems to be very tech-savvy, but sadly cut off from the harvests going on all around us. This is more true today than it was for our parents or grandparents, when the majority of Americans lived in a rural location. Gardeners today are more connected to the land than non-gardeners, but does one, as a gardener, have to grow something for the household to eat?

No, not really, but there is a lot to be said for the idea that we all need to be closer to the soil, closer to nature, and closer to the food we eat to know where it came from and how it got to our table. In the old days, even after clothes dryers were common, many people preferred to dry their clothes on clothes-lines, and anyone who has ever gone to bed in line-dried pajamas and sheets can tell you why. It was pure heaven. Line-drying exposed you to airborne pollen and other mild irritants and antigens in a kind of homeopathic dose, raising your system's resistance the same way eating local honey used to do, but that is nearly impossible now.

We are lucky to have friends who have a ranch near Aspen, and they send us a fantastic jar of honey from that ranch for Christmas every year, but when this is gone (always a sad day), our family's honey comes from Australia, of all places. And our clothes come hot and antiseptic from the dryer, and we have to take antihistamines, sometimes every day for some people. Is this an improvement? A sort of bucolic ideal is being explored contemporaneously and very interestingly by the poet Wendell Berry on his all-organic farm in Kentucky, essentially off the grid and producing everything he needs himself on his own land. The world's seven billion people can't live this way, because this sort of farming simply can't feed seven billion people; but it works for a few and is very hard to fault as a way of life or as a philosophy: it is simple, local, holistic, balanced, and environmentally committed. You have to admire it.

What can ordinary people do, who aren't lucky enough to have a self-contained farm in Kentucky? I think we can all grow something that attaches us to our land, whether that is a sprawling suburban garden, a small city plot, or the balcony of any apartment building.

Some people like a large vegetable garden, others like a tomato plant on a sunny balcony, others are happy with an herb cutting garden outside the back door or in a kitchen bay window. It almost does not matter. What does matter is that you watch a plant live and grow and give to you of its fullness before it perishes. You are part of its lifecycle and it becomes a part of you. I used to want to say, when I was younger and liked to say obnoxious things, that a gentleman should only burn the firewood that was produced on his own land or dropped from his own trees. And this was when I lived in Virginia on only a tiny piece of land. Though its large trees did drop quite a lot of firewood, that is an impossible standard to set for most people. Earlier too, I had declared that no self-respecting gentleman should drink a port that was younger than himself. This was an opinion formed in the common rooms of Oxford after much cautious and careful experimentation (okay, not that cautious, really), but one that has become increasingly difficult to hold to as time goes by, and is practically impossible now.

Anyway, the point is, anyone can grow a tomato plant or a few pots of herbs. Some people like to do a lot more. For myself, I like to have a few fruiting plants and I have just enough room for the smaller varieties of one peach tree, two cherry trees, two robust grape vines, two raspberry cane patches, and one (very small) fig tree. Though we live in southern New Jersey and have sprawling blueberry farms near us, I have never had luck with them, and have given up on them entirely. Likewise with apricots: our rabbits have a deplorable habit of girdling them in the winter; I have lost two and can't bear to lose another one, so I have reluctantly given up on them too. The birds get most of the fruit we do have, and what they miss, the squirrels and chipmunks strip clean, so very little of this makes its way to the kitchen table, but the point is that some of it does. And actually, flowering peach branches, forced to bloom in winter when the garden (and the gardener) are burdened and oppressed with snow and ice, is a glory not to be missed and nearly as good as a nice ripe peach on a hot August day.

Even modest gardens, as I say, can sustain a tomato plant (though I rarely can, thanks to my little rodent friends) and a basil plant, and what person above the age of ten has not noticed that store-bought tomatoes have no flavor at all and are simply not worth buying? Or to be more exact, the grape and cherry tomatoes are still produced with some flavor, but the large ones never are anymore. And we all know this is because they ship better if picked green and allowed to "ripen" (really, merely become red) in an unnatural way. And that is what happens, of course, when you want fresh tomatoes in February; you may have them, but they have to be shipped to you from the other side of the country (or world), and arrive with no flavor, having used up their own weight in fuel to get to your table. There, are you happy now? If not, simply grow your own. It's fun, inexpensive, defies the lords of agri-business, amuses the children, and tastes superb.

And speaking of basil, late October is the time to start thinking about harvesting all the basil plants before frost ruins them. We grow one plant per adult (or teenager), and that is ample, if you give it a sunny location such as most herbs require, to supply a year's worth of pesto, if you do not go crazy with the stuff and butter your toast with it, as has been known to happen at our house—it is that good. Of course, finding a sunny part of the garden not being used for anything is most unlikely for most of us, especially for something that does not flower gorgeously. But four basil plants for a family of four is really not a lot to ask.

In late summer, you pinch off the flowers when they appear, to promote taller, more vigorous growth; you can cut these into bits and put them in your salads, as they have an intense basil flavor. Before the final harvest, let them flower as much as they want, then pinch off all the flowers and strip off all the leaves; even the small stems are okay, as they are all going into a blender anyway. And here is a recipe for an out-of-this-world pesto. It's a bit fussy and many prefer simpler versions, but start with this and then you can personalize it or simplify it. The following ingredients are stuffed into a regular-sized blender in any order, though I pour the oil in last, as it helps pack the other ingredients down:

Basil Pesto

3 cups of roughly chopped basil leaves, flowers, and small stems

1 cup plus 2 Tbsp. freshly grated parmesan cheese

1½ cups toasted nuts (pine nuts are great, walnuts are much less expensive)

1 Tbsp. salt

9 cloves garlic (roasted for 20-30 minutes if you like, for a more mellow flavor)

1 Tbsp. freshly squeezed lemon juice

1 Tbsp. balsamic vinegar

½ Tbsp. freshly ground pepper

½ Tbsp. freshly ground nutmeg

2 cups of olive oil

Optional (but nice if you have either or both handy):

½ cup fresh mint leaves

½ cup fresh chives

Now the result of this is about seven cups of one of the world's most marvelous substances. Think of it as green gold and treasure it accordingly. You pour and scrape it into plastic cup-sized containers and keep them in the freezer; they last all winter and through to the next harvest. Harvesting four plants will mean many blenders-full and quite a mess, but it is heaven to have homemade pesto with pasta in the middle of winter. It can also be used with poultry, soups, gravies, paninis, and any grilled sandwich, or any bread for that matter, for those of us lucky enough not to have to go through life as a rail-thin super-model and who can still eat bread and pesto.

November

Moonlight Sonata

There are some definite benefits to being a "dynamo" who many times can't sleep past five in the morning. Sunrise this morning was an astonishing affair, with a broad turquoise sky streaked by striations of tangerine cloud, infused with the yellow citrus heat of the rising sun.

Hardly anyone was up to see this great light show, and I am so glad I didn't miss it myself. In the western sky, dropping low and fat toward the horizon, was an enormously full and ponderous silvery moon, looking like it was at any moment about to fall into the open arms of our large and frosty cardoons, made of the exact same shade of glimmering silver as the setting moon. Sometimes, when you see something like that, you just have to stop and stare; perhaps the lovely words of the 46th Psalm will come into your mind: "Be still, and know that I am God; I will be exalted among nations, I will be exalted in the earth." Being still is something I need to work on. To be sure, it is a bit easier to do early in the morning, before having a cup of coffee.

The full moon is an extraordinary sight to behold and it is no wonder that it has captivated and transfixed humans since before recorded history. Do you know about the old-fashioned moon names for the months of the year? Before there were the familiar calendar names—November and August and so on, which are largely Roman and post-Roman innovations—months were called by other names. Indeed, even before written history, the year was divided into lunar months by those observant enough to notice the celestial order of things, and each month's full moon was given a traditional, often local, name. The names were commonly associated with important things in the lives of the people, usually weather and food-gathering. This tradition persisted well into the modern era, and persists still in some places and among some peoples.

The early American colonists borrowed the Native American names and created some of their own. Different tribes had, of course, different naming conventions, as the weather or crop or hunting conditions of a given lunar month would be very different for a tribe in Florida than for a tribe in the Pacific Northwest. So there is no settled or agreed naming convention that applies nationwide, but the Algonquin names seemed to impress themselves upon early settlers in the region where we live.

The ones I am giving here were very common, and you might call them consensus names, though not universal. To avoid controversy and not wishing to be disrespectful to any other traditions, perhaps we can just think of them among ourselves as gardener's moons.

November's full moon, the moon I saw this morning, for example, was called the Beaver Moon or the Frosty Moon. "Frosty" is obvious, but why "Beaver"? Well, November was when you had to set the traps for beavers, before the swamps froze for winter, to ensure enough warm beaver pelts for the freezing months to come. Last month, October, was very widely known as the Hunter's Moon because game is fattened nicely then, and Native Americans and colonists alike needed to lay in as large a supply of meat as possible for winter. The Cold Moon of December needs no explanation, nor does the other name it was known by to many Native Americans, the Long Nights Moon.

January was the Wolf Moon, because that was when the wolves howled in hunger outside the villages and settlements. Some Native Americans called it the Snow Moon, but more commonly that name was used for February's full moon. Because hunting was so difficult in February and stored food supplies would be running low, February's moon was also often called the Hunger Moon. The spring moons show the relaxation of winter's icy grip. March was the Worm Moon, because the thawing ground meant the reappearance of earthworm casts and the birdlife that came with them. It was also called the Sap Moon to indicate the rising sap of sugar maples and the beginning of the syrup tapping season. April was picturesquely called the Pink Moon, for the reappearance of pink wild ground phlox, one of the forest's first blooming flowers. It was also called the Egg Moon or the Fish Moon for the renewed availability of birds' eggs and fish for food.

Every gardener will know why May was the Flower Moon, and some Native American tribes also called it the Corn Planting Moon to denote that important horticultural activity, on which so much tribal prosperity depended. June was the Strawberry Moon for reasons that will be obvious, but some Native American traditions coined it the Hot Moon or the Rose Moon. I'm going to go with Rose Moon myself: a perfect name for a nearly perfect flower and a perfect month in the garden. July was the Buck Moon, because that was when young bucks would be growing new antlers; it was also called Thunder Moon for the furious thunderstorms that are common in much of the country during that month. August was the Sturgeon Moon, because that was when the great fish of Lake Champlain and the Great Lakes were most readily caught. And September was very commonly called the Corn or Barley Moon, indicating that those crops were ripe for harvest then. Harvest Moon was the name given to the full moon that was closest to the autumn equinox; so it could fall in either September or October and, of course, was an important cultural reference in both Native American and colonial traditions.

Thinking of these things, my mind turns to the great Chief Seattle of the Duwamish people in the Pacific Northwest. He said that, as a young man, he had seen the ships of the Vancouver Expedition (1791-1795) as they explored Puget Sound. He gave his name to the city of Seattle, was of tall stature, and was celebrated as a furious warrior. He was also a famous orator, and made a very impactful speech in 1854 upon concluding a peace treaty with the U.S. government. It is worth looking this up and reading it in full, but here is one beautiful sentence from it: "There was a time when our people covered the land as the waves of a wind-ruffled sea cover its shell-paved floor, but that time long since passed away with the greatness of tribes that are now but a mournful memory."

That speech is still admired, and even revered, today for its beauty and its moving testament to the principles of ecology, ethics, and stewardship, things to which every serious gardener is fully alive. He said, "Humankind has not woven the web of life. We are but one thread within it. Whatever we do to the web, we do to ourselves." It is lovely, is it not? As obvious, arresting and lovely as the full moon itself!

Outside, It Is All Slipping Away

I am awakened early by a certain canine member of our household, who evidently feels I have had a sufficiently refreshing sleep and should now nobly bestir myself and cook his breakfast: chicken broth, steamed broccoli and chopped egg with kibble. I try to ignore him and go back to sleep, but without success. My mind begins churning through all the things I need to do and think about today, like the giant paddle wheel of a Mississippi steamer, roiling the broad, clear waters of my mind (as I like to think of them) with the muddy debris of mundane worry.

So I wearily clamber out of bed, diligently make the dog's breakfast as requested, clutch a cup of milky coffee in my hand, and peer outside, where it is just beginning to lighten up a bit. English weather again, I see, and that is a bad thing. The classic November sky looks like dark, weathered lead. When I fetch the papers, I feel the sharp tang of the raw, humid air. It is not raining, exactly, but just misting: that pervasive, insidious mist that gets in amongst your clothes and wets your skin just enough to be annoying but not enough for you to bother putting up an umbrella. If it were ten or fifteen degrees colder, this would be lovely snow, perhaps, but as it is, it is just irksome. Oxford and Cambridge share the patent on this precise kind of weather. I am familiar with it, because I marinated in it for the better part of three years.

I didn't mind it so much when out for an early morning row on the river or a long run, because it kept me cool. But it was bothersome to walk through on the many trips back and forth to lectures. Okay, perhaps I didn't really make *that* many trips back and forth to lectures, at least, not nearly as many as I was meant to, but still. You learn to wrap your face in your college scarf and ignore it, or if it turns to more serious rain, you have a stout English umbrella to put up against it. And not one of those flimsy, travel umbrellas either (unless, of course, you are in fact traveling), but a long, stout umbrella that gives good coverage and would never dare to invert. Today, I have just such an English umbrella that I love. It was given to me by some friends at the BBC and has a colorful map of the world printed on the inside, I suppose so that, if I get lost in a rainstorm, I will have the consolation of being able to indicate to myself exactly where I am.

Anyway, I would show up in the college Hall for breakfast every morning, ravenous as I always was in those days, damp and thoroughly misted over like everyone else. We had odd things for breakfast, things I never had heard of where I grew up. Like smoked kippers, which I actually grew to like in time, and other things, like haggis, which I certainly did not. The first time I saw a big dish of this revolting mess on the steam table, I asked the server what it was. "Coo, it's 'aggis, luv, try some. It'll soon put you right and make a man of you!" This, of course, was said in a broadly comic accent that all fans of Monty Python (and owners of trained parrots) will be familiar with. I asked an English friend what haggis was and he said, "Don't ask; it's too dreadful. It comes from Scotland." As if that fact explained everything I needed to know about that. To save you having to look this up, I will just tell you here that it is a savory pudding made out of a sheep's liver, heart, and lungs (eewww), which are chopped up with onion and oatmeal and then stuffed into the sheep's stomach and baked for three hours at least. If you were going out hunting in the Scottish highlands after breakfast, you would drench this mess with whisky, making it even more awful. It was said to put hair on your chest.

After a breakfast like this, you didn't care as much about the weather. And if you were a certain sort of Oxford don, you would trudge back to your quad, spired and carved out of mellow, honeyed Oxfordshire limestone, and climb up the broad stone staircase, deeply worn by centuries of undergraduates pounding up and down it, to your rooms. There, you would pour another scuttle of coal onto the fire, until it glowed like a heap of brightly lit rubies, and call out to your scout for a fresh pot of tea, very hot. And then you would go over to your desk, sweep aside the jumble of books and papers you had been working on late last night, and set about writing a fantastic novel about hobbits or Narnia or some such, which would delight the world for, oh, about a century or so. All fueled by smoked kippers, bangers and mash, baked beans, fried tomatoes and greasy streaky bacon, thoroughly disgusting haggis, cold toast, and strong, milky tea. A most improbable provenance. And not much gardening would be happening here, apart from when the don would throw his cold tea into his aging philodendron, high on a cluttered bookcase.

But returning to the modern day, in the diminishing glory of the garden in these dark, wet days of late fall, there is very little left to enjoy, unless you are willing to look very closely, and sometimes with a magnifying glass. Gone are the glories of late spring and high summer, when the garden was sheets and planes of color and growth. As we walk now through the dreary, wet and disheveled reality of the late autumn garden, we see very little to cheer the spirits. This morning, on the way to the car in the near dark, I notice a single, tiny yellow bloom on the forsythia bush, which makes me smile, and its small flare is answered across the way by the single, tiny white bloom on an azalea. Two of the indigo irises on the corner are blooming, echoed by a splendid dying display of half a dozen indigo clematis stars still spangling the column of the front porch. Here and there, a rose is still blooming, and these end-of-year roses, though very few in number, are perfect gems, as no pests survive to blemish them in any way. Each stage of life comes with its little compensations, does it not? A small vase of half a dozen of these exceptional blooms is heaven indoors, at your wife's bedside, when outside it is wet and dark, and it is all slipping away.

This past weekend, we were given a weather reprieve and Sunday was mild, lofting into the balmy sixties. We are definitely in the Christmas spirit here already, with amaryllises and paperwhite bulbs being forced on every warm radiator top (they love the heat) or sunny windowsill (prettier, but not as warm for them) in the house. The gardener is forced to consider aloud putting up the Christmas tree as an effort to bring the garden indoors, but the tentative venturing of this tepid opinion is met with a harsh rebuke from others in the household who won't hear of it this early, so that is that. Christmas must wait.

Meanwhile, in the world of the kitchen, these short dark days before the holidays begin to put one in mind of cooking wholesome things and storing them away for the winter. Some deep, atavistic impulse is surely at work in that, and we all feel it, notwithstanding that lovely fresh strawberries are available to us every day of the year at very low prices, and so are thousands of other products, so we do not need to prepare food seasonally any more. We can have asparagus year-round now, and not just for three weeks in May! It is amazing, but probably not very good, really, to fly strawberries and asparagus all around the world every day of the year so America's grocery stores are always packed with them. But now I am going to hop down off my little soapbox and prepare this lovely cake to get in the mood for the holidays. It's simple, classic, and far nicer than revolting haggis, I think you'll agree.

Lemon Cake with Marmalade Cranberry Sauce

For the cake:
1¾ cups flour
2 tsp. baking powder
¾ tsp. salt

¾ cup sugar

1½ Tsp. grated lemon zest

2 large eggs

¾ cup whole-milk yogurt

½ cup vegetable oil

½ tsp. vanilla extract

1 cup of marmalade cranberry sauce (see recipe below) or
    marmalade

For the frosting:

2 cups powdered sugar

2 Tbsp. softened butter

2 Tbsp. milk

½ tsp. vanilla extract

Pre-heat oven to 350 and grease and flour a standard bread loaf pan. Put the first three ingredients in a bowl and combine with a fork. Put the sugar and lemon zest in a larger bowl and knead them with your fingertips until the sugar is moistened and "lemonized." Whisk the eggs in a third bowl, then add the rest of the ingredients to the eggs and combine this wet mixture. Then combine the wet mixture with the sugar mixture. Finally, add the dry ingredients and stir until just mixed; do not over-mix. If you have kids around the place, get them to help you with all the mixing; they will love the process and become invested in the delicious result. Pour the batter into the bread pan and cook for 55-60 minutes, until the top is golden brown or a knife inserted into the center comes out clean. Allow to cool on a baker's rack for 15 minutes. Beat the ingredients for the frosting on medium speed until smooth, then frost the cooled loaf. You can serve this with vanilla ice cream and limoncello.

And here is the recipe for a wonderful sauce for the cake, or you could just use any marmalade, if you are pressed for time.

Marmalade Cranberry Sauce

3 packages fresh cranberries (about 36 ounces), washed and drained
½ cup sugar
½ cup orange juice (freshly squeezed if possible)
1½ cups port
36 ounces of marmalade

(Note: This recipe is for a double portion of the sauce, so halve it if you only want one portion.) Stew the cranberries in a saucepan with the sugar, orange juice, and port until they are tender and about half of them have begun to burst. Remove from heat and stir in 36 ounces of an inexpensive marmalade. Then allow this mixture to cool. It freezes well for future use, and will be a great accompaniment for Thanksgiving turkey.

Mint, Limoncello, and Good Things to Do

This morning, I took a short walk around the chilly garden. The roses are looking rather ragged and forlorn late in life. I find myself relating completely to these roses, as I am ragged and forlorn late in life too. We are on the cusp of our first hard frost of the year, and it's getting me down a bit, as happens every year at this time, when the garden gracefully gives up the ghost for another year.

For some of us, it's hard to keep our spirits up at this darkening time of the year. We recently set the clocks back and I grew depressed, as I always do on the first Monday after Daylight Savings, when I have to drive home in the pitch black. During the day, the color is also rapidly draining out of the landscape, which is hurrying into its dull green and dun gray combination, which is so tiresome to the eye through the long, dragging months of winter. I find that I simply must look for positive ways to stop being a seasonal drudge. And so I begin a mental list of good things to do, things that will take me out of myself.

On recent walks around our town, I have been picking up long ponderosa pine cones, and last weekend, I wired them together with florist wire into the shape of a large string of chili peppers; then I spray-painted them gold and wound red ribbon through them. I hung them on the bright white plantation shutters in the three windows in the reading room. Watch out Martha Stewart; you aren't the only one who can wield a can of gold spray paint! Also, my wife has switched out the blue hydrangeas in the reading room for the red and white poinsettias, so I guess the unofficial Advent season has quietly begun, and the house has more of a holiday air. I even listen covertly to occasional Christmas music, Celine Dion being a great favorite. I'm feeling better already!

My inner farmer has realized there are a few herbs left in the garden. I grow chives all over the yard, more for their purple golf-ball flowers than for their oniony leaves, and some autumns, I have brought in masses of cut chives and frozen them for winter soups, but find it hard to use up more than a little of that. And others in the household begin to complain about the many frost-bitten bags of chives taking up valuable freezer space. So this year, I am going to bring just one large clump inside after a severe haircut and general tidying up, and grow it indoors in a pot in a sunny window by the patio door. I will do the same with a small rosemary plant. Fresh rosemary is wonderful in pasta, in breads, on any poultry, and in soups. If your plant is producing faster than you can use it, harvest a lot of it, strip off the fragrant leaves whole, and then fry them in olive oil that is very hot, but not smoking. Drain the fried rosemary leaves on paper towel, and then freeze the fried leaves for use all winter; they are marvelous on almost anything.

Mint is easy to gather in this season. Practically any yard can support a plant or two of mint and it is very easy to grow. Actually, the problem with mint is that it is *too* easy to grow, and if you are not very vigilant, it will soon take over any sunny spot you give it with its invasive, shooting roots. So I don't have to spend all summer worrying about it, I plant it in the ground in the large plastic pots it comes in, and while this is not ideal for it, it will grow quite merrily this way and at least it cannot sucker as it would like. In November, I cut them down to the ground and take the cuttings to the basement to air-dry on spread-out newspaper. After a few weeks, I strip off all the dried leaves into a large bowl and crush them by hand. This can be used for making mint tea, hot or cold, and a few plants will easily see you through the winter. You can also use it to make mint sauce for your lamb, if you like mint sauce with your lamb. I lived in countries where they ate plenty of lamb with mint sauce, but now cannot bear the idea of either mint sauce or eating lamb. The twiggy stems that are left behind after the dried mint is stripped can be tied into bundles, and I keep these in a large basket by the fireplace. They burn very hot and keep the fire lively, plus they give off a wonderful minty aroma, not unnaturally. Waste not, want not, and we certainly get full value out of our mint around here.

Speaking of fragrant winter fires, I can't resist just saying that, as you go around your yard in winter pruning things and doing a general cleanup, some aromatherapy opportunities will crop up and help keep your spirits high. Russian sage should be cut back a third each winter, just like lavender, and the cuttings for both can be gathered and put in your firewood basket. Keep some string or twine handy to tie these into bundles or they make a great mess and attract the unwelcome attention of other people in the household, who sometimes make unkind remarks about one's efforts. I find that adding a festive bow to the bundles soothes the restless natives and helps keep unfriendly remarks to a minimum. A really great source for fragrant firewood is the huge amount of wood you take out of mature buddleias in winter, if you are lucky enough to have one or two of these about the place, as I am. These are cut back severely in February, and please do not be timid here. Be firm; tough love is what you should be thinking. Ours grows to twenty feet tall in summer and we cut it back to pollarded stumps about four feet high each February. And then we (I say we) chop up the cut stems for the fragrant hearth.

But where was I? Oh yes, why is the mint tea good to have around? It is delicious and fresh, and it is good to know you grew something yourself, however simple and easy, on your own land that you can enjoy in winter when you are feeling more than usually cut off from the land that sustains you. But also because it gives you an important component in solving the problem of how to make lemons a larger part of your life. In Tuscany, lemons have, of course, been an important part of the agricultural countryside for hundreds of years. Here, we tend to take them for granted. Italian limoncello is a miracle of intense and refreshing taste, and is drunk in Italy as an apéritif, a digestive, a dessert wine, and as a nightcap to settle your stomach before bed. In America, limoncello is available, but is rather expensive, considering what it is: just sweetened vodka infused with lemon. Making this yourself is surprisingly easy and satisfying, and is related to the topic of mint, which I will get back to in a moment.

Limoncello

6-8 medium lemons
3 cups vodka
3 cups water
One cup sugar

Peel the lemons, using an ordinary vegetable peeler, but be careful not to get any of the white pulp from the lemon rind, as this adds a bitter taste to the drink. Combine the peels from the lemons in a large jar with three cups of vodka, and let this stand for two weeks. Boil three cups water (or 2.5 cups if you want a stronger drink) and one cup sugar until the sugar is dissolved, then allow this simple syrup to cool; add to the vodka and lemon peel mixture, and let stand another week. Then drain the limoncello away and store in the freezer (discarding the peels). Serve in frozen shot glasses on a hot summer day, closing your eyes and thinking of Tuscany. The first time you make this, go buy a nice bottle of limoncello, preferably one with frosted glass or an interesting shape; you can keep this in the freezer and sample it while your own batch is brewing. Then use this bottle to house your own product thereafter.

Now, back to the mint. Once you have the peeled lemons left over from the limoncello process, you can squeeze them into a large pitcher and make another simple syrup, this time with a cup of water and half a cup of sugar. Add this hot syrup to the lemon juice. Take a large handful (about half a cup) of your fresh, dried mint, and pour four cups of hot water over this, allowing it to steep. For the steeping process, I use one of those French coffee presses, which works well to separate the tea from the dregs. When the mint tea turns a strong golden-green color, pour it into the pitcher with the lemon juice and sugar, then fill up the pitcher with water and chill. You will love the mint lemonade that results; it tastes so great and fresh, and you can drink it all winter. Kids, there's a special treat in the kitchen for you!

Fresh mint, limoncello, winter walks, roaring scented fires, and Christmas music—these are some of the good things that brighten our dark days at this time of year. But back to the Daylight Savings change, on the day I was talking about, it was a rather dull day that sloped toward a dark evening; just before the sun set at 4:55, it slipped below the dark cloud that almost covered the sky from horizon to horizon, leaving only a tiny band of clear sky in the west. When the sun fell into this clear band, it illuminated the entire canopy from horizon to horizon in a spectacular display of a dramatic purple and black ceiling, shot through with gorgeous red and orange flares and flourishes. It was breathtaking, and there is an object lesson of some kind in here somewhere, I feel sure, about hope or being surprised by grace and the advent of good things to come.

Qui Plantavit Florebit

It is a gray and foggy day, and I find my mind roaming far away and musing about the spirit of "place" in gardening: what will grow and how it grows in one's particular climate, temperature zone, soil conditions, etc. And it is only human nature to suppose jealously that the gardening grass is greener in another's garden. The weather I have to endure, we think, is awful, but somebody else—the rose fancier in Portland, say; or just about any gardener anywhere in England, that supposed gardening paradise; or the guy with the big koi pond and two acres of orchids in Hawaii—is lucky enough to enjoy the perfect gardening climate.

But no, this is simply absurd. Much though we might like to live in a perfect climate—where the rain never falls until after sundown, and by 9:00 p.m., the moonlight must appear in such a congenial spot—it is a mythical dream and the grass is not really greener elsewhere. Roses flourish in Portland, for example, because it rains there all the time or else is gray and dull, with just enough sun to keep the flowers from damp rot and to keep most (but not all) of the gardeners from going mad as a result of the rain and gloom and killing themselves from despair.

England, of course, has a perfectly atrocious climate, far too bitter in the winter and far too cold and wet in the summer. It does have two very fine days of weather each year, usually June 21 and 22, and it is well to make the most of them that you possibly can; I think it is actually provided for in the (unwritten) English constitution. Plants only fare well there because of the long summer days and the usually abundant moisture, both of which are decidedly mixed blessings. The less said about the long, dark winter nights there the better; that is what English pubs are for, as everyone knows. And the tropics are no picnic either, really. The ratio of flowers to verdure is completely out of whack and the whole garden is essentially scraped off every few years by ripping tropical storms, or else it is sluiced away in monsoonal downpours.

I loved the gardens I made in Colorado, but conditions there were actually very harsh. The combination of a high, dry location; extremely poor soil; and a short, intense growing season with long, bitter winters, late spring freezes, and early fall snows each year made for a gardening nail-biter every season. There were plenty of tragedies and heartaches to brood darkly over during the much-too-long winter months, when nothing much good was going on outside. Literally the first thing to leaf out in new bright green each year was the shrub oak, normally in the first week of *June,* which I think you will agree, leaves a lot to be desired from the gardener's point of view.

Where we live now, in southern New Jersey, is actually not so bad from the gardening point of view. As in the nation's capital, most southern plants grow here (azaleas, magnolias, even figs and camellias, if you want to be a bit risky), but we are far enough north to be able to grow the full range of northern plants as well. We have nicely defined seasons that wheel sharply from one to the other, with none of the back and forth shilly-shallying that plagued us in Colorado and which play merry hell with gardens. They were so bad that you could never really be said to have a decent run of spring or fall weather.

With us now, autumn runs right up until Christmas and the winter solstice, just like God intended it to do, and spring gets off to a good strong start just after the vernal equinox and never really looks back. Rain waters my garden most of the year; in a wet year, like this last one, I hardly drag the hoses out at all. Sunshine is plentiful, especially if you are blessed, as our garden is, with enough open ground (just) to satisfy your taste for sun-loving flowers, as most of the really beautiful flowers are.

The summer heat is rather hard on the grass and garden here, indeed, but not nearly so much so as in D.C., and of course, the further north you go, the less summer heat you have, but the more harsh the winter is on the other side of the calendar. Perhaps you have noticed this already? The fulcrum is set just about perfectly here—at least I think so, Dr. Pangloss—and our winter cold is definitely enough to give all the spring bulbs and flowering plants their needed shock of frost and to kill all the pests that are fortunately programmed to succumb to it, the dears, but not enough normally to do much damage to the plants or to force the poor gardener to break his back with the snow shovel very often.

With a bit of extra work, we can even manage to grow tender plants like dahlias, which come to us from sunny and warm Mexico and cannot over-winter outside here, and even tropicals if you like, such as the canna lilies we favor. I notice ruefully that some of them do fine in our more mild winters these days even without all the gardener's extra work, like the ones by the front door of the town bank on Main Street that grow in front of a warm, south-facing wall that channels heat into the ground. Similarly, we have a pleasing mix of southern and northern birdlife, plus all the migratory traffic that comes down the New Jersey Flyway and keeps things interesting for those of us with an eye on the wild world (that is, my dog and I).

The meaning of all this (for perceiving meaning through gardening is surely one of its subtle charms, otherwise you are just a sort of unproductive farmer, really) is that a plant should flourish where it is planted. For the gardener, it is to resist the dreamy infantilism of climatological envy (or other kinds of envy, for that matter), and to accept the conditions where you find yourself, glorying gratefully in their advantages and ameliorating their disadvantages diligently, patiently, and with a happy heart. All wherever you can and for as long as you can. *Qui plantavit florebit*—He who has planted will flourish!

Perpetual Thanksgiving

It is Thanksgiving week and is cold and rainy, very foggy. It's hard to be thankful when you are chilled to the bone by weather like that. I guess the best you can say is that it does have a certain enveloping mystery. It's a great backdrop for a movie or a clandestine meeting, if you happen to be an international spy or something of that sort. If you don't lead such a strenuous and worrying existence, you can just light a fire on a day like this and curl up with a favorite old book.

Every few years, I re-read Thoreau's classic *Walden*. Every time I read it, I get more out of it. Thinking of him reminds me of what he wrote a few years after *Walden* was published, in a letter to his friend Harrison Gray Otis Blake: "I am grateful for what I am and have. My thanksgiving is perpetual. It is surprising how contented one can be with nothing definite—only a sense of existence." My thanksgiving is perpetual—what a lovely concept. If you want to work that into a grace or toast before your Thanksgiving feast, you could do far worse. Much the same sort of idea was, I think, intended by the great English gardener Gertrude Jekyll, who said that the consummate achievement of a garden is "to lift up the heart in a spirit of praise and thankfulness."

Another thing to do when it's forty-five degrees and foggy is to get an eggnog latte from Starbucks. Imagine our luck, living on the one planet in the universe that has eggnog lattes! What are the chances of that?! The first sip reminds me of every eggnog latte I have ever had, most often at airports around the world when completing my last pre-Christmas travel and heading home with a light and happy heart. The lattes also, of course, remind me of every sip of eggnog I had as a child and invoke the memory and feeling of what it is to be a child at Christmas, the pure magic excitement of it all. I would lie in my bed downstairs, from which I could see the curved stairwell lined with beautiful, gleaming, polished walnut paneling that reflected the mellow glow of the Christmas tree lights in the living room upstairs. It is odd how a sip of latte conjures up that whole complex of memory and emotion, and odd too how that one latte can motivate you to get going on the holiday decorations.

While I worked outside on general garden cleanup and Christmas lights, my wife unpacked about fifteen Christmas boxes, giving the house already a decidedly festive air. I dug up all the dahlias and planted seventy hyacinth bulbs along the walk back to the side yard; they don't look too plump, but I think they will be all right. I threw away the annual chrysanthemums that had been decorating the front and back porches. How spruced up the house and garden now look, with some of the dead and blasted vegetation cut away, the earth clean and dark for winter. The golden leaves under the maples in the front of the house are about a foot deep and are fun to walk through, as one did as a child. Cosimo was delirious out in the yard, positively whimpering with joy, and would not let me get more than ten feet away from him, the dear old thing.

We noticed on a nearby street that there is one grand, bearded iris blooming, in late November of all things, defying the advancing dark and cold with its absurdly gorgeous, orchidaceous bloom. I saw it as my son and I went off to run errands this morning, and it cheered me up enormously. And I also noticed that the grand white azalea by our front porch, what was in the old days called a "Delaware Valley white azalea," has mischievously opened precisely one white bloom to say goodbye to summer. The white rhododendron outside the family room window has opened just a single white answering bloom. What can these quiet floral semaphores imply? And meanwhile, the heartiest of the last roses are putting forth their last tentative blooms, while the serious frost yet holds off. Though not for long, as a hard frost is predicted for this weekend, the first of many very cold nights to come, no doubt.

In fact, on Saturday, we were treated to one of the earliest snowfalls in the region since the Civil War. We only received a slight dusting, which was merely atmospheric and allowed us to light our first fire of the year. We had our daughter home from college for Thanksgiving, and she mostly hung about the house over the weekend, at one point wrapped up in a blanket, drinking tea and watching the snowflakes come tumbling picturesquely down. It is good for her to have family cocooning time, even though she is usually so far away, and we loved having her home for the break. She and her brother went out for sushi Saturday night, and we remembered to be grateful they get along so well. Sunday, when I dropped her off at the airport to go back to Texas, it was very sad. Melancholy plucks hard at the heartstrings, more and more each year, I find.

Like many people, we are thankful to have a healthy family, plenty of food, and a solid roof over our heads, and that makes us want to do something for others who are living with more distress. So we all got up early on Sunday before the melancholy airport run and made the monthly batch of frozen casseroles for our church's food drive for the area's homeless shelters. Leaves are falling in earnest now. We did a second light raking this past weekend and put fertilizer down. I was home with a bad cold in the middle of last week, so I mowed, likely for the last time this fall; made pesto, also for the last time; and pottered about the house feeling a bit sorry for myself, as one does with a cold. I disconnected the hoses and turned off the water supply to the outdoor taps. We are not quite ready for Christmas, but we are ready for winter, sort of, come what may. Our Thanksgiving holiday is now officially over, our daughter has gone back to school, and we are burrowed in against the cold. But the perpetual thanksgiving goes on, blending naturally into the light of the Christmas season.

December

Feasting with Thanks

People who are moved by the Christmas spirit are definitely divided into two groups: those who listen to Christmas music before Thanksgiving, and those who think this is quite wicked and are adamant about waiting and taking their holidays in the proper order.

I confess I am in the former camp and, if truth be told, have even secretly started to listen to Christmas carols after *Labor Day*, when in my view it is perfectly legal, so long as it is done discreetly and in the privacy of your own automobile. Today, I was humming a carol and thinking of how winter is definitely and grimly bearing down on us, with a nice arctic blast of air that has cut right through the garden, leaving a pall.

The impatiens have all now completely collapsed, the grass had a crispy crunch when I went out to get the papers, and even a rhododendron or two were droopy. Brrrrr, that's how you know it's really cold here, when the rhododendrons droop like that. Our leaves are mostly down, raked up, and carted away, though our town still looks lovely, with quite a bit of remaining color here and there. A single giant purple clematis flower has opened and flung itself defiantly into the teeth of the oncoming winter, and across the patio, a single bold pink gerbera daisy has bloomed; a few roses are straggling along in sporadic bloom, as they will almost until Christmas week at our place.

Every once in a while, not often, but just enough to keep me in my place, my wife has the fun of saying, "You know, for a Rhodes Scholar, you're not really all that bright, darling." The "darling" just manages to make the comment respectable, and I think that's a deft touch. The last time I heard this was a few days ago, when I used our electric hedge trimmer and carelessly cut through the hot cord. In case you ever wondered what *that* would be like, let me tell you. It is quite exciting: there is a tremendous explosion with smoke and flames and sparks shooting out everywhere; it's all extremely stunning and impressive. Plus, as I say, it tends to elicit unwelcome and unhelpful marital speeches, cautions, you-should-be-more-carefuls, and the like. I am on my second electric hedge trimmer now, and treat this one with much more care.

One does not want to be electrocuted more than once while pottering about in the garden, after all; it is amazing how rapidly wisdom enters in, occasionally.

But I am in high spirits all the same, as I have bought a replacement trimmer, as I said, and this weekend, I tried a new thing. I used it to cut down by degrees all the dead or near-dead things in the garden in furtherance of my new theory of mulching-in-place. This is an admittedly experimental gardening practice, but it is derided scornfully by other members of the household as "messy gardening." I, on the other hand, find it more environmentally sound and, frankly, quite a lot easier. Must be getting old. Or soft in the head, perhaps. Anyway, that went all right, and amazingly, I managed not to cut any bits of myself off in the process or to cut the power cord with the trimmer again.

But we really must come inside and get cracking on the holiday cooking, so here is the recipe for some outstanding dressing. This can be for Thanksgiving or Christmas and can be served with or without a roasted bird. The sausage makes it very hearty, so it can accompany a holiday feast or stand on its own. We make it all winter.

Chicken Sausage Dressing

1 baguette or similar loaf of French bread

2 crisp apples

2 stalks celery

8 Tbsp. butter

1 medium yellow onion

1 lb. of chicken sausage, without casings

4 oz. Portobello mushrooms

1½ cups chopped Italian parsley

3 eggs

16 oz. chicken stock

1½ Tbsp. chicken base (or 4 Tbsp. chicken bouillon powder)

1 Tbsp. diced thyme leaves (no stems)

½ tsp. freshly ground pepper

1/8 tsp. cayenne pepper

1/8 tsp. freshly ground nutmeg

4 oz. cognac or bourbon (optional, but preferred)

1 clove garlic, finely minced

5 oz. pecans, finely chopped

Cut the loaf into half-inch slices, brown these on both sides under the broiler of your oven, and then cut the toasts into half-inch cubes. Peel and core two large apples; any will do, but crisp ones are better and locally grown ones will have a great starchy crispness. "Honey Crisps" are perfect and they are just going out of season at this time of year, but they are worth looking out for. Cut them into a half-inch dice too. Cut two stalks of celery lengthwise and then cut them into a half-inch dice; brown the celery in two tablespoons of the butter. Dice two onions and brown them also in three tablespoons of the butter. Brown the chicken sausage. Chop the Portobello mushrooms and brown them in three more ounces of butter; add a little water if the mushrooms absorb the butter too quickly. Chop the flat Italian parsley. Lightly beat three eggs. Put all the foregoing ingredients into a large pasta bowl and toss, mixing well.

In a medium-sized saucepan, create a fragrant broth by combining the chicken stock, chicken base or bouillon, fresh thyme, ground pepper, cayenne, ground nutmeg, cognac or bourbon, and the garlic. We have also used aged tequila in lieu of the bourbon or cognac, and this works well too. Simmer the broth for 10 minutes to allow the flavors to combine. Once the broth has cooled somewhat, pour it over the ingredients in the pasta bowl and toss all the ingredients well. Butter a large casserole dish and put the stuffing in it. Cover with tin foil and cook at 350 degrees for 30 minutes; remove the tin foil and cook for 15 more minutes. While that is cooking, toast the pecans and, immediately before serving, sprinkle the toasted pecans over the top. If you like, you can double this recipe and freeze half for later use.

And here is a recipe for the best garlic mashed potatoes ever, while we are on the topic of holiday food.

Garlic Mashed Potatoes

2 bulbs garlic
1 Tbsp. olive oil
3 lbs. of potatoes (or 2 lbs. potatoes plus 1 lb. sweet potatoes)
1 Tbsp. plus 1 tsp. salt
½ tsp. freshly ground pepper
4 oz. whipping cream
8 oz. melted butter
1/3 cup chopped parsley or cilantro
1 tsp. coarse sea salt
2/3 cup Japanese bread crumbs (such as Panko)
2/3 cup freshly grated parmesan

Cut off the pointed ends of the garlic bulbs, drizzle them with the olive oil, and bake them for 30 minutes at 350 degrees; allow them to cool, then squeeze out the pulp and put it into a blender. While the garlic is roasting, peel and quarter the potatoes (or, if you prefer a bright orange color and a slightly more interesting taste, potatoes and sweet potatoes). In a large stock pot, boil the potatoes with the tablespoon of salt, 20-25 minutes or until tender. Mash the potatoes by hand (or, better, put them through a ricer) in a large bowl. To the garlic in the blender add the teaspoon of salt, the ground pepper, the whipping cream, the butter, and the parsley or cilantro. Blend this together, then add it to the potatoes until it is all combined. Spoon into a buttered baking dish. Mix together the sea salt, bread crumbs and cheese; sprinkle the bread crumb mixture over the potatoes for a crispy topping. Bake at 350 for 40 minutes. This recipe may likewise be doubled and half of it frozen for another occasion.

In this recipe, we are consciously breaking the rules with garlic and roasting it for a flavor twist. What, you didn't know there were rules about garlic? Well there are, but luckily, they are simple. It's called "the king of herbs" for its delicious flavor and the fine savor it adds to so many foods. It also is wonderful as a medicine, having strong anti-oxidant powers and boosting the immune system. It is one of the critical, versatile, and health-giving components of a Mediterranean diet, but it has earned a place in all the cuisines of the world. And here are the simple rules:

Mince it. Chopping raw garlic releases a sulfur-based compound called alliin and an enzyme called alliinase; these then combine and create alliicin, which is what gives garlic its strong flavor and boosts its health benefits. Mincing is better than chopping and using a garlic press is best of all.

Wait 10 minutes. This allows the alliicin to form. What's the rush? You have other food prep to do anyway, so give the garlic time to breathe.

Don't overcook it. Do not cook the garlic for more than 10-15 minutes on low to medium heat, or you will deactivate the healthful enzyme. It is powerful enough to do its flavor magic in so short a time.

Garlic is a very powerful ally in the kitchen. Follow these three simple rules and you will maximize its power, taste, and healthfulness.

We made both of the above dishes for Thanksgiving this year and they were big hits. The other day, I was putting up Christmas lights, and in late morning, it started to snow: big fat flakes that could not have been more atmospheric. It was very festive and seemed tailor-made for the season.

In the reading room these days, I am sailing stately through James' *The Wings of the Dove*, getting so much more out of it now as an older reader than when I first read it as a much younger man. His prose is masterful, but let's be honest, it's just too dense, really; it makes me feel a bit like the Emperor Joseph II, who supposedly said to Mozart on hearing "The Abduction from the Seraglio" for the first time: "That is too fine for my ears — there are too many notes!" Oh yes, I know the elegant, rarefied writing of this particular book adds a special horror to the morally monstrous story line, but still, it is a bit thick. If I have just a single glass of wine while reading him and my perception is not totally acute, I quickly lose the thread of the narrative and can scarcely tell what he is rabitting on about.

Then December arrived on a dark but mild morning at 6:30 a.m., the sky just lightening. By seven, it was a tropical sunrise — surprisingly mild and humid, the sky a beautiful shade of tangerine, but instead of the tropical turquoise, here it was more of a purple bruise color. It was sixty-three degrees at 8:00 a.m., but then fell to fifty-three degrees and rainy by the afternoon, and near-freezes are suggested for the next few nights. And so December comes on.

Life Is Real, Cold Is Good
How fast the light drains out of the northern hemisphere in December. It is only 5:20 p.m., and already it is nearly as dark as darkest night, as

the northern world slides down the slippery slope of the winter solstice. At seven this morning, the sky was just barely lightening. It snowed here Sunday, and much of Canada and the U.S. are gripped in a bitterly cold winter storm. Inside, we finished decorating for Christmas over the weekend and everything looks very festive at last.

We still have a small vase of the last autumn irises that will open a bloom or two every day, and an astounding 'Jaguar' amaryllis has erupted into bloom in our reading room, without leaves and on a bare stalk over a yard high. Of course, this one was a gift, so to my consternation, I cannot take any credit for its amazing performance, having had nothing at all to do with it.

The house was quiet this morning and nothing much is going on in the garden, which is only enlivened by a rabbit for Cosimo to chase every now and then; the constant one-note from the cardinals, whose cheery "peet" can be heard distinctly from inside; and the resident groups of Carolina wrens—one group in the pyracantha, one in the yew by the garage, and a new group in the wisteria, now large enough to provide sufficient shelter. They fly from the pyracantha to the garage to the wisteria and back again, paying each other holiday visits and twittering about the neighborhood gossip in a friendly way that is charming to see.

In the cold of the morning, I went outside to see if there was *anything* left in the garden that could be used to put a bouquet together. Not much, just the last of the roses and a few mums in sheltered spots. Mums really are good value, I think, though they are sometimes looked down on as common by gardening snobs. Not by the Japanese, of course, who have almost a reverence and religion for them, and glory in their beauty and hardiness in ways we could well learn from. They are so varied and interesting, practically pest-free, and bring color to the autumn garden when almost everything else is finished; plus, they have such a long season of bloom. What's not to like?

Gardeners, though generally a cheerful and steady lot, don't like to miss a chance to complain about the weather. And gardeners love to complain about the cold, even more than the heat, but perhaps less than the wreckage caused in the garden by a long hard drought or blast of late spring hail. For myself, I like the cold in winter, on the whole, and it brings the gardener many good things. A hard freeze kills off lots of weeds and a huge variety of insect pests that blight the garden during the entire growing season, and thank goodness that it does. The battle with bugs and weeds never ends, but we would not even stand a chance of staying on top of these tasks if the world were not destroyed and renewed in this seasonal way. Plus, the action of repeated freezes and thaws breaks up the soil and reduces the compost and mulch to the valuable components of a healthy soil, saving the gardener weeks of back-breaking labor.

When the garden is denuded of its luxurious summer growth and all the bushes are stripped bare, the gardener can learn a lot about the fundamental design of the garden. The underlying structure is candidly, perhaps cruelly, revealed. Try this experiment: the next time the garden is rimed with frost or etched in its outline by a light fresh snowfall, put on some warm clothes and go out and study it. What are your garden's bones? Where does its design look weak or fall apart a bit? What are the main features, plant-scape and hardscape, that give it structure and integrity? How do the foundational shapes flow through your garden landscape, or is it all just a big mash-up that can only look good when the plants return and cover up the underlying lack of design?

Just as tomatoes and other vegetables need a set number of hot days in summer to ripen fully, so do many plants—especially spring flowering bulbs—need a requisite number of cold days to bloom, so think of every bitter winter day as so many more tulips, daffodils and crocuses safely in the bank.

And of course, it is not the case that you can't enjoy the garden in winter. Far from it; many gardens are spectacular in winter and well worth the time to visit, including possibly your own. Whole books have been written about how to plan your garden so it looks great in winter, either through color or structure, and the gardener should not feel limited to being a three-season gardener. Some of my best days in this garden have been on mild winter days, when you can get outside and tend to light chores like pruning and general cleanup. Days like these are not to be missed.

Finally, it is not a terrible thing for the gardener to be forced to loaf for a little bit of the year; and of course there is always Mexico, Arizona and Florida, you know, if you are dying for hot sun and want to see some blazing bougainvillea when you wake up in the morning. Your own garden may be perfectly beautiful, but even beauty needs to take a break, and there is something to be said for even the most beautiful of movie stars, for example, not lingering too long on the stage, for fear people will get tired of the gorgeousness of the overall effect. Change does us all good, really, garden and gardener alike.

Driving in to work yesterday, I was forced off my usual route by a road construction detour, onto a quiet suburban street I think I had never traveled before, and there I saw a most surprising sight: in the front yard of a house was a very large cherry tree (at least, I think it was a cherry tree; it certainly looked like one) that was almost fully in bloom; not 100%, but more than 80%. It was a blizzard of white-pink, *in December*, creating a kind of Fellini-esque cinematic moment, something that could have been in *Amarcord*, perhaps. How does something like that happen? It is funny how life sprinkles little surprises like these around the world; I remind myself to look for them more intently. So an epiphany descends, unexpectedly, during a hassled commute to work, and changes everything.

Yesterday, I hadn't slept well and so got up early; as I came into the dark reading room, I noticed the computer was running our family slide show as a screensaver, so I sat down with a cup of coffee and watched in the dark room for about an hour. Sometimes we have to be made to observe the good things that fill our lives so abundantly. We get so caught up in all the day to day, worrying about all the little things that beset us, that we often lose sight of the big picture: that the lives we are living are great gifts that unfold beautifully and truly, just as they should. It is funny how these clarifying moments come upon us unawares. Advent is the time of joyful waiting and preparation, we are told, of confident hope in the present darkness, when we reflect that life is real and a gift, beautiful but fleeting.

Our house is decorated as charmingly as never before, with all the Christmas lights twinkling cheerfully. In these days, I get up early and drink lots of milky coffee and read whatever I feel like until it is time to go off to work with a happier heart. Christmas will soon be upon us in glorious earnest.

Solstice Pancakes, Focaccia

The solstice has come, and the earth has tipped over its axis, taking us minutely back toward the light. The sun rose today to peer weakly through the holly tree, the one by our driveway, in the extreme southeast corner of our property. We have had such a cold December, in the twenties almost every night, that even the rhododendrons have been drooping dejectedly. So our attention turns to indoor gardening. I planted several paperwhites in potting soil this weekend. Is there anything that says "winter" better than the hard, crisp, mineral scent of paperwhites? Many do not like this scent and find it too strong and not sweet enough, but I love it. That scent, and the fresh white flowers on a cold windowsill that looks out on bleak drifts of fresh snow in the garden: that is a perfect vignette of winter for me. We also have one single gerbera daisy in bloom in the mudroom, in a pot holding a large dracaena that winters there, and that is about it.

Saturday, my son and Cosimo and I drove to the airport to pick up my daughter, who is back from college for the second time, and what a thrill it is to have her home again. Sunday morning, I found her flip-flops in the middle of the reading room floor where everyone can conveniently trip over them, just like the old days, and was exasperated for a second until I thought how right it felt to see them there again, and I wisely held my tongue. Smart, no?

Speaking of things, like kids' flip-flops all over the place, that you don't want but can definitely live with, how do you feel about cultivating weeds in your garden? I mean, on purpose. At some point in a gardener's life, we must ask ourselves whether some decorative weeds should be allowed in the garden. Most gardeners fiercely think not, some are more flexible, and some like a bit of a wild look. I am in the latter category. And this is probably a good place to remember that it takes all kinds to make a world.

Once, I got to be part of a gardening team that was conducting an interesting experiment. Like many towns on the East Coast, we have plenty of rain and all of the storm-water runoff issues that come with it. Our town has large swales, or catchment areas, that hold storm runoff until it can drain off into the watershed of the Delaware River. We planted one of these huge catchments with a vast plantation of all-native plants: weeds, shrubs, and trees. The idea was to create a totally native area that was very diverse and dense, and would help with the storm-water runoff while creating a diverse wildlife and bird habitat. I walked by it the other day, several years after we planted it, and what a wonderful success it has been: dense and tangled, thick and prosperous, and no doubt sheltering a lot of creatures whose habitat is otherwise under great pressure.

Certainly some thistles can be very beautiful, and some native flower species that are very vigorous and not very flowery are hard to tell from weeds. In my garden, I don't have weeds, in general. That is, I have plenty of them, but I don't actually *cultivate* them. They are there against my will. But I do make a few exceptions. I have to say I have liked seeing tall wands of dill going to seed in robust gardens, as I once saw at Kew, and I do grow cardoons. They look like monstrous thistles on steroids (though they are actually a member of the artichoke family); I like them precisely because they are so arresting in appearance and have large, intensely violet flowers on a sort of artichoke knob. These flowers are very unusual and have a strong perfume that is strangely attractive and off-putting at the same time. They do look like weeds, but really interesting weeds, in short, or at least I think so; but another member of my household is unreasonably prejudiced against them, so I try to temper my enthusiasm, or else grow them covertly in the interest of pacific household relations.

The prejudice of this important person extends also to mulleins, my only other exception to the weed rule. If it is an exception. Just because you see mulleins growing by the roadside and on hardscrabble hillsides around the country does not mean they are weeds. They grow very tall—I once had a stupendous one that grew to ten feet—and they have numerous small yellow flowers on their bloom spike. Their leaves are large, soft, and a beautiful green-gray. They form large basal rosettes in their first year and send up their bloom spikes in their second year. That is to say, they are biennials. I like to have three of them in a row to define the long herbaceous border by our driveway. But I only want them the year they bloom, or rather, I should say I want them every year but they only bloom biennially, which means I have to find year-old replacements each fall. And that means I have to go mullein-hunting when I am able to slip my leash and other members of the household do not know that weed-hunting is afoot, or else go despite their open scorn.

This year, still smarting from ridicule from you-know-who when I set off on my annual mullein safari, I went to the railroad tracks in town, where I had noticed some very vigorous specimens growing. To my surprise, at first all I could find was last year's and this year's flowering spikes, now dead, and no little first-years at all. Then, finally, I found two, but could not for the life of me find a third. So I came home with the pair, and scrounged up a pretty meager third specimen in the corner of our yard, and then planted these without much expectation of future glory, but who knows. Hope springs eternal.

Sunday, I got up early and wrapped a bunch of presents, then made a wonderful new thing to have for breakfast. It's an eggy, sort of brioche pancake that was quite marvelous, so I decided to call it a Swiss solstice pancake, but you can call it whatever you wish. Just do, by all means, try this at least once; it is one of those rare dishes that is terribly easy, very unusual, and extremely impressive in appearance and sophistication. We do not get to use many such recipes in a lifetime, so do enjoy it.

Swiss Solstice Pancake

3 Tbsp. butter
2 eggs, beaten
½ cup flour
½ cup milk
1 tsp. sugar
1/4 tsp. salt
Garnish: Juice of 1 lemon and powdered sugar, plus marmalade
     or jam

Pre-heat oven to 425. Put butter in a 9- or 10-inch glass pie pan and put in oven until it melts. I use a pie plate with scalloped edges, and this is perfect, because as the edges of the brioche pancake puff up, they have the scalloped edges that makes this dish appear even more beautiful. Whisk everything else together (except the garnish, of course) and pour into the hot, buttery pan. Bake 18-20 minutes until the edges are puffy and evenly browned and the middle part of the pancake is cooked through. Sprinkle with lemon juice and sugar. Or, richer, slather pieces of the pancake with marmalade or jam like a crêpe.

That night we had two made-from-scratch pizzas for dinner: one was chicken sausage with red sauce and one was turkey barbecue with a red pepper and roasted eggplant sauce, and wow, were they good. Homemade pizzas are a great foil for heavy holiday food, when you want something tasty but not too fussy, something everyone can pitch in and help make. The key is to start with a simple Italian bread dough that you can make focaccia with, which is also how you make a pizza crust. What, you have never made a pizza crust from scratch? Well, it is time, it is time.

Classic Focaccia
(Olive Oil Bread and Pizza Dough)

2 packages of yeast (5 oz.)
2 cups warm skim milk
2 tsp. salt
1 tsp. sugar
6 Tbsp. olive oil, plus more
5 cups flour, plus more
1 egg white
1 tsp. sea salt
2 Tbsp. sesame seeds

Dissolve the yeast in the milk, then add the salt and the sugar. Stir and let sit until the growing yeast gives the mixture a beige and frothy surface. Then add the olive oil and stir again. Put 5 cups of unbleached white flour in a large mixing bowl and pour in the yeast mixture while stirring. Once this mixture forms into a dough, turn it out onto a flour-dusted countertop and knead it for several minutes, until it has a smooth, elastic consistency. Add more flour if it is too moist. Form it into a ball, slice the ball in half, and place each half in its own bowl that has been oiled with olive oil, turn once, and then cover. Allow to rest in a warm place until it doubles in size, about 45 minutes.

Then take each ball out, dust it with flour, and roll it out into a circle about a half-inch thick (thinner if you are making pizza, but the rest of these instructions are for the bread). With a sharp knife, make a few cuts in the top of the dough so it can expand when baking without splitting. Make a wash of equal amounts egg white and warm water whisked together, and paint this on the surface of the round with a small brush. Sprinkle sea salt and sesame seeds over the round. (If you are freezing one or both rounds for future use, stop here and put them in the freezer.) Allow the rounds to rest again, for 20 minutes.

Bake at 450 degrees in the top third of the oven on an oiled sheet for 25-30 minutes or until brown. Time this so the bread is warm when you sit down to dinner and offer liberal amounts of pesto for spreading, and you will be amazed by the goodwill that arises. You can also use butter, of course, or just eat it plain.

Family have all gathered, we are stocked up on holiday food, flip-flops are actually on our daughter's feet for now, presents are all (nearly) wrapped and all just in time, as Christmas is here!

❁

White Christmas

It was a very White Christmas after all. It started snowing hard on Christmas Eve and went on all day and night, dropping nearly two feet of the stuff, the heaviest snow since we have lived here. I wrapped the last presents like mad, worrying about my wife out in the blizzard, buying them faster than I could wrap them, but somehow, it all came together as it always does. That is a minor Christmas miracle in itself. On Christmas Eve, we opened a few presents and had cheese fondue in the reading room, followed by a disk of video from Christmases when our children were small. Tears of laughter all round. Then chocolate fondue in the reading room for dessert, and then we all fell into bed rather late.

On the great day, I was up at 7:30, baked a Christmas Stollen and put a kringle in the oven to warm, treasured Scandinavian traditions from my childhood, and eventually everyone else got up, and we started in on the presents. Then we had our favorite Christmas egg casserole. Kids (younger kids) like to help with the Stollen, but make this before Christmas Day, as it is much too involved (as I discovered) for the great day itself; and you can make the egg soufflé the night before too.

Christmas Stollen

5½ cups flour (more if the dough is sticky and too like cookie dough)

4 tsp. baking powder

1½ cups sugar

1 tsp. salt

1 tsp. mace

1 tsp. ground cardamom

1 tsp. ground cinnamon

1 tsp. freshly ground nutmeg

8-10 oz. slivered almonds, toasted and ground
1½ sticks unsalted butter

16 oz. softened cream cheese
2 eggs
1 tsp. vanilla extract
1 tsp. almond extract
50 ml cognac (the size of an airplane bottle)

½ cup currants
½ cup golden raisins
½ cup dried cherries, chopped
½ cup dried pineapple, chopped
The peel of one lemon (not the white part), chopped fine
2 7-oz. tubes of almond paste (marzipan)
One tube of any cookie icing for decorating

Let the cream cheese and butter come to room temperature and put to one side. Then sift together the dry ingredients in the first group. Add the almonds, then cut in the butter with a pastry knife until the mixture resembles coarse sand.

In a blender, cream together the ingredients in the second group. Pour this into a bowl and stir in the dried fruit. Gradually add the wet mixture to the dry mixture until everything is well blended.

Work the dough into a ball and turn it out onto a lightly floured surface. Knead it for a few minutes, just until the dough is smooth and elastic. Divide the dough into two halves. Shape one half of it into an oval about ten inches long and eight inches wide and about one inch thick. With the edge of a blunt butter knife, crease it lengthwise, just off-center. Roll out one of the tubes of almond paste to a little smaller than the crease, then lay the rolled-out almond paste on top of the larger half of the Stollen, next to the crease. Fold the smaller side of the Stollen over the larger side and place it on a greased baking sheet. The traditional idea, you see, is that the folded, lumpy bread resembles the bundle of the infant Jesus.

Brush it lightly with melted butter before baking. Repeat for the second loaf. Makes two large loaves or four small ones. Bake at 350 for about 50-55 minutes. If it gets too brown, cover it with aluminum foil. Allow to cool before decorating it with the cookie icing. The loaves can be prepared in advance and then frozen, to be cooked later. One way to serve the bread is toasted with vanilla ice cream; then you can go completely off the deep end (it is Christmas, after all) by pairing it with a glass of Madeira from V. Sattui in the Napa Valley. Oh. My. God.

Christmas Egg and Cheddar Soufflé

1 lb. grated white cheddar
½ lb. sausage, cooked and drained
½ lb. good quality bacon, cooked and drained
Half a baguette of bread, cubed

9 eggs, beaten
3 cups whole milk
1 tsp. salt
1½ tsp. dry mustard

Spread the first four ingredients in a greased 9x13 baking dish. Pour the next four ingredients on top and refrigerate overnight.

Bake at 350 degrees for 40-50 minutes and allow to rest ten minutes before serving. Serves 6-8.

And then we left the kitchen in a mess and hurried off to noon Mass. Afterwards, I took Cosimo for a long Christmas walk around a pond not far from our house. It is a bit warmer today, though there is still a lot of snow on the ground, and the only color in the landscape (other than the cheerful Christmas lights everywhere) is the startling red of the holly berries and an occasional fly-by of our pair of cardinals. Which reminds me that, as we were lying in bad last night and falling asleep with the fire flickering in our bedroom, we could hear our vigilant neighborhood owl outside, hooting a friendly Merry Christmas to all.

Afterword

It is early spring in the garden again. This has been a remarkably dry and warm spring, with a high two days ago in the nineties, and last night it was eighty at 6:30 when I got home from work; perfect weather to go sit on the patio with a glass of wine and watch the dozen or so turkeys who live nearby swoop in at twilight to roost in the high trees at the back of our house. Across the fence that defines our backyard is a band about half a mile thick of dense and wild forested land. Well, I say wild forest. It is a sort of greenbelt, really; just the sort of untouched, scrubby, and tangled lowland forest that must have covered most of southern New Jersey at one time, with the exception of the mysterious and far more wonderful and atmospheric Pine Barrens. But the tangled forest here is still a lovely amenity, dressed in its fresh new verdure at this time of year. Most of our windows on the back of the house look out onto this vast green space teeming with lowland wildlife, birdlife especially. Yesterday, we were having coffee and saw a large, but timid, wild turkey slowly pick his way daintily and surreptitiously across the backyard.

But the dryness and heat of this spring have dramatically advanced the general timetable of things, and spring has now descended like a sudden storm. As you drive around our beautiful old town, you see huge swaths of frilly white and pink dogwoods, often juxtaposed with the brilliant purple of the Oklahoma redbuds and underplanted with early azaleas or tulips, often both, for impressive dashes of brilliant color, all set off against the fresh green backdrop of newly unfurled foliage.

Not long ago, the wildly popular painter Thomas Kincade died. He called himself "The Painter of Light," and he became enormously successful commercially, owing to his luminous depictions of old-fashioned cottages and houses set in gorgeous, old-style gardens and villages. His art was very retro and sentimental, but he connected with a longing for things as they were in the old days, or as they were the way we idealize the old days to have been. Norman Rockwell developed a wide commercial and popular audience in a similar way, in another time. The reason I mention Kincade is that our town often reminds me of his artistic vision. It is a very old town, settled a century before the Revolutionary War disturbed the peace of the Delaware Valley, and its old, gracious homes are set far back on huge lots and are deeply surrounded by gorgeous gardens. With a bit of atmospheric fog in winter, or seen in the gauzy light and haze of spring greenery, you can almost hear the sound of horses clip-clopping down the broad, cobbled streets, and the creak of their wagons, delivering milk or ice, coal or groceries.

We have lived here eight years now. The first year after we moved here, a national magazine named our town America's best small town, period, and strolling around its streets on a gorgeous spring day like today, you can see why. You could point a camera in any direction and publish the result in a sentimental calendar of old-fashioned, small town life. Our house, for example, is a 125-year-old Arts and Crafts bungalow built in the Swiss style, and as such, must be one of the earliest Arts and Crafts houses in America, as that architectural style only came to these shores from England in the 1880s. When it was built, I suppose it was very avant-garde; now it looks charmingly dated, with a granite-block first story, soaring and intersecting A-frame axes, the steeply canted roofs supported by heavy carved corbels and gracious old brick chimney blocks that vent the house's five fireplaces. It is set in an acre of old gardens, which it has been my great joy and satisfaction to tend for these eight years. In retrospect, it was probably far too much for one person, without help and with a difficult day job and a demanding family growing up on the premises, but there you are.

Gardens do not last forever, and indeed that is part of their charm. They are a work that is endlessly in progress, never finished; they change daily, and over time, they change dramatically or perish altogether. They are mutable and ephemeral; it is their nature. Gardeners do not last forever either, as you have probably reflected, but that is not really my subject here, although I guess indirectly it is. We move about far more often these days than families used to, and gardeners do not generally get to garden in one place for decades and decades. Who would want to anyway; that would be so boring. Our jobs and our families and our health histories, or whatever, move us in different directions, so that we must love the gardens we tend fully and well, we gardeners, and be prepared to leave them when the time comes, hopefully with a full and happy heart and with the satisfaction of having done a good job. And without regrets, if that is possible.

For those who make a life practice of gardening interiorly, this is rather easier than it is for others. For us, gardening is not so much about the garden itself as it is about what is going on inside ourselves. That way, when we move on, the garden goes with us. That is, if your garden is interior, it is by definition portable, and it does not cease to exist because you happen to live somewhere else. It goes on inside you. The same is true for family, love, friendship, and many of the other good things in this life, in the unlikely event that you have lived this long without yet noticing that. And isn't this remarkable portability of the good things in life itself one of life's very good things?

But still, as our time here draws to an end, I have been on vigilant alert for incipient melancholy in these few final weeks, as I do each routine, practiced, and well-loved chore for the last time. I planted this summer's crop of dahlias, for example, that I will not see bloom, and likewise scores of canna lilies that will be blooming at their finest in the fierce heat of July when I will not be here to marvel over them once more. But what a feeling of satisfaction I have this spring to see the lovely wisteria, which I have carefully coaxed to grow up a corner of this fine old house and then scramble twenty more feet over the front of the garage, now finally old and established enough to bloom. And to add to my intense satisfaction, blooming with it is the pink clematis that I paired with it, its pink spangles entwined with the purple racemes and the two of them perfectly synchronous. Amazing. Just as I planned it, for once. The clematis is exactly the same color signature as the whitish-pink of the pink dogwood just a few feet away on the patio, so the overall scheme was a satisfying success. For me, that is remarkable, as my plans rarely come off so perfectly, and I am so glad I lived in this house long enough to see its fulfillment. They are going to look well together for a very long time, with any luck.

I love wisteria, as I have written elsewhere, and I rejoice that in our town it grows like the Chinese weed it of course is. In some of our wooded greenbelts, it is positively rampant, covering the spring woodland like a huge and very lumpy purple blanket. Sometimes it clambers up tall trees until they are completely smothered in drooping violet. Just a block from our house, there is a garden with a giant skeleton of a dead spruce in it, at least fifty feet high, perhaps sixty. It has never been cut down because it is completely smothered by a vast and venerable wisteria vine and, for two weeks each spring, that tree is a giant purple spruce that looks like a bizarre tree in a Dr. Seuss book. It is fantastic.

In another part of our town, there is a farmer's market stand on a corner lot, whose surrounding acres provide the produce that is sold at the stand. Every fall, they plant row after row of cabbages there, and they grow all winter. I have never really cared for cabbage, either the edible or the ornamental kind, but I must admit they are a bit of tonic to look at in the depth of winter—they are so bright and hardy in the otherwise bleak landscape. Then in spring, for some reason, they sometimes let them go to flower and seed. So right now, they are all topped with tall, waving, yellow flower fronds and are looking rather bizarre, in point of fact. And right across the street from them is one of those greenbelts with a rumpled coverlet of purple wisteria, so that the intense combination of acres of yellow competing with acres of purple is far, far overdone and someone should call the police really, it's much too much.

And a further word about dogwoods. They are one of the many great things about being American. These delicate, beautiful woodland creatures are native to our eastern forests, which they fill with their graceful growing habits and the beautiful white or pink flowers that open on their bare and delicately fanned stems. They are evidently afflicted by a terrible blight that is slowly but surely killing off the American dogwood (*Cornus florida*), and I suppose a terrible time may come when they are all gone at last. But until then, I think we should go on planting them as long as we can, and that is why I chose to plant the beautiful pink dogwood in the center of our patio, doomed as it perhaps may be (and as perhaps we all are). It is gorgeous enough for me, and there is time enough yet for beauty in the land, come whatever may. Perhaps in the future, our impoverished descendants may only be able to plant the blight-resistant Korean dogwood, and that would be a shame. These Korean dogwoods certainly have their partisans and their considerable virtues—they are disease resistant, more vigorous bloomers and have a winningly compact growing habit—but they simply do not, in my opinion, have the elegance of the American variety, and of course, they bloom with their dense pelt of green leaves, which is far less beautiful to my mind.

Returning to my own garden, this spring the bluebells have excelled themselves, forming big, fat clumps that are more like daylilies in size than bluebells. Whatever can have gotten into them? They are blooming so profusely that, for once, I was able to cut enough for vase after vase in the house, paired with dark blue irises and purple honesty for the last indoor displays from this garden that we shall have, while still leaving plenty of them outside to rejoice passersby. As the very first irises are now opening, I have to confess a pang of melancholy that I will not be here next month to see the May zenith of this garden, when irises, roses, and peonies are all at the top of their form together, the triple crown of this garden, as it is for so many.

Still, the gardener must move on to other gardens and to other schemes and challenges. All that I learned here and remember from here will go with me, and often, usually as I am falling asleep at night, my mind will roam familiarly through this garden, as it does in others where it knows its way well, restlessly checking each plant in turn and in each season, love mingled with loss, joy mingled with affection, always questing. Today I walked alone through this lovely old house where we have lived together longer than anywhere else in our family's life. Now it is empty and clean, and ready for another family.

For just one more day, it is still ours. It is beautiful inside, but very bare. Every room rings with memory, and I pause in each in turn, with a full heart. I tend dangerously toward the sentimental in life and was so proud of myself for not indulging in it until now. But now, now I am giving way a bit, as of course we must in life. Inevitably, we think of our children and how much of their lives are lived in each of the homes we make for them, what a large part of their lives each home is, and the cataract of memory cascades from year to year, flowing from child to child, from home to garden, and back to home again. And then I turn, and lock the door one final time.

The last I see of this garden is the pink and white of the coolly elegant, gesturing dogwoods against the dark green of the hedgerow at the back of the glorious garden, looking serene and everlasting.

About the Author

David Jensen was born in Chicago and was raised in a small town in Western Colorado. He was educated at small country high schools in Colorado and South Australia and graduated from the University of Denver, with a degree in history and political science. After that, he studied in England for three years as a Rhodes Scholar and has a law degree from Oxford University.

After returning to the US, he was a legislative staff member in the United States Senate for eleven years and served in the administration of President George H.W. Bush as Deputy Assistant Secretary for International Economic Policy for the U.S. Department of Commerce. A long career in the media industry followed, and today he is an international television executive for major telecommunications companies.

He began gardening at the age of nine and has gone on doing so for nearly half a century. His first book, *The Garden Interior: A Year of Inspired Beauty*, is a garden memoir about years of gardening on a beautiful property in the Mid-Atlantic region. He lives and gardens now, with his wife Deb, at their homes in Denver and in Scottsdale. His motto as a gardener is *"Qui plantavit florebit"* ("He who has planted, will flourish").

Printed in the USA
CPSIA information can be obtained
at www.ICGtesting.com
JSHW022313220524
63639JS00004B/257

9 781630 476823